PRESERVE AND CREATE
Essays in Marxist Literary Criticism

AIMS MONOGRAM SERIES NO. 4

PRESERVE
AND CREATE

ESSAYS IN MARXIST LITERARY CRITICISM

Selected and Edited by

GAYLORD C. LEROY
Temple University

and

URSULA BEITZ
Institute for Literary History
Academy of Sciences of the German Democratic Republic
Berlin

HUMANITIES PRESS
New York   1973

Library of Congress Catalog Card Number: 72-75793

ISBN Number: 391-00233 3

Printed in the United States of America

PREFACE

For a decade now, newly radicalized students of literature have been groping for a relevant approach, for the most part unaware of advances in literary scholarship in the European socialist countries. The irony of that situation gives rise to the present anthology, an attempt to make a portion of this vital movement available to the American reader.

The essays we have selected should be looked upon as part of a collective effort to design new tools for criticism. The effort is still in its beginnings; we are in the first stages of a movement of criticism and scholarship that can be expected to increase in scope of reference and persuasive force in the years ahead.

In selecting the articles, one of our purposes was to represent approaches to literature that may have a model function for us. We would hope that all the articles will be read at least partly with the question in mind: what use can be made of this approach to literary study by students in the United States?

The articles in Part One are concerned with such matters as levels of meaning in art (Lukacs, "Appearance and Essence"), a Marxist approach to the universality of appeal in literature (Petrov, "The Generally Human"), the question of relevance in literature from the past (Weimann, "Past Significance and Present Meaning"), the disastrous consequences of criticism that partitions art off from society and history (Weimann, "Point of View"), and the cognitive function of art (Gay, "Truth in Art and Truth in Life").

At a time when Marx and Freud have made us aware of continents of behavior unsuspected by the everyday consciousness, Lukacs' concern with levels of meaning has a special urgency. In this first essay, it might also be mentioned, we enter at once into a sphere of controversy in Marxist scholarship. (In "The Brecht-Lukacs Debate" in Part Three, Mittenzwei presents in passing a differing interpretation of Lukacs' principle of appearance and essence.)

In dealing with the so-called "universal" themes in literature, Petrov attempts to avoid the connotations of a timeless human nature, but to avoid at the same time the notion that human nature is so

i

infinitely malleable that the critic can be concerned only with what is specific to a given time and place. These questions, as Petrov indicates, have a bearing on the important Marxist concept of the "typical."

For illustrative material in "Past Significance and Present Meaning" Robert Weimann goes to Shakespeare (specifically to *Hamlet*), but what he has to say offers guidelines for a Marxist approach to literature in any genre and from any period of the past. Readers looking for specific ways in which Marxist criticism can achieve "relevance" will be able to make good use of this essay. Also in this essay: a class analysis of the New Criticism.

Approaching the question of relevance from a different angle in "Point of View in Fiction," Weimann examines one kind of formalist criticism in the United States in an effort to show that the dimension of society and history must be brought into the field of vision.

In dealing with the cognitive function of art, Gay argues that there is always some kind of connection between truth in art and truth in life, but that this connection can have a variety of forms, from very close to very tenuous. In other words, he combats both the notion that the truth of art and the truth of life are identical, and the contrary notion that we need not bother about the connections between the two. At the end of the article, Gay throws out hints that might point to a literary history using the relationship between truth in art and truth in life as an essential thread.

Part Two is devoted to the Marxist theory of modernism. Here Mittenzwei develops a fundamental principle of Marxist aesthetics having to do with the relationship between the individual and the social. In order to create character, he argues, an understanding of this relationship is indispensable. Mittenzwei works out the implications of his proposition by examining major trends in drama, in particular the psychological play and the theater of the absurd.

In Zhantieva's essay on Joyce's *Ulysses* we have a kind of Marxist criticism not yet too common, the extended examination of a single work. Making different use of the proposition concerning the relationship between the individual and the social, Zhantieva considers both the world view—the "vision of reality"—and the formal characteristics of *Ulysses*.

The subject of Part Three is revolutionary-socialist literature. In "Partisanship," Pracht and Neubert, developing a thesis that true-blue representatives of our literary establishment will reject out of hand, make a case for the relationship between revolutionary art and party leadership.

In "The Brecht-Lukacs Debate" Mittenzwei gives an account of the head-on collision between two of the most eminent Marxist critics, both committed to the development of a specific Marxist aesthetic. Their subject: what constitutes revolutionary literature (socialist realism)?

In "Socialist Realism," Pracht gives an indication of the concerns of a criticism in support of the new socialist literature. He touches also upon questions of alienation, myth, levels of difficulty, and ways to take possession through art of a new man "conscious of his powers."

The selection of Elisabeth Simons is an inner-party document, developed in the Institute for the Social Sciences of the Central Committee of the Socialist Unity Party (German Democratic Republic). A working paper not intended primarily for publication, this document gives us a glimpse of what is involved in conscious direction of the artistic process. The concept of conscious direction itself (as opposed to "spontaneity") is fundamental for the Leninist outlook; it is a principle very much at the heart of the class struggle in ideology and aesthetics in our time. In this essay we see the importance of conferences and working collectives in the evolution of new critical policy. The essay touches upon a number of subjects treated in a different connection in earlier articles, the relationship between the individual and the social (Mittenzwei on drama), the question of cognition and artistic truth (Gay), the concern with the portrayal of the new man "conscious of his powers" (Pracht). Positions are developed also with regard to a variety of other subjects, for example, the theme of decadence in art; also the Kafka controversy, where Simons takes exception to the position of Ernst Fischer. Throughout the article, one observes the twin concern with (a) ideological clarity and (b) artistic mastery. Of special interest also in the Simons article is the insight provided into the continuity of the struggle against two opposing deviations, that of dogmatism (sectarianism, schematism) on the one hand, and revisionism on the other. In any new situation, one or the other of these deviations may manifest itself in a new guise.

If in the above remarks we have had in mind especially the student of literature, we believe nevertheless that the essays have much to offer the general reader. The themes introduced are of importance to everyone. How do we use the past in the service of the present? what are the distinctions between an understanding confined to the surface and one that penetrates to deeper levels? what is the connection between the timeless and the historically specific? what do we know? by what means? how do the arts help?—these questions are not only for the specialist. The same goes for the modernism articles, with their profound comment on the nature of the modern world and elements of the breakdown of the humanist tradition. The same goes also surely for the essays in Part Three, devoted as they are to the struggle to create a new socialist reality. In offering some insight into the operation of conscious direction in the sphere of social and artistic processes, the concluding essays introduce a key Leninist principle whose influence on world history we can already see to be incalculable.

The editors will not try to express their many debts. To Eva LeRoy—translator and adviser. To Willi Beitz—senior mentor. To the Writers Union in Moscow, to many individuals in the field of literary scholarship in the German Democratic Republic (and in the other East European socialist countries, whose production was represented in an earlier, more compendious version of this anthology). Also to Temple University for its support of a kind of scholarship universities do not always approve. To the Louis M. Rabinowitz Foundation, which underwrote part of the cost of translation for this and the earlier version. To the American Institute for Marxist Studies, whose director, Dr. Herbert Aptheker, offered many kinds of indispensable support.

May, 1972

Gaylord C. LeRoy
Ursula Beitz

CONTENTS

PRESERVE AND CREATE

Essays in Marxist Literary Criticism

CURRENT DIRECTIONS

INTRODUCTION

Many signs point to the likelihood of an advance in Marxist criticism and scholarship in this country. Dissatisfaction with the existing state of affairs is widespread. At the New University Conference meetings and now even at the Modern Language Conference and elsewhere, probes are constantly being made for new radical directions. When it comes to the interpretation of our own literature, much of the work we will have to do ourselves without expecting too much help from elsewhere. On the other hand, we should know as much as we can about developments in Marxist criticism elsewhere, especially from countries where many people are devoting the major part of their time to this work. Because of the legacy of McCarthyism and the Cold War, we have a culture lag in this area of Marxist scholarship as in others. The selections presented in this anthology are offered as a sample of some of the advances now being made mainly in two leading socialist countries, the USSR and the GDR. In the introductions, the editors will attempt to indicate some highlights of the contemporary development of Marxist criticism.

The most significant difference between bourgeois and Marxist criticism has to do with the relationship between literature and reality. For Marxist criticism this is a matter of central importance. It plays a much smaller role in bourgeois criticism. A common view in the United States is that the relationship between art and reality is something each student should be free to deal with in whatever way he pleases; it is not really the concern of the critic. Questions bearing upon the real world are rather the concern of the philosopher or social scientist, or maybe of the private citizen, not the critic. His job is to describe the means through which a certain interpretation of reality is turned into art. We are dealing here with a formalist trend. Formalism has many meanings, but one of them is precisely what we encounter here, namely, a one-sided concern with the form of art as opposed to its content. The trend cannot be understood except in terms of the class character of the dominant culture. It is a trend that parallels in literary study the condition that can be somewhat more easily identified in the social sciences, where everything possible is done to make unavailable a revolutionary view of our time. This can be accomplished in the humanities by turning away from the investigation of social reality, and one of the most convenient ways to do this is to concentrate on form rather than the artistic insight, or content.

When we say that the relationship between literature and reality is important for the Marxist critic, we do not mean that one goes to literature for illustration of knowledge that can be derived just as well from other sources, from the sciences or Marxist theory, for example. On the contrary, one looks to the arts as an independent way of discovering and knowing the truth about man and society; the knowledge that comes from this source is unique and indispensable, not simply a substitute for some other kind of knowledge.

Nor is this central function of literature detachable from questions of literary form, style, construction. The old stereotype of Marxist criticism as concerned only with social and class content and neglectful of formal considerations is kept alive now mainly as part of the arsenal of anti-communist propaganda. The Marxist critic is concerned with "realized" content, that is, with content achieved through unique formal means. He is concerned, that is, not only with content but also with the formal techniques the writer uses to create character, develop episodes and scenes, find the most effective embodiment for his theme, relate elements of the work to its structure as a whole, create emphasis, and so on.

When we study the relationship between literature and reality, we can view the literary work as a "model" of the real world. The kinds of relationship between the model and what it refers to must be almost infinite. The student of literature needs to be able to tell what kind of model he is dealing with and what are the important kinds of relationship between the model and the real world. Beginning students are often clumsy when it comes to determining what the model relationship is. Conversely, a person skilled in literary interpretation senses this almost at once.

An important function of the model in "realist" literature is to communicate some grasp of the major conflicts within the individual and society and of forces that bring about social change—matters that tend to be hidden in a social formation marked by structural opaqueness. In order to determine whether a given literary work possesses such qualities as these, the critic would want to make use of whatever insights Marxist theory can contribute. This does not mean, to repeat, that he would expect to find in the literature simply an illustration of understanding that could be achieved just as well by means of the theory alone. Yet at the same time the interpretation of a literary work, with its element of discovery, will have some relationship to knowledge that comes from Marxist theory. This relationship will be varied, the insight derived from the literature being sometimes ahead of what can be learned from social theory, sometimes behind it, and sometimes obliquely related to it. (The relationship in other words will be not mechanistic but dialectical.)

In *Studies in European Realism*, Lukacs has much to say about how such writers as Balzac, Stendhal, and Tolstoy, much more than Zola, were able to grasp the essential forces of their time. In the recent work on aesthetics, he uses the concept of "defetishization" to get at the same issues.[1] Here he is making an extension of a term that Marx and Engels took over from primitive religion and used for social analysis when they talked about the attribution of magical qualities to inert objects —the fetishism of commodities or of money. Lukacs points out that in its appearance society has in fact a fetishized character; an art that does not go deeper than the surface embodies a "capitulation to fetishism." He adds that T. S. Eliot's poetry in large part represents capitulation to the fetishized world of monopoly capitalism, and he speaks of the nihilism, cynicism, despair, and mystification that commonly result from capitulation of this kind.[2] On the other hand, art may have the function of penetrating beyond the surface and thus "defetishizing" reality. He speaks of Balzac and Tolstoy as writers whose main function throughout their work was to clarify and restore the integrity of man by stripping off appearances and making the reader aware of deeper levels of truth. Lukacs proposes that the question of whether an artistic work removes the cloak of fetishism or retains it may be thought of as a main criterion for distinguishing between progressive and reactionary art. He is here getting at something similar to what Brecht had in mind when he said an important function of art was to penetrate to the causal nexus in society.

In the article on appearance and essence in the present anthology, Lukacs puts the matter in still another way. He describes it as one of the functions of art to throw some light on the relationship between what appears on the surface and underlying causation. It is a matter of exploring the relationship between appearance and essence. The goal of art, Lukacs says, is neither a faithful presentation of surface phenomena nor the rendering of an essence independent of surface. The goal rather is an all-embracing interpretation of a complex totality in which surface and essence appear in different roles as insight deepens. One expects from art both a rendering of the surface phenomena of life and some degree of penetration to the meaning that lies behind appearances.

As Mittenzwei points out in Part Three, Lukacs' formulation of the problem in terms of appearance and essence creates the danger of thinking in terms of a static reality—even a static "essence." Mittenzwei believes that in some of his work Lukacs loses sight of the fact that the deepest reality is to be understood in terms of contradiction and movement; the consequences, Mittenzwei implies, were of some moment. But that comes later.

To show the implications of an art that is able to penetrate to the causal nexus, one might examine the literary treatment of a period of economic depression. In the actual depression of the 30s many were injured by a sense of personal inadequacy, whereas in fact what was at fault had nothing to do with personal inadequacy; the fault lay in the breakdown of a particular economic system. What is needed is a literature of the depression that would make at least this feature of the causal nexus plain. This does not mean that the function of literature would be to provide an economic analysis of the breakdown of the system. If that were so, then literature would merely be illustrating truths that could be arrived at by other means (in this instance, economics). What can be expected is that in the literary study of actual men and women who endure an economic depression there should be some insight into the tragedy of self-recrimination in a situation where true causes have little to do with personal inadequacy but inhere rather in an obsolescent social mechanism. Some depression novels were able to give this kind of understanding, others not.

The case is somewhat similar with war. Is war treated as the manifestation of aggressive drives in the individual? As an upheaval in the state of nature? Or is there understanding of the degree to which modern wars have their sources either in the contradictions of the existing system or the struggle between systems, one dying, the other being born? And once again we have to repeat that what should be expected is not simply an analysis of the nature of modern war; if we asked that, again, we would be seeking in literature an illustration of modes of cognition that belong properly to other disciplines. What is wanted is a treatment of the concrete experience of the individual man in the wars of our time that will have a new quality of depth and perception because the fate of the individual is related to a grasp of the causal nexus of the life experience in which he is engaged. The same goes for fascism, whether in the Hitler-Mussolini period, or the incipient fascism in the United States today. Are the roots of fascism understood? Did Camus understand them when he wrote *The Plague?* Did Robert Penn Warren when he wrote *All the King's Men?* As above, what is wanted is not a social-historical exposition of the causation of fascism in our time. What is called for is rather that the interpretation of the lives of men and women affected by or involved in these currents of history should have the kind of depth of comprehension made possible only when the writer himself has insight into the causal nexus.

Consideration of the causal nexus leads to the concept of type. The term is used for characters in whom particular traits are combined with a high level of generalization. We can speak also of typical situations in literature; those would be marked by the same combination of the particular and the general. One would like a better term, since the typical in Marxist criticism has a meaning that conflicts with our use of the term. The typical, for one thing, has no necessary connection with the average. Hamlet, Petrov remarks in the article below, represents a grasp of the typical on the part of Shakespeare in that the central forces of the epoch were brought into conflict in his person; we see in him the collision between the past and a new and different world that is coming into being. But it is not to be supposed that this conflict was articulated in the average man of Shakespeare's age. Similarly Don Quixote represents penetration to the typical on the part of Cervantes. Here again we have the collision between two epochs in world history, the chivalric past and the utilitarian future. But again it seems unlikely that the conflict appeared in many contemporaries. On the contrary, was it not the genius of Cervantes that enabled him to penetrate to the typical of which his contemporaries were unaware? What this means is that the far-out or exceptional may serve as well as everyday experience to disclose the general significance of social conflicts or situations. If we are to understand, for example, why a protagonist behaves in a certain way in a given situation, unusual happenings may serve as well as those drawn from everyday life.

The typical does not mean the familiar, since it may well imply discovery. The writer, as was said, may be the first to disclose the typical or representative character of a certain kind of person or situation. It is not simply a matter of giving us a new insight into what is already understood. It is not a matter of giving us illustration of generalizations that we can achieve by extra-literary means. It is—or may be—an act of discovery that cannot be achieved by any other means at all. As a form of discovery, the typical may be related not only to past and present but also to the future. Discovery of the meaning beneath appearance discloses possibilities that would otherwise be unknown. Again, in some instances (and perhaps especially in the lyric) the typical may be reached through direct expression of the artist's individuality. When he expresses himself, he expresses something essential in the age. Further, the insights associated with the typical cannot be separated from the artistic context in which they appear. If one should attempt to separate them, it would be on the assumption that art serves as a convenient vehicle for a message that could also be conveyed separately.

Since all these meanings are in conflict with what is suggested by the term typical in our own literary tradition, one would welcome a different term. The closest term is the "universal," but it is not a good term to use for our purposes because it suggests the kind of unchanging reality one associates with philosophic idealism. It is hard to think of a single term that would do. What one has in mind is representative significance achieved in part though comprehension of historical change, a comprehension that cannot be reached except through the capacity to penetrate to the causal nexus.

How does the "generally human" relate to the typical? Here one has in mind behavior that persists throughout different historical epochs. We have examples in passions associated with class society, the struggle against exploitation, the Promethean theme, and the striving for freedom and happiness, on the positive side; and servility, avarice, and so on, on the negative. Surely we have significant generalizations about man in literature that deals with traits of this kind. Do these characteristics then enter into the concept of the typical? And what then about the relationship to the "universal" (a bourgeois category)? Petrov deals with these questions in his article on "The Generally Human."

Because of the concern with the reality criterion, Marxist criticism gives a good deal more stress to the element of historical concreteness than is customary in bourgeois literary study. The bourgeois outlook leads to stress on the timeless; Marxism, in contrast, gives attention mainly to the historically concrete. Of course for the Marxist critic the importance of literature that associates itself with a specific time and place is not to be made into an absolute. Literature of the first order will often have a high degree of generalization and rather little historical concreteness. Further, the proportion of historical concreteness is something that differs from period to period, genre to genre. More is expected from realist literature than from romantic, more from prose than from poetry, more from some kinds of prose than from others. Parables, maxims, and the Sermon on the Mount have a high degree of general significance and rather little built-in historical concreteness. Still, when all is said and done, it remains true that stress on the timeless is a leading feature of bourgeois criticism, as we see in the archetypal and myth criticism now in fashion. And we should never lose sight of the fact that this stress on the timeless at the expense of the historically conditioned has a class character.

It is to the *interest* of the dominant class to stress permanence, not change. In a study of Faulkner, for example, the Marxist critic would want to know among other things about the relationship of his work to an historically concrete situation in 20th-century America. How does he see the position of the Negro in this concrete context? What is his understanding of the relationship between the South and the industrial Northeast in this particular epoch of history? If Faulkner is interpreted simply as a depository of symbols having to do with the general condition of man (the myth criticism approach), these urgent questions will be by-passed. For these reasons the Marxist critic will keep coming back to his sense of the importance of taking account of the dimension of historical concreteness.

In the period of transition from romanticism to critical realism, a distinctive feature of the new movement in art was the effort to connect a visionary and perhaps timeless conception of human possibilities (as in romanticism) with the concrete circumstances of here and now. Marxists regard the change as a step forward in the development of literature. Introduction of the element of historical concreteness is one of the subjects treated in Lukacs' *The Historical Novel*. Here Lukacs studies the new historical sense that developed in the early 19th century. With the French Revolution and the Napoleonic wars, history for the first time became part of the consciousness of masses of men. Mass armies replaced mercenary armies, so that people were drawn into the events of their epoch and came to think of their own experience as historically conditioned. In the 19th century also, capitalism came to be thought of as representing an historical era in human development. Lukacs speaks of the contribution of Condorcet and Hegel to the development of thinking in terms of historical process.

The reality principle in Marxist criticism entails a break with leading assumptions of bourgeois literary study. For one thing, it requires a different approach to history. In "Past Significance and Present Meaning in Literary History," Robert Weimann takes note of the rejection of the historical method in the West during the past 30 years and sets out to reassess the possibilities of the historical study of literature. The rejection of literary history itself, he observes, is part of the larger crisis in Western society.

The New Criticism began as a formalist revolt against 19th-century positivism. There can be no question of a return to positivist assumptions, but the tradition of historical inquiry is not to be identified with its positivist variant. As an alternative to formalism, Weimann advances the conception of a dialectical approach to literary history. It will maintain a tension between past and present by exploring the unity and contradiction between past significance and present meaning. The question at issue is how the literature of the past is to relate to the present. The problem cannot be solved, it is argued, except through a rapprochement between literary criticism and historical scholarship; the past significance of a literary work is indivisible from its present meaning and its chances for survival into the future.

Weimann supports his argument with a discussion of how Shakespeare's plays are to be staged. Two common approaches to Shakespeare are necessarily unsatisfactory, he says. The first is that of the scholar-antiquarian who concerns himself mainly with the defense of the text against adaptation that might be suspected of infidelity to the Renaissance frame of reference. His mistake is to sacrifice present meaning to past significance. But equally unsatisfactory is the approach of the producer who stresses present meaning at the cost of past significance. In his work the modern tone will be certain to jar with a text "whose verbal and poetic structures are conditioned by a different system of references."

What is needed, then, is to maintain the connection between the historical and the modern point of view. The producer must have both worlds as points of reference. He must make the play as Elizabethan as is possible without abandoning its meaning for us, and as full of meaning for us as is possible without abandoning its Elizabethan character. In short, his task is to combine in a new unity the maximum amount of historical and contemporary significance.

In the discussion of two performances of *Hamlet* in the German Democratic Republic, Weimann tells of how, in the first, stress was put upon a world out of joint and on Hamlet's realization that this world must be changed. Hamlet himself came forward as a representative of a new era, not lacking in capacity for action, but held up by the question of force; he could not bring himself to use force which he had seen only in its abuse. He shrank from this and searched for a bloodless solution. Weimann's comment is that this interpretation had a great deal of present meaning but did not fit well with the text of the Renaissance play.

In the second performance, Hamlet was presented as a representative of values that were utopian in his time but have remained relevant into our own day, and he was pitted against powers frightfully evil and dangerous, as was made clear even in the interpretation of Polonius, Osric, and Rosencrantz and Guildenstern. The play presented then the contradiction between an advanced view of man and mighty powers which stood in the way of implementing this view. In this performance the past significance turned out to have maximum meaning for today without doing violence to the text.

The principle concerning past significance and present meaning would apply to literature of any genre and from any period of the past. One implication is that readings of past literature must, to some extent, differ according to time and place and with each succeeding generation. Each new performance of an historical play should have in it certain elements of discovery.

In his article on "Point of View in Fiction," Weimann deals with the question of the degree to which formalist criticism can be assimilated as part of a Marxist method. He gives an account of both the purely technical concept of "focus of narration" (use of the first person, the omniscient author, and so on) and the concept of the author's "standpoint," something having to do with the author's attitude toward his materials (ironic, detached, sympathetic, etc.). Weimann is at pains to show that if the first concept is purely technical, the second requires historical and social considerations. But he shows also that the two concepts are interrelated. The author's attitude toward his materials (the author's "standpoint") makes sense only when it is rendered through the particular focus of narration, and conversely the focus of narration becomes meaningful only as it helps to "create content," that is, to communicate the author's sense of the meaning of his materials.

Throughout the article Weimann's purpose is to show that point of view must be studied in such a way as to require reference to a given state of society in a given stage of historical development. His accomplishment is to force history and society into the field of vision of the critic. Only when the critic takes into account the inter-relationship between the social and technical points of view, he asserts, will we be able to overcome "the frustrations of forty years of formalism." The technical point of view must not be abstracted from the complex dialectic in which it operates as only one element. One cannot understand the technical point of view without understanding the narrator's relationship to the raw materials of his story—that is, to the world itself. The student of fiction, therefore, must concern himself with more than aesthetic method. He must achieve an historical perspective that will enable him to grasp the interplay between the materials of the narrative and the focus of narration. A conclusion to which the Weimann essay leads is that we can make use of a great deal of formalist criticism provided that we relate what we learn from this source to the Marxist understanding of the relationship between literature and social reality.

Since for Marxist criticism art constitutes a unique form of cognition, the question of artistic truth inevitably assumes central importance. Bourgeois criticism in its present state tends to reject the cognitive function of art. The *Journal of Aesthetics and Art Criticism* runs articles in practically every issue to demonstrate that no sane man can take seriously the cognitive function of art. The matter is always proved to the satisfaction of the writer, but then the next issue presents another article in which the matter is proved once more. This would be inexplicable if one did not understand the class character of the thinking manifested in such articles. Those who represent the outlook of an historically obsolescent class are not able to understand social reality, they do not wish to understand it, they seek to make the understanding unavailable. All this takes place generally on an unconscious level. Marxist critics, at the other extreme, seek to work with two fundamental insights: (a) Literature and the arts are important for, among other things, some kind of profound penetration into the truth of life. (b) We cannot approach the truth of art in the way we approach other kinds of truth.

Truth in general has to do with harmony between a statement or proposition and what is represented or asserted, but in artistic truth we do not usually deal with propositions. Yet one is concerned with the relationship between the second reality of art and the real world. The relationship can be of a great many kinds (as we recall if we think of art as a model). The truth may be found at many possible levels of generalization. In documentary art a fairly direct relationship between the content of the artistic work and the real world is often to be expected. But a novel commonly does not have reference to particular happenings so much as to larger social relations, historic processes, aspects of social practice, and so on. As a matter of fact even Peter Weiss' *The Investigation*, a documentary play, has a model relationship not merely to Ausschwitz but to the nature of German imperialism and the continuity between the Hitler period and the ruling class in West Germany today.

In pursuit of the model function of art, one would not generally explore the connection between details (plot, episode, character) and corresponding materials in the real world. The model character is more likely to lie in the internal structure of the artistic work—that is, the inter-relationship between character, episode, background, tone, theme and all the rest; the task, when all this has been grasped, would be to explore the relationship between this structure of materials and the structure of the segment of social reality which it interprets or in some way discovers. Obviously great tact is required of a person who is going to set out to understand first of all what the internal structure of the artistic work is and then to examine its relationship to the real world. We must keep it in mind, furthermore, that truth for the Marxist has a class character; that is, when it comes to the truth in regard to man in society, only those who are identified with an historically progressive class are able to approach an objective understanding of what the reality is. To adopt the outlook of a class whose interest requires it to impede social advance is to condemn oneself to bias and falsification. (If you want examples of bias in the social sciences and humanities, go to bourgeois scholars who think of themselves as bastions of objectivity.) Artistic truth includes aesthetic evaluation—that is, the representation of various features of social reality as attractive, contemptible, abhorrent, etc. Here again we see that the matter cannot be thought of except in terms of a class position. For a truthful aesthetic evaluation of the acquisitive entrepreneur in capitalist society, or of proletarian solidarity, a revolutionary class position is indispensable.

If, unlike most literary scholars in the American establishment, one takes the concept of artistic truth seriously, what is to be said about the subjective element in art? What about the artist's unique way of seeing, imagining, dreaming? This uniqueness (the subjective element) is often enough regarded as the main distinction of the artist; it is felt to be the secret of artistic creation, and no great effort is made to relate the subjective to its opposing principle, the objective content of art. Everyone has his own truth—that is the general assumption. Again we should take note of the class character of this view. An expression of the unrestricted relativism of bourgeois thinking in our time, it serves the interest of the dominant class by sustaining an intellectual climate in which literature cannot be taken seriously as an instrument for the discovery of truth about the real world.

The Marxist position in contrast affirms the interconnection between the subjective and objective function of art, as we see in the article by Gay. In order to discover the relationship between the truth of art and the truth of life, Gay analyzes the interplay between the subjective and the objective element in art. Throughout the article, he insists on the central role of the subjective (imagination, fantasy, etc.). Art should never be thought of as a mere copy of objective reality. At the same time, however, Gay separates himself from the position of critics who assert that freedom of the imagination is to be thought of as untrammeled. Gay sums up his point about the subjective and objective elements of art (that is, the unique creative contribution of the artist as opposed to imitation of the real world) by saying that we need a duet. Artistic truth cannot be understood apart from a dialectical interchange between subjective and objective. But we cannot speak prescriptively about the proportions, for this is an area where you get the widest variety between the two extremes.

These considerations provide Gay with a key to the relationship between truth of art and truth of life. The truth of art, he asserts, must not be thought of as identical with the truth of life. To suppose the two to be identical would lead inevitably to a tyranny of fact accompanied by the notion that the role of art is merely to supply a copy of external reality; it would mean denial of the creative principle in art. The great works of literature would then have merely the status of historical documents. But neither is it possible to consider the truth of art as wholly separate from the truth of life. Artistic illusion may penetrate to the truth of life or it may obscure or mystify it. The bond between artistic truth and the truth of life may take a wide variety of forms but can never be broken, and the nature of the bond is a matter of supreme importance. Gay breaks with bourgeois critics who sanction artistic illusion without examining the nature of this bond. If the bond becomes too twisted or fragile, we can no longer talk about a given work as having artistic truth.

Marxism has much to contribute to an understanding of advance and decline in the arts. We can best get at this if we think of the principles applicable to advance and decline in social consciousness. Historical materialism supplies us with criteria that apply. An advance in social consciousness (or at any rate the potential for such an advance) comes in periods when man's command over the processes of nature and society moves forward, generally in association with new initiatives on the part of an historically progressive class. At such times major kinds of false consciousness (those associated with religion or the feudal class structure, for example) are removed. Decline in social consciousness comes with the intensification of old forms of false consciousness or the introduction of new forms. One of the most important of these is accelerating capitalist alienation, having its source both in unforeseen effects of the spontaneous development of capitalism and in a deliberate manipulation of social consciousness on the part of the ruling class whose interests lead it to block the path of revolutionary change.

The Renaissance was a period of rapid advance in social consciousness, with the stripping away of religious and feudal modes of thinking, revolt against the intellectual dictatorship of the church, new discoveries concerning the potential for freedom and power in man and a new sense of man's responsibility for himself. The Enlightenment brought a new stage in the revolt against the dictatorship of the feudal and absolutist past with the development of philosophic materialism and the new historical consciousness associated with it. Romanticism constitutes still another period of development in social consciousness, especially as to what man has the power to achieve, both individually and collectively. In romanticism this new sense of human powers was developed largely through the imagination and communicated through image and symbol. The new awareness is to be thought of as a transformation of consciousness growing out of the age of the industrial and French revolutions. (Hence the affinity between romantic literature and certain prognoses for the literature of a socialist society.)

It is clear at the same time that the advance in social consciousness in the period of the Renaissance and of the Enlightenment is partial and qualified. It does not go beyond the false consciousness associated with a class view; the time is still far off when conditions will be ready for the leap in consciousness that comes with an understanding of the relationship between material forces in society and the capacities of the reason. In the period of romanticism, the great advance in consciousness is accompanied by a revulsion against the life-destroying feature of the emerging capitalist society. This is expressed in a retreat from problems of the real world—a retreat that leads to a new interest in nature, or to the far-off in time and place, or to a preoccupation with the supernatural. Here a certain decline in social consciousness accompanies the advance.

In the Victorian period, we have already taken note of the principle of advance in the shift from romanticism to critical realism with its effort to relate the ideal to the actual. But this is an advance offset by many trends that indicate the curbing of social consciousness, if not a decline. One of these is the shift from the effort to solve problems in the real world to an effort to solve them in the domain of art. The influence of Schiller is important here, and the art for art's sake movement is affected by this trend. Another trend is the effort to solve the problems through utopian thinking or through the establishment of isolated utopian societies. A third trend is abandonment of the search for "harmonious man." With Balzac, according to Lukacs, we witness the tendency to renounce the effort to depict harmonious man; he seeks instead to portray a "disharmonious, mutilated life, a life that mercilessly crushes and—which is worse—unwittingly distorts, corrupts and drags into the mud all that is great and beautiful in man." For some, like Balzac, capitalist society becomes "a great cemetery of murdered human genuineness and greatness." Capitalism "forces men to become either cashiers or embezzlers, that is to say, either exploited fools or scoundrels." Writers become chroniclers of an iron age. Hope for a struggle against the system collapses. Hence the profound elegiac and pessimistic note in much of 19th-century literature.[3]

With the crisis of imperialism in the last third of the 19th century, the decline in social consciousness as regards man's nature becomes the dominant trend in ruling-class culture and has remained so to the present. The entire literature of modernism shows the results of this decline, as will be seen in Part Two. But at the same time the new revolutionary movement associated with the beginnings of scientific socialism introduces an advance in social consciousness that represents one of the greatest of human achievements.

Observations of this kind are tentative and provisional. Of course it is understood that no simple connection exists between the level of achievement in the arts and advance and decline in social consciousness. In certain respects there seems even to be no advance whatsoever in the arts. Marx and Engels called attention to the fact that in some ways Homer seems never to have been rivalled. But all the same, if it is true that part of the function of art is to penetrate to the truth about reality, then movements of advance and decline in social consciousness must necessarily have an effect on artistic development. They do not tell the whole story, but they do tell something. While we are still far from a theory that will take account of the complexities of advance and decline in the arts, insights concerning changes in social consciousness that derive from historical materialism constitute one factor that has to be taken into account. The reality principle in Marxist criticism does provide some input for a theory bearing upon this question.

This survey of trends in Marxist criticism points up the need for an initiative in Marxist scholarship. The work will be done not by intellectuals separated from activism but rather by those who assume the responsibilities of the revolutionary intellectual outside as well as within the university. They have much to do. Their job is to combat ruling-class brainwashing in every area and in this way break up the almost totalitarian control of the mind; to make clear the nature of capitalist crisis and of the transitional period between capitalism and socialism; to demonstrate the difference between socialist and bourgeois concepts of democracy, equality, and freedom; to help with the definition of revolutionary strategy; and in general to demonstrate the authority of the Marxist world view and so help develop a revolutionary consciousness. Besides all this there is important work to be done in each of the university disciplines, philosophy, social sciences, literature and the arts, etc. Since all the disciplines are permeated with ruling-class ideology, the totality of the subject matter must be re-interpreted from the point of view of historical materialism. The potential of this work for breaking the hold of ruling-class ideology is boundless. In our own discipline, we have seen some of the needs. We need better understanding of history and a new concentration on the relationship between literature and history. We need a scholarship that will supply the foundation for fuller comprehension of the various insights that come from recognition of the reality principle, whether we concern ourselves with the principles of advance and decline in the arts, or the question of artistic truth, or the model character of literature.

REFERENCES

1. Georg Lukacs, *Aesthetik* (Neuwied am Rhein, 1967).
2. *Ibid.*, pp. 697-8.
3. Georg Lukacs, "Das Ideal des harmonischen Menschen in der buergerlichen Aesthetik," *Essays ueber Realismus* (Berlin, 1948), pp. 5-23.

APPEARANCE AND ESSENCE

When we want to clarify some of the most important aspects of literary creativity, immediately we are confronted with the question: what is this reality which the literary work must reflect faithfully? Here the negative part of the answer is of primary importance: this reality does not consist only of the surface of the outer world that has been perceived immediately, not only of the passing accidental appearances. While centering artistic theory on realism, Marxist aesthetics is clearly opposed to any trend which limits itself to the photographic reproduction of the immediately perceived surface of the outer world. On this question, Marxist aesthetics does not have anything radically new to say but merely raises onto the highest level of awareness what has always been the central point of theory and practice for the great artists of the past.

However, Marxist aesthetics is just as strongly opposed to another false extreme of development, namely, to the concept, born of the belief that it is wrong to copy reality, that artistic forms are independent of this surface reality. It leads to ascribing, in the theory and practice of art, absolute independence to artistic forms, to taking as an end in itself the perfection of forms or their perfectibility, and thus to become separated from reality itself, to behave independently of it, to assume the right to transform radically and to stylize this reality. This is a struggle in which Marxism continues and develops the views of the really great artists of world literature, the view that art aims at a faithful and true representation of total reality. Art is just as removed from photographic copying as from empty playing around with abstract forms.

Understood thus, the essence of art raises an important question of the theory of cognition in dialectic materialism, that of essence and appearance. Bourgeois thought and consequently bourgeois aesthetics could never solve this problem. Any theory of naturalism unites essence and appearance in a mechanistic, undialectical way and in this sad mixture essence becomes necessarily beclouded or, as in most cases, it disappears altogether. The idealist philosophers of art do sometimes see clearly the opposition of essence and appearance but lacking dialectics or because of their imperfect, idealistic dialectics they see only this opposition and are unaware of the dialectical unity of the contradictions within the opposition. (Schiller in his extraordinarily interesting and thorough aesthetic studies as well as in his poetry offers us a clear example of this problem.) In periods of decadence literature and literary theory present both of the following false trends: instead of a real investigation of essence, there is a play with superficial analogies but these analogies leave reality out of consideration just as much as in the representation of reality by idealist classical authors. Then these empty constructions are covered over with naturalistic and impressionistic details and the organically homogeneous parts are brought into a pseudo-unity through a kind of mystifying "Weltanschauung."

The true dialectic of essence and appearance rests on the fact that both are equally forces of objective reality, both are products of reality and not only of man's consciousness. However—and this is an important tenet of dialectic cognition—reality has different degrees. We have the fleeting, ephemeral reality of the surface, of the moment, and also deeper elements and trends of reality which come back repeatedly according to law although they vary with the changing circumstances. This dialectic penetrates the whole of reality in such a way that in this context essence and appearance are relative to each other: what seemed to us the essence of appearances when we were digging below the surface of immediate experience becomes with deeper analysis an appearance which conceals another, a new essence. And so on, ad infinitum.

True art, then, tends to be deep and all-embracing. It tries to seize life in its complex totality, that is, to explore at the greatest possible depth the essential forces hidden behind the appearances, but it does not represent them in the abstract, detached from the appearances or confronting them; on the contrary, art represents the living dialectical process in which essence turns into appearance, reveals itself in the appearance; it also shows the other side of the same process, when the appearance in its mobility reveals its own essence. These single impulses do not have only a dialectical movement but they also react constantly to each other, they are the impulse of an uninterrupted process. True art, then, always represents the whole of man's life, in its movement and development.

Since the dialectical creation encompasses the general and the particular in a mobile unity, it is clear that the characteristic of this creation must manifest itself also in the specifically artistic forms. Contrary to science, which separates this motion into its abstract components and aims at formulating the laws of the interaction of these elements, art brings to us this motion as motion and makes us grasp it in its living unity. One of the most important categories of this artistic synthesis is the type. It is not by chance that Marx and Engels put great stress on this concept when they defined true realism. As Engels writes, "in my opinion realism means, besides fidelity in the details, the true representation of typical characters in typical circumstances."[1]

But Engels observes that this typicality should not be opposed to the non-recurring nature of phenomena and that no abstract generalization should be drawn from it: ". . . each one is a type but at the same time a definite unique being, a 'such a one,' as old Hegel expressed it, and this is as it should be."[2]

Thus, according to Marx and Engels, the type is not the abstract type of the classical tragedy, not the form of Schiller's idealizing generalization and even less what the Zola and post-Zola school of writers and critics said it was: the average. The type is characterized by the fact that all the prominent features of that dynamic unity in which true literature reflects life run together in their contradictory unity and that in these contradictions the most important social, ethical and spiritual contradictions of an epoch are woven into a living unity. The representation of the average, on the contrary, has as a necessary consequence that these contradictions, always reflecting the great problems of the epoch, appear toned down, weakened in the soul and fate of an average man and thus lose their essential traits. In the representation of the type, in "typical" art, concreteness and conformity with law, the continuing human and the historically determined, the individual and the social are fused into unity. The most important trends of social development find an adequate artistic expression in the creation of types, in the revelation of typical characters and typical situations.

To these general remarks we must add one more point: Marx and Engels saw in Shakespeare and Balzac (and not, we shall note, in Schiller, on the one hand, or Zola on the other) the artistic realistic trend which corresponded best to their aesthetics. In extolling these eminent writers, they show that the Marxist concept of realism has nothing to do with the photographic reproduction of daily life. Marxist aesthetics requires only that the essence conceived by the writer

should not be represented abstractly, but as the essence of the phenomena in which surging life is organically hidden and out of which it
grows. But, in our opinion, it is not at all necessary that the typified
phenomenon be created out of daily life or even out of real life. That
is, even the most extravagant play of the poetic imagination, even the
farthest reaching fantasy in the representation of phenomena, is completely compatible with the Marxist concept of realism. It is not by
accident that some fantastic tales by Balzac or E. T. A. Hoffmann
count among the works which Marx rated very high.

Naturally there are different kinds of fantasy and imagination.
When we are trying to find here the principle of evaluation, we always have to return to the main thesis of materialist dialectic, the
reflection of reality.

Marxist aesthetics denies the realistic character of a world drawn
in naturalistic detail and demands that in representing this world the
essential moving forces should be expressed. Hence it takes it for granted
that the fantastic tales of Balzac and Hoffmann constitute high points
of realist literature since in them, precisely with the help of imaginative representation, these essential forces are portrayed. The Marxist
concept of realism is the realism of artistically typified essence. This
is the dialectical application of the theory of reflection in the field of
aesthetics. And it is not by accident that precisely the concept of type
is what makes this special feature of Marxist aesthetics so evident. On
the one hand, the type provides the artistic, unique solution to the
dialectic of essence and appearance; on the other, it refers back to the
socio-historical process which when it is faithfully reflected gives us
the best realist art. This Marxist definition of realism continues the
line followed by the great masters of realism, like Fielding, in their
artistic practice. They called themselves historians of bourgeois life,
historians of private life. But Marx goes farther in regard to the relationship of great realist art with historical reality and values the results
they achieved even more highly than the great realists themselves. In
a conversation with his son-in-law Paul Lafargue, the eminent French
socialist writer, he said: "Balzac was not only the historian of the society of his time but also the prophetic creator of characters who were
still at the embryo stage under Louis Philippe and who developed fully
only after his death, under Napoleon I."[3]

All these claims reveal the definite and profound objectivity of
Marxist aesthetics. According to this conception the dominant trait of

the great realist is the passionate, devoted attempt to grasp and represent reality as it objectively is in its essence. In this respect, many misconceptions are common. Some say that Marxist aesthetics underestimates the role of the subject, the influence of the subjective artistic factor in the creation of works of art. Others confuse Marx with those popularizers who are theoretically caught in naturalistic traditions and who present as Marxist the false objectivism of these traditions. But, as we saw, one of the central problems of the Marxist world view is the dialectics of essence and appearance, the revelation of the essence cleared from the entanglement of contradictory appearances. If we do not believe that the artist "creates" out of nothing something radically new but if we recognize that he uncovers an essence that exists independently of him but is not accessible to anybody and sometimes has long been hidden even from very great artists, it does not mean that the artistic creativity disappears or is even in the least diminished. Thus when Marxist aesthetics sees the main value of artistic creation in the fact that the artist stresses in his works the social process, makes it visible and accessible, when in these works the self-knowledge, the awareness of social development is portrayed, this all does not signify that the activity of the creative artist is undervalued but on the contrary that it is raised to a higher and more legitimate point than ever before.

As elsewhere, Marxism does not bring us something "radically new." Plato's aesthetics, in the theory of the aesthetic reflection of ideas, had already touched upon this problem. But Marxism puts here aesthetic truth in its correct position, after it had been thrown upside down by the great idealists. As we have seen above, Marxism on the one hand does not admit of the complete opposition of essence and appearance, but looks for essence within the appearance and for appearance in its organic relationship to essence. On the other hand, for Marxism the aesthetic grasping of essence, of the idea, is not a simple and at the same time definitive act, but it is itself a process, a movement, a gradual approach toward the essential reality, for the deepest, the most essential reality is only a part of that same general reality to which surface phenomena also belong.

REFERENCES

1. Letter to Miss Harkness, April, 1888.
2. Letter to M. Kautsky, November 26, 1885.
3. Cf. *Karl Marx als Denker, Mensch und Revolutionär*, edited by D. Rjazanov, Marxistische Bibliothek, vol. 4, (Vienna-Berlin, 1928), p. 97.

REALISM – THE GENERALLY HUMAN

A literary type will frequently give us an image of a particular person and at the same time present a generalization that applies, we might almost say, to the whole of mankind. In the type something that is common to everyone is presented in a concrete social-historical form. It is the combination of the two, the particularized social-historical person and the "universal," that explains the lasting significance of great literary creations. As Belinski remarked, human life, no matter what form it takes, is comprehensible to all because its transient forms are combined with changeless elements. In writing of Pushkin, Belinski said that the true poet, no matter what his degree of artistic importance, but more especially the great poet, does not invent something entirely new; rather, he gives artistic form to that which is common to all mankind. That is why people find in the poet's creations something that has seemed long familiar to them, or something they have felt vaguely or indistinctly pre-sensed, something for which they could not previously form a clear image or find words; the poet's contribution was to give expression to this. The reader is often surprised that it did not enter his head to create something similar, it appears so simple and easy. Writing in which people do not recognize something of their own in this way but where instead everything seems to be the creation of the poet, will not generally be of great importance.

We have here the clue to the significance of the "generally human" in literary types. The tragic love of Goethe's Werther or of Julia Saint-Pré in Rousseau's *La Nouvelle Héloïse* is particular and individual; yet, if it were only that, it would not have made all Europe weep. In *Die Leiden des jungen Werthers* Goethe presents a conflict between personality and society in the framework of the old feudal order in Germany at the end of the 18th century. But Goethe said to Eckermann that Werther does not really belong to a particular stage in the development of world culture but rather to the life development of each particular person who must find a place for himself within the oppressive conditions of an outdated world. Happiness destroyed, a career ruined, a wish unfulfilled—these are not the misfortunes of a particular epoch but of every person. We cannot agree with Goethe that the experience of Werther can be torn away so completely from a particular stage in the development of culture, specifically from the feudal order which in his time represented the outdated world; yet in the drama of Werther's love and in the problems of his developing personality, arising as they did in a particular concrete-historical context, there was in fact a significance common to all mankind. The story has meaning for contemporary man despite the fact that the historical conditions of Goethe's Werther have long since passed away. Could we not say that similar conditions exist in the "outdated world" of contemporary capitalism, though to be sure in a very different historical context?

In Goethe's Werther what is common to all mankind has a high significance which everyone recognizes. But we must not think that the generally human always appears in forms removed from everyday experience. We have it in Sancho Panza and in the grave-digger in *Hamlet*, as also in the "simple soul" of Félicité in Flaubert's story. The generally human appears in many forms, dependent on the fullness and depth of insight of which the writer is capable. Much depends upon the degree of talent and on the author's knowledge of life. Shakespeare abounds in types having this kind of universal significance. The same is true of Tolstoy (Natasha Rostova, Pierre, Andrey Bolkonsky), Turgeniev, and Chekhov.

Progressive writers have always believed that the creation of the generally human in this sense was the most important problem of their creative work. Tolstoy wrote of how even foreigners recognized themselves in the characters created by Dostoyevsky. The deeper we probe, Tolstoy said, the more familiar are the characters we create. The breadth and depth of generalization in depiction of the generally human, then, is a chief secret of literary excellence. Heinrich Heine put it well when he said that every man contains a universe which is born with him and dies with him; under every gravestone there lies the whole world history.

Some literary types of great importance, however, do not represent a phenomenon that is necessarily widespread in actual life. We do not feel that Hamlet and Don Quixote could have represented the majority of people in their time. In what sense is it correct, then, to speak of their generalizing significance? What is the representative quality in them? The generally human in types like these lies in qualities inherent in a majority of people of different historical periods but usually stifled or suppressed, often by the harshness of life under the conditions of an exploiting society.

It would be entirely wrong to associate the generally human with positive qualities alone, particularly when we are speaking of a pre-socialist society. In the society of his own day, Engels remarked, based as it was on class antagonisms and class domination, there was little possibility of manifesting purely human feelings toward other people. During the long history of antagonistic society humanity developed, side by side with positive qualities, much that was bad, warped, negative. Petty bourgeois characteristics, for example, have their national forms and yet remain traits that are to be found everywhere and in people from many different strata of the society.

Or consider Lenin's remark about Oblomov, "There was such a type, Oblomov, in Russian life. All he did was to lie in bed and make plans. A great deal of time has passed since then. Russia has made three revolutions and yet the Oblomovs are still here with us, for Oblomov wasn't only a landowner but also a peasant, and not only a peasant but an intellectual, and not only an intellectual but a worker and a Communist. It suffices to look at ourselves, the way we conduct meetings, the way we work in committees, in order to say that old Oblomov is still here and it will take a great deal of washing, cleaning, pulling about and flogging him till something good comes of him."

Oblomovism is not a phenomenon restricted to Russian life alone; it is met with in various forms in the historical development of other nations also, as for example among the French rentiers as described by Maupassant.

We must not fall into the vulgar-sociological error of thinking that the characteristics of a given person are to be related only to his own class and time. Some of the less attractive traits of man appear throughout the whole development of the pre-socialist "pre-history" of humanity from the beginning of civilization up to the present. Miserliness and money-grubbing, for example, are found in ancient literature, in Shakespeare's Shylock, Molière's Harpagon, in Pushkin's miserly knight, in Gogol's Plushkin, Balzac's Gobsec, and so on. Each of these characters bears traits of his time and class and also something that belongs to proprietary society of all periods.

In proprietary society humanity falls into the laboring masses and the exploiting classes. The private ownership of the means of production, the exploitation of man by man, the mercenary interests and the monstrous egoism of the ruling classes, the policy of oppression of the laboring masses, the social and spiritual fraud perpetrated against them, this policy carried on over a period of many centuries by the slave-owning, feudal, and capitalist state and by the church, daily created in the spiritual and moral development of millions of people all kinds of prejudices, a wolfish psychology, vices, base feelings and drives, all that Marx called "the inhuman" in man. Class society created the lackey as a particular social and moral-psychological type. With the dominance of private property, Marx said, people characteristically try to subject those around them to an alien force in order to use them for their own mercenary ends, with the result that man is constantly being degraded. A multitude of characters in world literature show us that this "inhuman man" is a typical phenomenon in the life of an exploiting society.

People commonly underestimate the degree to which inhumanity, having its main source in exploiting classes, has penetrated into the thoughts and feelings of the popular masses. "The whole people was infected with a low, servile, miserable, mercenary spirit," writes Engels about the Germany of the end of the eighteenth century. Gogol shows how serfdom poisoned the masters and slaves alike, made them witless, and debased them to a semi-beastlike existence. Or let us recall the morals and manners of the peasantry living under capitalist conditions as these are portrayed in the novels of Zola and Balzac, or in the stories of Chekhov and Bunin. The hard conditions of life and work of the popular masses, the cultural backwardness and darkness which the exploiters and the church made use of in their own interest, the corrupting influence of proprietary relations, all this contributed to the spreading of vice and prejudice among the people. Engels pointed out that even in revolutionary periods one must contend with the backwardness of the masses.

We must not be misled by false patriotism or a simplified social didactics, as used to be seen in some of our studies. Patriotic feelings did not prevent Engels from observing that traits of German philistinism could be found even in the great Goethe; Engels knew the social-historical origin of these traits and was convinced that in time they would disappear from the German character.

The human qualities in man, as Marx said, have appeared most conspicuously in the laboring classes. It was labor that made man of man, separating him from the rest of the animal world; in the later stage of evolution, it was labor that provided the source of what was most truly human in man. In the struggle against social oppression, the popular masses developed moral norms which now form the basis of the universal moral ideal. The best traits of man in every country are formed first of all among the people. Consider the way Belinski time and again wrote about the wisdom and moral fortitude of the popular masses in Russia. Despite unfavorable conditions, human qualities have been developed in the people to a measurelessly greater degree than among the ruling classes. Similarly, human qualities appeared most conspicuously among those representatives of the ruling classes who drew near to the people and responded to their influence. We have striking evidence of this in Pushkin and Tolstoy. In those historical periods when ruling classes played a progressive role, their foremost representatives reflected the hopes of the popular masses.

The history of literature makes it clear that, despite negative qualities formed in the world of exploitation, the protest and the struggle of the laboring masses brought gradual awareness of man's social essence and of his right to freedom and happiness. Spiritual qualities were formed which were to lead eventually to the attainment of true freedom with the triumph of the socialist revolution. The artistic reflection of this process is widespread in world literature.

World literature gives even greater evidence, though, of what might be called the destruction of personality, of that spiritual impoverishment of man and the unavoidable shrinking of the "I" of which Gorky wrote. Consider the destruction of man's reason, the impoverishment of soul and heart, and the pettiness in thought and feeling that have been part of bourgeois-individualistic society. Under these conditions, man has commonly lost definiteness and independence of character and has become poor, limited, egoistical. We have another example in the conception of petty-bourgeois felicity in those "happy endings" that signify compromise with life, or forfeiture of high ideals and the loss of human dignity, all of which has been portrayed for us by Chekhov.

It is impossible to imagine that those two processes took place on parallel lines which did not cross. On the contrary, throughout history, in every nation and class, and in the personality of every man, the two opposing forces struggle and clash; the human and that which is alien or inimical to it exist everywhere in a state of contradiction.

In actual life this struggle is unending; sometimes it achieves world-wide historical significance, and at other times it goes on unnoticed in the inner micro-world of some particular man. Artistic literature provides us with the opportunity of observing the concrete manifestations of this struggle in man.

A question might be asked as to whether this understanding of the generally human takes us back to bourgeois-liberal views in art and literature, especially to the notion that there exists a general essence of man apart from class and historical period. In writing of Feuerbach's conception of man's nature, Engels said that the Marxist must always bear in mind the concrete world in which a man lives and the class struggle in which he is engaged. In his article on Count Heyden Lenin said that to picture man outside the class struggle corresponded to bourgeois-liberal conceptions necessarily alien to Marxism.

But the vulgar-sociological reduction of man to what we can understand from an immediate historical class situation is also alien to Marxism. If the literary type were reduced to matters of class, then artistic works would have only an historical importance for us. What interest would we have in reading *Eugene Onegin* if the humanity and tragic experience of the poem belonged entirely to an historical situation alien to us? What interest would we have in reading of Goncharov's Oblomov, the landowner turned into a personification of idleness, if we did not find in it general truths as to how a man at any time can lower himself and stagnate and even die spiritually and morally before his physical death? What interest would we find in *Dead Souls* if it really dealt only with a land-holding, serf-owning society?

The fact is that the works of classical art exert an influence upon us because they combine universal content with concrete social-historical forms. Eventually the particulars of time and place are superseded, "aufgehoben" (in the Hegelian sense), but the universal in the literature of the past continues to live and to touch contemporary man. Marx showed this when he wrote about the riddle of Greek art and poetry. The difficulty, he said, does not lie in understanding that Greek art is connected with certain forms of social development. What is difficult to understand is that it continues to give artistic pleasure and still serves as a norm and unattainable model. In seeking a solution to this riddle, Marx observed that though a man cannot turn back to childhood without becoming childish, yet the innocence of the child may still gladden his heart and he may still wish to recapture, at a different stage, the true essence of childhood. Hence the eternal charm of an art that so wonderfully represents the childhood of human society. Marx was here describing a "generally human" quality in Greek art. He appears not to have been afraid of falling into a vulgar error.

Flaubert once voiced disapproval of Taine because the latter viewed every literary masterpiece merely as an historical document. Many of our own scholars deserve a similar reproach. The trouble is not only that they are insufficiently concerned with questions of artistic form but also that in examining the social-historical element they frequently do not see the universal content of literary types. This can only lead to an impoverishment of the classical heritage.

ROBERT WEIMANN

PAST SIGNIFICANCE AND PRESENT MEANING
IN LITERARY HISTORY

Over the last 30 years the critique of the historical method has, in the West, achieved considerable dimensions, but perhaps the time has now come to reassess the nature and the object of this critique, and from there to proceed to some reappraisal of the possibilities and limitations of literary history. If, in the United States, the historical study of literature is to achieve a new sense of direction and purpose, it must first be prepared to face (with all that this implies) the full extent of the crisis of its discipline. This crisis is in many ways a symptom of the larger crisis of Western society, in which the revolutionary idea of change, organic and dialectical concepts of evolution, and the liberal and humanist traditions of progress are all, in various degrees, affected. In recent years the consciousness of this wider background of crisis seems once more to be gaining ground, and perhaps the conjecture may be hazarded that a new interest in historical method can only benefit from an awareness of its present background. Such awareness may indeed facilitate the first steps towards reopening, in the realm of literary history, the question of method and purpose from an angle which defines itself, at the outset, beyond the assumptions of formalist criticism.

Among the recent adverse forces which the historical study of literature saw itself confronted with, the New Criticism was certainly not the least important. But while the anti-historical direction of its influence can scarcely be doubted, this does not mean that its critique of literary history did not raise a number of very important questions. Now that the New Criticism has itself become part of the history of criticism, the neohumanist and formalist revolt against positivism, as well as its consequences, can more nearly be seen in perspective. At this date we certainly cannot go back to the nineteenth-century tradition of historical philology. But for all those who have felt that the theory and practice of formalism do not offer any valid alternative, the demise of positivism can never mean the end of literary history. A new method of literary history will reject the uncritical study of sources, influences and biographical data as an end in itself; but it will

30

also refuse to accept the new critical indictment of the 'extrinsic' approach, precisely because the much recommended 'intrinsic' study of literature has shown itself equally incapable of coping with the challenge of a new literary history.

Any serious reappraisal of the aims and methods of literary history, then, would have to dispense with antiquarian as well as formalist assumptions. It would have to pursue a more dialectical method, for which the work of art, even when it imitates reality, is seen to be more than merely the reflection or expression of a past age or society. There would still be room for an approach to literature as past mimesis, but not at the cost of present morality. Thus, the customary distinction between the 'extrinsic' and the 'intrinsic' approaches would appear to be almost as irrelevant as the similar one between the pastness of the work and its present 'autonomy.' From this angle, history would then be seen as a comprehensive process which includes the present as well as the past: a process which is a continuum and as such as indivisible as the aesthetic experience, which appeals to the whole nature of man as a historical being. In this *process* and in this *nature* both the extrinsic and the intrinsic interact: change and value constitute a relationship which corresponds to a similar tension, in the work of art, between what is past and what is present. Literary history has to embrace this necessary tension, and conceive of its object in terms of both the unity and the contradiction of mimesis and morality, of past significance and present meaning.

I

As indicated, a new approach to the historical study of literature cannot pass by, and indeed must not underrate, the theoretical positions from which the New Criticism has challenged the methods of traditional literary history. This is not the place for a full survey of new critical opinion on the subject, but perhaps a few illustrations will suffice to bring out its main direction and emphasis. Even when, with some effort, the new critics would retain a grudging modicum of respect for the "intense and precise labors of the Victorian philologists

in the service of authenticity and other forms of factuality,"[1] their
rejection of historical antiquarianism was as consistent as it was complete. If this had entailed a formulated alternative in historical method,
there might have been more to be said for their polemics, especially
for their attacks on the academic accumulation of unrelated historical
facts, and even their scarcely concealed scorn for those mechanistic
"exercises relating literature to various kinds of influence—social, political, economic, climatic, national, regional, traditional, psychological, and genealogical."[2] Such polemics, of course, were almost as vigor-
ous in Britain and Europe, as in F. R. Leavis' protests against "the
usual compilation . . .—names, titles, dates, 'facts about,' irrelevancies,
superficial comments, and labor-saving descriptions."[3]

These attacks (which were also aimed at "the verbose inanities of
tendencies," historical *Zeitgeist*, etc., and which were echoed by a good
many literal critics) are too well-known to call for further documentation. They were all more or less explicitly based on certain theoretical
assumptions which, reduced to their common denominator, can perhaps best be phrased negatively: They saw "the great mistake of the
scientific-historical scholarship" in the fact that it "had allied itself
with the physical sciences of the nineteenth century."[4] The most dis-
reputable symptoms of such *mésalliance* were diagnosed in "the whole
underlying assumption that literature should be explained by the methods of the natural sciences, by causality, by such external determining forces as . . . *race, milieu, moment*."[5] Such 'scienticism,' it was
argued, was behind both the "study of causal antecedents and origins"
and the use of "quantitative methods of science: statistics, charts, and
graphs."[6]

Again, this is not the place to open the vast question of the relation of historical scholarship and natural science, and in any case an
answer to this question would have to show, as many scholars and
critics have done, that literary criticism is not an exact science. But
even though the early battle in "the revolt against positivism" was in
many ways justified, later new critical polemics tended both to com-
placency and to ingenuousness. Even while the enemy was routed, the
attacks continued to be directed at a straw man who supposedly still
believed in the methodological identity of history and mechanical
physics. Although positivism was dead, its specter was not allowed
to find rest. These polemics, which served as a comfortable *alibi* for the
anti-historical bias of the newer criticism, were questionable in several
respects.

In the first place, the attack against the mechanistic aspects of nine-teenth-century literary scholarship never paused to consider that the tradition of historical inquiry was much older than, and never solely identical with, the pseudo-scientific pose of some latter-day philologists. The rise of historical criticism can (roughly) be traced in the decline of the social and theoretical presuppositions of natural law, and dates from, say, Vico's *La Scienza Nuova* (1725), the work of Leibniz, Shaftesbury, the French enlightenment and, in its fully de-veloped form, from Herder's *Ideen zur Philosophie der Geschichte der Menschheit* (1784/91). It finds its mature expression in Goethe's own "sense of the past and the present as one," for him a "powerful and overwhelming feeling," which could hardly "be expressed wonder-fully enough."[7] This is a poet's statement which corresponds to Schiller's attempt, in his theory of *Universalgeschichte*, "to connect the past with the present": "das Vergangene mit dem Gegenwärtigen zu verknüp-fen."[8] From here, through Hegel, this tradition of historical thought branched off in two directions. On the one hand there was the *geis-teswissenschaftliche* idealism of Dilthey and the later historians of *His-torismus*, Ernst Troeltsch and Friedrich Meinecke, whose philosophy of history certainly contained elements of irrationalism, but not of mechanism. On the other hand it was, in the context of revolutionary materialism, carried on by Engels and especially Marx, who in his well-known comment on classical Greek art argued that certain great works of art can only arise at an early or undeveloped stage of social develop-ment, and that "the charm of their art for us" is not opposed to their historical origins; so that the true "difficulty" of the historian's task lies not in the fact that "the Greek epic and Greek art are connected with certain social forms of development," but rather that these works of art "still offer aesthetic pleasure to us and in some respect serve as norm and unattainable standard."[9]

It was an illusion, therefore, to assume that the indictment of phil-ological positivism could refute the tradition of historical inquiry at large. At the time when Hippolyte Taine was developing his deter-minism in terms of the *moment*, the *race* and the *milieu* (1863), the more dialectical concepts of historical criticism were perhaps over-shadowed by what Nietzsche contemptuously called the reign of "that blind force of facts"[10] but they certainly had not ceased to be avail-able. There was, from the point of view of method, a tradition in which "the past and the present" could be considered "as one" and in which the present "charm" (and meaning) of great art, its norm

and standard, might well be reconciled with a thorough understanding of its past genesis.

If it was undiscriminating to charge the historical approach with
the abuse of "the methods of the natural sciences," then it was no less
questionable, in the fourth decade of the twentieth century, to conceive of these methods solely or mainly in terms of nineteenth-century
ideas of causality and such mechanistic assumptions as "that the world
was reflected with perfect literalness in the will-less mind of the observer."[11] Again and again the literary historian was warned to keep
away from the methods of science—but of a science which was hope-
lessly out of date. Nor was there, on the side of the critics, any cu-
riosity as to whether the method of historiography itself had not (like
that of modern science) developed considerably. By now to condemn
the writing of history on the charge that it adopts the methods of the
natural sciences (*which* "natural sciences"?) has become meaningless,
if not downright complacent. At any rate (and this is not the place
to say more) it ignores a great deal in modern physics; for instance
the tendency among physicists in recent years to speak of their science
in terms which (as a distinguished historian notes) suggest an "identity of aim between scientists and historians" and even "more striking
analogies between the physical universe and the world of the historian."[12] It may be that in the light of such statements and recent
insights into the nature of "the two cultures" (and how "dangerous"
it is "to have two cultures which can't or don't communicate"[13]) the
responsible literary critic will have to be more and more wary of stressing the irreconcilability of the two disciplines.

To say this is not to minimize the basic differences in method, and
is emphatically no apology for positivism, but it may help us to recover
a more sober perspective, from which the nineteenth century's "serene
unification of scientific conscience" can be viewed with less ambiguity
than Cleanth Brooks betrays in the context of this phrase. Whatever
its shortcomings, historical philology was the intellectually most coherent movement in nineteenth-century scholarship, and it is with some
feeling of respect that one would wish to see *the necessary criticism*
based on more facts and less arrogance. It would take more detailed
investigation into the method and practice of nineteenth-century literary history to assess the degree to which the attempts at historical
syntheses were actually thwarted by the pseudo-scientific pose. Not
that the "blind power of facts" (Nietzsche) can ever be admired again,

but on the basis of a recent study of traditional literary history in America[14] one is inclined to think that the really important works are less seriously affected by the mechanism of uncritical research than is commonly assumed by the critics of positivism. A sober reassessment of these works (some of which, by the way, are eminently readable) would, among other things, reveal a startling contrast to the much more analytical and experimental prose of the New Criticism.[15]

If the new critical attitude towards historical scholarship was somewhat ambiguous, it was also, of course, not uniform. The various critics reacted rather differently, and there were quite a number of protests (some of them undoubtedly sincere) "that the literary historian and the critic need to work together" and that both functions should, ideally, be united "in one and the same man."[16] But, as the main works in the tradition of historical inquiry were generally treated with more condescension than knowledge and as their results were, in the practical business of criticism, usually ignored, such protests often rang hollow. So whereas the critics did not offer any theoretical alternative, there developed and spread a climate of critical opinion in which historical scholarship seemed *per se* hostile to critical evaluation. Likewise, the genetic approach seemed *per se* to be an expression of relativism; the study of the writer's background and biography seemed *per se* to be a symptom of the "intentional fallacy"; etc. As in the forties and early fifties the New Criticism reaped its academic triumphs and one scholarly journal after the other thinned the volume of its historical contributions, it must have appeared to many that the study of literary genesis could only detract from and never add to the critical approach to literature as a serious art form. Small wonder, when even the most thoughtful observers approached the relations of "History and Criticism" as "something unavoidably problematic, part of a troublesome opposition which runs through all our experience."[17] Such an opposition was in many quarters not merely taken for granted; it was justified by, and elaborated into, the theory of "absolute" criteria of evaluation. It was an "absolutism" by which the (undoubted) "relativism" of the traditional literary historian was, unfortunately, not overcome but relegated to a series of opposites, among which change and value, development and order, history and aesthetics, past significance and present meaning, appeared more irreconcilable than ever before.

II

However, it would be a gross over-simplification to imply that the new critical critique of traditional literary history was entirely based on a series of formalist fallacies. Nor would one wish to minimize the extent to which the virtue of close textual analysis can survive the decline of the dogma of the autonomy of literature, thereby making a very considerable contribution to the most recent *rapprochement* of literary criticism and historical scholarship. And in the work of critics such as F. R. Leavis, Yvor Winters and Kenneth Burke, these possibilities reach as far back as the thirties and forties. For whatever the degree of the failure of the New Criticism in the field of literary history, even in its heyday a number of serious issues were raised and several very penetrating questions were asked, which a new approach would not wish easily to dismiss.

Among them, the question of relevance was foremost. Inspiring the attack on historical antiquarianism, it asserted the need for a new consciousness of "the relation between antique fact and poetic value."[18] The simplest and the most straightforward form in which the problem was posed was one in which the purpose of literary history was defined from the angle of the present. A history of English literature, F. R. Leavis wrote, "will be undertaken because the works of certain poets are judged to be of lasting value—of value in the present."[19] From this position, which may be said to stress one aspect of one basic truth, the need for evaluation was articulated with a new sense of urgency: If the criteria for a history of literature somehow correspond to a living system of values, then an awareness of these values would indeed seem to be *one* prerequisite for historical studies. F. R. Leavis (without bothering much about the emphasis carried by our cautious italics) put this quite bluntly: "Such a history, then, could be accomplished only by a writer interested in, and intelligent about, the present. It would, for one thing, be an attempt to establish a perspective, to determine what of English poetry of the past is, or ought to be, alive for us now."[20]

The strength of this position consisted in the fact *that* (not in the

method *how*) the literature of the past was related to what was felt
to be "alive" in the present. When the interests of contemporary literature can find an echo in the literature of the past, then there needs
must exist some community of poetic values (and, we should add, of
historical moments). Even when this community was defined solely in
terms of "modern" values, it comprised, and had to be defined in terms
of, a sense of tradition. But then, again, "tradition" was taken as a
mode of relating (rather than *correlating*) past poetry to present practice. F. R. Leavis and most of the new critics still behaved as if their
literary history virtually had the choice between past significance and
present meaning—*their* choice being, of course, in favor of the latter.

The result, even though it satisfied current aesthetic assumptions,
was not very helpful in establishing criteria by which a new approach
to literary history might have prospered: F. R. Leavis' *The Great
Tradition* (1948) just as Cleanth Brooks' *Modern Poetry and the Tradition* (1947) yielded the proof that by and large the historical community of values had been defined solely in terms of "modern" meaning. Here were two accomplished critics, both of them certainly "interested in, and intelligent about, the present," and both venturing into
literary history, but with a result that somehow defeated the very aims
and functions of this discipline. To be sure, neither critic had intended
to write anything like a history of the English novel or a history of
English poetry—as they are "or ought to be, alive for us now." But the
historical elements of tradition which they recommended were so much
at odds with the history of English literature as an actual process of
possibilities (a process, that is, of both developments *and* values), that
not even the rudiments for a future synthesis of history and aesthetics
were laid. (In this, Leavis and Brooks followed the critical theory and
practice of T. S. Eliot, who however—interestingly enough—had defined the idea of tradition much less exclusively and more 'historically,'
when he said that tradition involves "the historical sense" with its "perception, not only of the pastness of the past, but of its presence."[21])

To take up only one example, the criteria by which Leavis defined
the great tradition of the English novel were not merely narrow and
exclusive, but also confusing. To dismiss, usually in the form of a footnote, Defoe (without mentioning *Robinson Crusoe*) as well as Thack-
eray, Scott and Hardy may perhaps be legitimate for one who wishes
to bring out the undoubted greatness of George Eliot, Henry James
and Joseph Conrad. But in this context to introduce such concepts as

"historical importance" or "the important lines of English literary history" is entirely to beg the question not merely of literary history, but of a workable synthesis of criticism and history. If Leavis states his "reason for not including Dickens in the line of great novelists" and then proceeds to assure us that he is "a great genius and is permanently among the classics";[22] if he gives a mere "note" to Emily Brontë "because [her] astonishing work seems to me a kind of sport," and then continues to say that "out of her a minor tradition comes . . .";[23] if Fielding is rejected as "simple" and then is said to have "made Jane Austen possible by opening the central tradition of English fiction"[24] —then there must be something wrong with a criticism which conceives of "tradition" not historically, not as a process of both developments *and* values, but in terms of three or four major modern novelists. Again, the complex relationship between past significance and present meaning is overlooked. It is ignored or replaced by a concept of tradition which can conceive of no unity and of no living interplay between the past world of the English novel and its present reception, but which judges everything in terms of "the significant few" major novelists. (Leavis touches on the real problem, which he prefers not to go into, when he says: "To be important historically is not, of course, to be necessarily one of the significant few."[25])

But to raise these objections is not to dispute the relevance of a concept of value, which (for Leavis) is seen "in terms of that human awareness . . . of the possibilities of life."[26] Nor can such a concept of value be anything but critical; that is, it will evaluate the literature of the past not "as a record of past customs, past habits, past manners, past fashions in taste,"[27] or anything which is in the nature of a museum. If, as the New Criticism was perfectly justified to insist, literature is properly understood as literature and not as a medium of sociological reference and exemplification, then indeed the poetic value of a work of literature is not easily to be abstracted from its ideological or biographical significance. To elucidate the latter is not in itself identical with an awareness of the former. And to achieve this awareness, it is certainly not enough to assume "that the specific problem of reading and judging literature is completely met in the process of learning the meaning of words, the political and philosophical allusions, the mental climate in which the poem originated, etc., etc."[28]

The most valuable contribution of the New Criticism, then, was to raise (if not to answer) the question as to the function and the criteria of literary history. To stress the need for evaluation involved an awareness of both, the necessity of selection and the importance of achieving a point of view from which to select and hence to evaluate. In the words of W. K. Wimsatt: "We are bound to have a point of view in literary criticism, and that point of view, though it may have been shaped by tradition, is bound to be our own. . . . Our judgments of the past cannot be discontinuous with our experience or insulated from it."[29] The realization of one's own point of view as both distinct from, and shaped by, the past finally called for a recognition that the object of evaluation was (just as its 'subject,' its ego) part of a more comprehensive process of tradition and experience. Such an approach could conceive of history not only "in its several antecedents or causal relations to the writing of literature" but it could also raise the question "whether antecedents themselves, if viewed in a certain light, do not become meanings."[31]

But to answer this question already involved a break with the formalist dogma of the autonomy of the work of art. This paved the way towards the more recent *rapprochement* between literary criticism and historical scholarship which reveals the extent to which the virtues of close textual analysis can survive the decline of formalism. The inevitable compromises so characteristic of the late fifties and the sixties, need not detain us here. Obviously there are plenty of ways and means through which historical concepts such as, say, the author as "The Necessary Stylist" (Mark Spilka) can be reintroduced, and the whole question of rhetoric can be smuggled into the discussion of the purists. Once the "implied author" is conceived as a "core of norms and choices," a "choosing, evaluating person" who attempts "consciously to impose his fictional world upon the reader," the "strategy of point of view" (Percy Lubbock) can no longer be divorced from the world of history and sociology. This is a far cry from the formalist ghost of "the affective fallacy"; and even though *The Rhetoric of Fiction* still dismisses the "social and psychological forces that affect authors and readers," it again points to what is potentially the historical meaning in the narrative structure of point of view. Similar tendencies have for some time been noticed in the interpretation of imagery, another domain of formalist interpretation, where there is a tendency to widen the scope of the term image and to stress its subject-matter or "tenor" as opposed to its "vehicle," the real subject of the discourse as opposed to the adventitious and imported image.[32] It surely is a sign of the times when a critic of the stature of W. K. Wimsatt produces a historical monograph on the portraits of Alexander Pope, or when Cleanth Brooks, former explicator of "paradox" and "irony," now writes at great length on the geographical theme and background of Yoknapatawpha County. To recognize "that a writer's choice of a subject is an aesthetic decision"[33] prepares the way for a deeper understanding of history as part of the literary theme. The renewed interest in thematics, like that in poetic, personality and rhetoric, is an indication of far-reaching transitions and changes in critical doctrine. Themselves part of history, they reopen the neglected dimensions of change and society by which literary history can now be discussed more profitably in terms of what it can and what it cannot accomplish.

III

A dialectical approach, which is conscious of its own social function, will have to consider the problem of literary history from an angle where literature *is* history, and history is an element of literary structure and aesthetic experience. What is needed is not simply an act of combination between the literary historian's approach ("A is derived from X") and that of the critic ("A is better than Y"). It is not good enough to have—in F. W. Bateson's sense—a "more intimate co-operation" of their efforts, or anything less than an integration in method and purpose. To say that the historian is concerned with a task like "A is derived from X" is in itself a somewhat superficial formula; but even if this is read as a symbol of the genetic approach, it will not do merely to combine or to *link* the study of genesis with the critical evaluation of the art-work. One has to be contained in the other, and the historical sense of the critic needs to be quite indistinguishable from the critical sense of the historian.

A postulate like this may sound presumptuous and, perhaps, over-optimistic, but really the object and the function of literary history can demand no less. Let us for a moment ask the question: What *is* the object of the literary historian as critic? Is it the work of art as it is experienced today? Or is it the work of art in *statu nascendi*, in the contemporary context of its genesis and original audience? To ask the question is to draw attention to both the unity and the contradiction of the past world of the art-work and the present world of its reception; or, in other words, to suggest that the historian's task (and the pastness of the work) cannot be separated from the critic's task (and the work of art as a present experience). Obviously, we cannot afford to isolate these two necessary aspects: Merely to do the former is to fall back into some kind of antiquarianism; merely to do the latter is to run all the risks of misunderstanding and distortion that the New Criticism was guilty of so often. The one alternative will finally reduce literary history to a study of origins and influences, a mere *Entstehungsgeschichte;* the other reduces the discipline to a series of modern appreciations, a mere *Wirkungsgeschichte.* Neither is (as an alternative) acceptable: In the last resort, for literary history to study past significance makes no sense without an awareness of present meaning, and an awareness of present meaning is incoherent without the study of past significance.

Thus the object of the literary historian as critic is necessarily complex. It involves both genesis and value, development and order, the work of art as a product of the past and the work of art as an experience in the present. To stress these two dimensions of the art-work in terms of their interrelationships is to argue for more than just expediency (in the sense that an awareness of history might prevent us from making a mistake or overlooking an anachronism in interpretation). The point that has to be made is not that the historian (or the critic) had better do his job thoroughly. The point is that these two dimensions are inherent in the work of art, and that the study of genesis and the pursuit of evaluation find an equivalent in the similar relationship, which is a historical *and* an aesthetic one, between the mimesis and the morality of the work of art itself. Or, to make this point from a somewhat different angle, one might refer to two basic functions of literature: On the one hand the work of art as a product of its time, a mirror of its age, a historical reflection of the society (to which both the author and original audience belonged). On the other hand, it is surely no idealism to assume that the work of art is not merely a product, but a 'producer' of its age; not merely a mirror of the past, but a lamp to the future. Incidentally, it was Karl Marx who pointed out that art is one of the "besondre Weisen der Produktion"[34]—the "special forms of production"—in the sense that the work of art can produce its audience, and influence their values and attitudes.

In order to distinguish these two basic functions of literature one might call them, although this is to over-simplify, the mimetic and the moral. (The over-simplification does not bring out that actually each is correlated to the other: the moral element is implicit in *mimesis* as representation, just as the sensuous nature of representation and imitation points to the only process through which morality can be translated into art.) But if we for the present purpose accept this convenient distinction of terms, it may be said that the twofold function of art calls for a corresponding activity of the historian as critic and of the critic as historian. Once the work of art is seen as both imitation and creation, it must be conceived as not merely a product of the past, but also as a 'producer' of the future. And while the former function is involved in the genesis (and is rooted in the past world of the artwork), the latter function is realized in both the past world and the present world of its reception: It is rooted in a creative capacity for 'production,' which transcends the very time and age that are object of the *mimesis*. Thus, the 'mimetic' (the historical) and the 'moral' (the ever present) functions interact: The literary historian as critic approaches an object in which *Zeitlichkeit* and *Überzeitlichkeit*, time and 'timelessness,' can be fused into one.

This is the very stuff that literary history is made of. The past significance of the work of art, its background and origins, is in the last resort indivisible from its present meaning and its survival into the future. The literary historian is confronted with more than the coexistence of these aspects: he has to face both their contradiction and unity. But to say this is not to make a new and particularly sophisticated demand on the historian of literature. Eventually, this is the same problem that, some 350 years ago, Ben Jonson faced, when he paid his highly complex tribute to his dead rival's work as "a Monument, without a tomb"; Shakespeare's work, he said, was "for all time," but at the same time (or even before this) he also remarked that Shakespeare was the "Soul of the Age."[35] Jonson's epitaph can hardly be said to anticipate the systematic approach of a modern literary history, but the basic problem, which is a dialectical one, is there quite clearly. It is the problem of origin and survival or, in a different light, of a great work as the product of its age and the 'producer' of its future. For the modern literary historian to grasp the dialectics of *Zeitlichkeit* und *Überzeitlichkeit* calls for an awareness of the art-work as having both a past and a present dimension (as well as a present and a future existence). And it calls for a perception from this awareness, that these dimensions are, as an object of literary history, simultaneous in their interaction and tension.

The task of the literary historian, consequently, cannot be abstracted from either the genetic or the functional aspects of literature. For the historical study of origins helps to assess the continuity of, or the degree of change in, its social functions; while the study of its present functions can, in its turn, help us to appreciate the potential richness of the original constellation of its origin. In this sense, history can be studied as meaning: the structure of the work of art is potentially inherent in its genesis, but in society it becomes functional only in terms of a human and social experience. Structure is intimately linked up with both its genesis and its affective relations, yet more than either. It is correlated to both its past genesis and its present functioning, and to work out the full measure of this correlation is to become conscious of the necessary complexity of structure as history.

IV

But to discuss this correlation in terms of history and aesthetics yields only very general results which do not by themselves suggest a more practical application of theory. In order to illustrate some of the issues involved, we propose to raise the problem in the more practical context of the historical, critical and theatrical interpretation of Shakespearean drama. Although here the gulf that separates the critical and the historical approaches has in recent years been considerably narrowed, there still exist an astonishing number of conflicting assumptions as to what are the aims and methods of literary inquiry into a great work of the past. Among these, the unresolved tension between past genesis and present meaning looms large, although as a problem of method it has hardly been perceived or discussed.

At the risk of repetition, the basic problem may perhaps again be phrased in terms of the question which we have asked above: What is the object of a historical and critical approach to Shakespeare? What does the literary historian as critic mean when he refers to *Hamlet?* Presumably the answer would still be quite different according to whether the person in question would wish to stress the importance of historical research or the priority of critical judgment. On the one hand (in terms of historical research) the answer would preferably be: the Renaissance play. Hamlet, according to this approach, will be a historical figure, the play's message an Elizabethan one in the sense that its past significance is to be explored without (explicit) reference to its modern meaning. On the other hand (and this would be the more critical approach) the answer would involve a different object which is primarily related not to the Elizabethan theater or even the Elizabethan text, but to the modern sensibility that it is meant to evoke. From this angle, an interpretation (or a theatrical production) would be authentic as long as it achieves the tone and tenor of our own age: Hamlet will be a modern symbol and the play's message a contemporary one in the sense that in the last resort its present meaning has priority over its past significance.

Actually, the two points of reference may not be so diametrically opposed, but the contradiction involved is an objective one. No matter what the approach is, there remains a historical text in the hands of modern readers (or actors); on the one hand the Elizabethan context and meaning, on the other the modern understanding and interpretation. There is no getting away from this inevitable tension between the historical and the modern points of view, and no one-sided solution is feasible. The most learned and historically-minded scholar cannot physically become an Elizabethan; he cannot recreate the Globe or visualize the original production. Even if he conceived of Shakespeare's drama as being enacted in the theater, he would still be influenced by his own experience of the modern stage, its twentieth-century audience and actors and their social relationships that are quite different from those which, in Shakespeare's Globe, then constituted part of the play's meaning.

The underlying contradiction is not an academic one, and the more we think of it in terms of practical interpretation (including the theatrical interpretation of Shakespeare on the modern stage) the clearer the theoretical implications will emerge. Since today it is just as impossible to understand Shakespeare without a modern interpretation as it is to have an interpretation without Shakespeare, we cannot proceed from either a genuine Elizabethan production (and this already contained an interpretation of the text) or from one which makes us believe that *Hamlet* is a modern play. Today *any* Shakespeare interpretation has to come to terms with the tension between historical values and modern evaluations. But this contradiction is not necessarily frustrating, and the way it is solved constitutes the most essential decision of both historical criticism and serious theatrical interpretation. Viewed from the angle of the drama as work of the theater, this contradiction involves an inevitable tension between the mimetic (or expressive) and the affective aspects, between the significance of what Shakespeare's work reflected or expressed in plot and character, and the changing impact of this on the affect of the contemporary spectator. But to recreate the mimetic and the expressive dimensions is impossible without reference to Shakespeare's world and his intentions; to reassess their affective and moral effects is impossible without reference to our audience and our world.

For the literary historian and critic the question, then, is not *whether or not* to accept both worlds as points of reference, but rather *how* to relate them so as to obtain their maximum dimensions. To put it like this may appear provocatively superficial, but to resolve the contradiction one cannot minimize the conflicting elements when each is —in its different world—so inevitable and necessary. The "maximum dimensions," then, can mean no more and no less than this: To have as much as possible of both historical significance and contemporary meaning merged into a new unity. Of course there is no easy formula as to how this synthesis of historical values and modern evaluations can be achieved. But in order to grasp its dialectic, it is as well to remember that it is not entirely a case of opposites. On the contrary, it would be a grave mistake to overlook those many points of contact and identity, where, say, Shakespeare's Renaissance values can today be considered valid. This area of identity or interaction, however, is not simply given; it will be enlarged from a contemporary point of view which can conceive its own social direction as historical in the sense that it affirms both the revulsions and the links of contact between the past and the future. In the last resort this relationship involves a social and a methodological position from which both the change and the continuity can be accepted as part of a meaningful movement in history. In the present reception of Renaissance drama, therefore, the area of identity will radically differ between, say, a Marxist interpretation and one based on the premises of Jacques Maritain's neoscholasticism. Where the Renaissance heritage is not repudiated, there is bound to be a wide range of living contact, so that the "historical" element can be viewed as part of a wider configuration in which the present reproduction of past art is one way of bringing about a meaningful future.

Nor is this area of identity, which of course is also one of humanity and derives from man's anthropological status, confined to the Renaissance tradition. We are all, the great dramatists of the past, their contemporary producers and critics, characters in history; our own points of reference are, like our predecessors', products of history. In this, our present values emerge from the same historical process which is both reflected in, and accelerated by, Shakespeare's contribution. This is quite obvious in the history of literature which can only be written in reference to a scheme of values that (among other things) has to be abstracted from its great objects, including Shakespeare's dramas. Their greatness has been confirmed by the very contribution they have made in furnishing us with criteria by which to judge, and to judge not only modern plays but also the history of the drama as a whole.

Since such area of identity may be accepted as given, the relationship between Shakespeare's vision and its modern perspectives cannot simply be described as one of conflict or opposition. The difference between his world and ours is obvious enough, but it does not exclude some kind of concurrence. As Arnold Kettle has remarked, "the best way to emphasize the value of Shakespeare in *our* changing world is to see him in *his*, recognizing that the two worlds, though very different, are at the same time a unity."[36] This unity is at the basis of all our veneration for Shakespeare; without it, the impact of his work would not be possible. At the same, this unity does not preclude a contradiction which is at the basis of all our conflicting interpretations. In very much over-simplified terms: the unity creates the need of our interpretations of *Shakespeare;* the contradiction accounts for the need of our *interpretations* of Shakespeare. But actually each is contained in the other, and the interpretation as a whole can only succeed when these two aspects are inextricably welded into one. (By himself the modern historian can, as we have seen, according to his point of view either enhance or reduce the sphere of unity or the area of contradiction, but he can never entirely annihilate either.)

Once this relationship (although here still over-simplified) is understood more deeply, the historical study of literature has gained at least two negative standards of evaluation, but they may have some practical use for judging not only the literary but also the theatrical interpretation of the great drama of the past. For in the theater as elsewhere, the modernized classic is no more acceptable than the museum version. This may not be saying anything new, but perhaps it helps to recover certain assumptions which might prove practicable to both the theater director and the historical scholar. If the rift between them could thus be narrowed, the present theatrical reception of Shakespeare need be neither academic nor irresponsible. In modern Shakespearean productions, then, Hamlet need not become a hippy in order to convince, nor would it be necessary, as Martin Walser thinks it is, to produce "the old play" in order "to show us what things were like formerly." If the past can be conceived neither in its identity with, nor in its isolation from, the present, a historical perspective could evolve which might be both theatrically effective and convincing to the scholar. No topical effects are wanted, but a sense of history which can discover permanence; the past in the present but also the present in the past. Hence the 'timeless' would result through a sense of time and history. It is in this sense that Shakespeare is "for all time" precisely because he was the "Soul of the Age." In this view, a historical vision can be made to yield a contemporary meaning. Its past significance was achieved because, at the time, it was contemporary and *then* incorporated the experience of the present. The meaning of literary history today can best be discovered through this past present, or that part of it which—although past—is still present and meaningful in a contemporary frame of reference. Thus, past significance and present meaning engage in a relationship which, in its interdependence, may illuminate either—the past work as against its present reception, and the contemporary interpretation against the historical significance of the work of art.

V

These points of method and evaluation open up a host of practical questions which do not very well bear a generalized treatment. Instead, two examples may perhaps serve which, despite their obvious limitations, can illustrate some of the more immediate problems of

producing Shakespeare's meaning from a specifically modern perspective. The illustration is taken from the GDR, the play is *Hamlet*, the
theatres being Deutsches Theater, Berlin (formerly Max Reinhardt's)
and Stadtische Theater, Karl-Marx-Stadt. Their productions of *Hamlet*
were first presented in 1964 and were still running in 1966. Nor were
they the only productions of *Hamlet* in this country.

Let us first look at the Berlin production (directed by Wolfgang
Heinz). Even before its flexibly managed stage was revealed in black,
with a huge tapestry in the rear displaying a Boschian vision of a world
'out of joint' a reading of the play's story was printed out like a sub-
title on an oversized play-bill attached to the front curtain. There it
was announced as "a tragedy which shows how Hamlet, called upon
to avenge the murder of his father, comes to learn that he lives in a
murderous world; how he begins to understand that this world has
to be changed, and how and why he is defeated." Although this syn-
opsis seemed reminiscent of some of Brecht's epic devices, the general
style of the production was more conservative, yet straightforward and
lucid. As the first scenes unrolled, it became clear that the "state" was
shown "to be disjoint and out of frame" (I,2,20) with "some strange
eruption" (I,1,69) imminent. Against this Hamlet (Horst Drinda) entered as the representative of a new era, and his task was not conceived
to be premature. Nor was his frame of mind that of a coward or a
weakling. On the contrary, his capacity for action and self-defense
was stressed; this was especially so in the "To be or not to be" speech
which was delivered with sword in hand by a man determined to meet
the danger of a possible ambush. Nor did the physical preparedness
exclude the inward concentration and self-searching; these were
brought out by the other great monologues, and also in his encounter
with the ghost: The ghost, in shining black armour, stood right behind Hamlet who, in a trance of intuition and surprise, himself spoke
the words that are assigned to the spirit. But as the Prince was so noble
in mind and full of fortitude, why then did he delay the "eruption"
that was so ripe? The answer, as the production suggested it, was not
quite convincing: Hamlet's problem turned out to be that of how to
use the force which had been known to him only by its abuse. He
shrinks away from it, searches for a bloodless solution and thereby
misses his opportunity. Feudal Fortinbras, the unprincipled warrior
who has no such scruples, can take over.

Although this concept was brought across with an admirable intelligence which allowed for both precision and pathos, the production got itself entangled into several contradictions. The Danish court, Horatio and the soldiers were all conceived in close reference to the Renaissance text. So was Hamlet, except for the interpretation of his central dilemma. To discuss the strategic use of force may yield excellent lessons, but here it amounted to a modern perspective which did not square with the Renaissance vision. It was, partly, a case of moral versus mimesis, and the modern interpretation could not find room enough in the structure of the play itself. Consequently, two passages from *Measure for Measure* had to be grafted upon Schlegel's text, and the play had to come to an end *despite*, rather than *through*, Fortinbras' arrival. (If you assume that Shakespeare's age is one in which "the ruling feudal class" is ripe to be overthrown, a triumphant feudal usurper must indeed be embarrassing.) But as the *historical* assumption was questionable in the first place, its *dramatic* correlative could not be discovered in terms of Shakespearean mimesis and expression. Consequently, *in this aspect* a modern perspective (and the contemporary "affect") had to be produced against, rather than from, the Renaissance intention and expression.

Apart from that, the Berlin production contained many admirable things; the fine ensemble acting and a swift sense of movement produced beautiful results in such moments as the play within the play, which—as most of the larger court scenes—was satisfying in many respects. In this, the larger stage of the Deutsches Theater had a natural advantage over the much smaller one in Karl-Marx-Stadt. There the director (Hans-Dieter Mäde) had to break up the proscenium line in order to provide for an additional entrance area; but in spite of the utmost economy the lively movement of the players' full orchestra had to be toned down almost to the requirements of a chamber recital. In the midst of this, sudden flashes of strength had a powerful, but sometimes inordinate effect. This was all the more so since Hamlet (Jürgen Hentsch) was most consistently seen as the Renaissance prince and Wittenberg humanist. This indeed was the courtier, the soldier, the scholar; not an existentialist or a frustrated revolutionary, but one whose historical stature allowed subdued contemporary pathos. The breadth of the generalization was such that Hamlet emerged as a Renaissance representative of values which—although utopian at the time —have remained relevant to this day.

These values were defined entirely in terms of Hamlet's dramatic speech and action. In this, the various relationships were extremely well differentiated; his attitude towards Horatio, the soldiers, the gravedigger and Fortinbras' captain had none of the flippancy, arrogance and cynicism that he displayed at court. This differentiation was based on a careful reading of the text, and its use as a means of defining the character's personality yielded a result both immediate and convincing. Nothing was vague; for at court Hamlet challenged adverse forces that were shown (and that he knew) to be dangerous and frightfully real: Polonius was less of a fool (though not nearly so brilliantly acted as in Berlin); Osric more vicious than ridiculous and, above all, Rosencrantz and Guildenstern had nothing clownish about them: two clever students going in for a courtly kind of careerism (hence resulted superb drama in the flute-playing scene!).

Thus, Hamlet's tragedy resulted not from any modernized dilemma, but from a contradiction, built up from the text itself, between his advanced view of man (as defined in monologues and relationships) and the over-mighty courtly powers that thwarted his plans and ideas about the world and how "to set it right" (I,5,490). To bring out this meaning, not a single line had to be altered, and no scene was transposed or forced into some topical context. In that sense, it remained a Renaissance play whose modern perspective was achieved not by ignoring or distorting but by probing its historical content more deeply. This implied an approach to history as a living continuum; in this view, the Renaissance world could be brought into a meaningful relationship with the present, and Elizabethan pathos had not to be disowned as modern bathos. Hamlet was no "immature" neurotic attempting "to escape from the complexities of adult living" (L. C. Knights), but was shown as a hero, and the reserve and the consistency with which this was done, were admirable. The surprising thing was that, from a purely theatrical point of view, it was all so rewarding. The director's hand was omnipresent, yet unobtrusive; his concept simple, but not superficial. The absence of anything sensational or merely pretentious was an engaging feature in an ensemble of actors whose strength was a perfect *unisono* rather than the *solo* virtuosity of any one star. Despite the considerable difference in approach and the various degrees of success, the Berlin and the Karl-Marx-Stadt productions both drew from similar areas of strength. The quality of this strength, in the last instance, resulted from a philosophy of history which, through the consciousness of its own consciousness, can achieve a more objective assessment of the works of the past. It is an approach to history which, thanks to its consciousness of the present, can afford to take the past seriously. The partisan nature of this consciousness and its achievement of objectivity do not preclude each other. On the contrary, they very much interact, to the benefit of a living theatre which, in the great drama of the past, can find more than repetition, namely: discovery. In *Hamlet*, the discovery was made possible by the willingness to take the hero's historical background seriously and to explore the position and the dilemma of the humanist in terms of his contrasting social relationships. The resulting figure was neither an "ambassador of death" (as Mr. Wilson Knight sees him) nor the "fundamentally immature" adolescent (that L. C. Knights has observed). It was a figure which, through its historical significance, was made to yield a contemporary meaning.

REFERENCES

This paper uses and develops further the theoretical assumptions that govern the present writer's previous work, especially *New Criticism und die Entwicklung bürgerlicher Literaturwissenschaft* (Halle, 1962); but also *Drama und Wirklichkeit in der Shakespearezeit* (Halle, 1958) and the more recent *Shakespeare und die Tradition des Volkstheaters* (Berlin, 1967). Some of these assumptions have also gone into several articles, of which two are accessible in English: "The Soul of the Age: Towards a Historical Approach to Shakespeare," *Shakespeare in a Changing World*, ed. Arnold Kettle (London, 1964) pp. 17-24; "Shakespeare on the Modern Stage: Past Significance and Present Meaning," *Shakespeare Survey 20* (1967), 113-120. There is one article in German which the present paper alludes to (but does not actually draw on) when it refers to the recent crisis of American literary history: "Tradition und Krise amerikanischer Literaturhistorie. Zu ihrer Methodologie und Geschichte," *Weimarer Beiträge* XI (1965), 394-435.

1. William K. Wimsatt/Cleanth Brooks, *Literary Criticism: A Short History* (New York, 1957), p. 537.
2. *Ibid.*, p. 543.
3. F. R. Leavis, "Criticism and Literary History," *The Importance of Scrutiny*, ed. Eric Bentley (New York, 1964), p. 12.
4. Lionel Trilling, "The Sense of the Past," *The Liberal Imagination*, Mercury Books ed. (London, 1961), p. 182.
5. René Wellek, "The Revolt against Positivism in Recent European Literary Scholarship," *Concepts of Criticism*, ed. Stephen G. Nichols (New Haven and London, 1963), p. 256.
6. *Ibid.*, p. 257.
7. J. W. Goethe, *Dichtung und Wahrheit* (14 Buch); cf. *Werke* ("Jubiläums-Ausgabe").
8. Friedrich Schiller, *Was heisst und zu welchem Ende studiert man Univer-*

salgeschichte?; cf. *Schillers sämtliche Werke* ("Säkularrausgabe"), XIII, 528.

9. Karl Marx, "Einleitung zur Kritik der politischen Ökonomie," cf. Marx/Engels, *Werke* (Dietz edition), XIII, 641.

10. Friedrich Nietzsche, *Vom Nutzen und Nachteil der Historie für das Leben,* (Kröners Taschenausgabe, XXXVII (Leipzig, [1933]), p. 70.

11. Cf. Trilling, *The Liberal Imagination,* p. 182.

12. E. H. Carr, *What Is History?* (London, 1962), pp. 80, 66. Contrasting modern and nineteenth-century assumptions of method, Carr writes (p. 55): "Nowadays both scientists and historians entertain the more modest hope of advancing progressively from one fragmentary hypothesis to another, isolating their facts through the medium of their interpretations, and testing their interpretations by the facts; and ways in which they go about it do not seem to me essentially different."

13. C. P. Snow, *The Two Cultures: And A Second Look,* Mentor ed. (New York, 1964), p. 90. Snow raises a vast question which has been asked, independently, in the distinguished work of Jacob Bronowski (see, e.g., *Science and Human Values* [London, 1961], pp. 50, et passim), in the writings of A. N. Whitehead, G. H. Hardy, et al.

14. See my article "Tradition und Krise amerikanischer Literaturhistorie" (cf. above, footnote to title), where the traditions of Moses Coit Tyler and Vernon Louis Parrington are discussed.

15. Ironically, when one pauses to consider that it "was precisely this scientific pose, conscious or unconscious, that constituted one of the main strengths of the New Criticism" (J. H. Raleigh, "The New Criticism as an Historical Phenomenon," *Comparative Literature* XI [1959/60], p. 23). The irony of it was noticed by at least one critic who—finding in Allen Tate's work "so deep a hatred of science and positivism, not to say democracy"—saw "a certain irony in his position, since the very textual analysis he defended was an aping of scientific method and rigor" (Alfred Kazin, *On Native Grounds,* Overseas ed., [New York 1942], p. 361.

16. Cleanth Brooks, "A Note on the Limits of 'History' and the Limits of 'Criticism,'" *The Sewanee Review,* LXI (1953), p. 132.

17. W. K. Wimsatt, "History and Criticism: A Problematic Relationship," *The Verbal Icon. Studies in the Meaning of Poetry* (Louisville, Ky., 1954), p. 253.

18. Brooks/Wimsatt, *Literary Criticism,* p. 537.

19. Leavis, "Criticism and Literary History," p. 13.

20. *Ibid.,* p. 14.

21. T. S. Eliot, "Tradition and The Individual Talent," *Selected Essays: 1917-1932* (London, 1932), p. 14.

22. F. R. Leavis, *The Great Tradition,* Penguin ed. (Harmondsworth, 1962), p. 29.

23. *Ibid.,* p. 38.

24. *Ibid.,* p. 11.

25. *Ibid.* There seems to be a similar contradiction, of which Cleanth Brooks is probably aware, when he says "that we need to revise drastically our conventional *estimate* of the *course* of English poetry." ("Criticism, History, and Critical Relativism," *The Well Wrought Urn* [New York, 1957], p. 224 (my italics.) At any rate, this is too facile a way of correlating value ("estimate") and development ("course").

26. Leavis, *The Great Tradition,* p. 10.

27. Cleanth Brooks, "The Quick and the Dead. A Comment on Humanistic Studies," *The Humanities: An Appraisal,* ed. Julian Harris (Univ. of Wisconsin Press, 1950), p. 5.

PAST SIGNIFICANCE AND PRESENT MEANING

PAST SIGNIFICANCE AND PRESENT MEANING   53

28. Cleanth Brooks, "Literary History vs. Criticism," *The Kenyon Review*, II (1940), p. 407.

29. Wimsatt, "History and Criticism," p. 258.

30. *Ibid.*, p. 254.

31. Wayne C. Booth, *The Rhetoric of Fiction* (Chicago, 1961), p. 74 and p. ix. See also Mark Spilka, "The Necessary Stylist: A New Critical Revision," *Modern Fiction Studies*, VI (1960/61), p. 285.

32. See the discussion of theories of metaphor in my *New Criticism und die Entwicklung bürgerlicher Literaturwissenschaft*, pp. 220-277; there is a much shorter French version in *Recherches internationales*, VIII (1964), no. 43 (mai-juin), pp. 201-211.

33. Harry Levin, "Thematics and Criticism," *The Disciplines of Criticism*, ed Peter Demetz et al. (New Haven and London, 1968), p. 145.

34. Karl Marx/Friedrich Engels, *Kleine Ökonomische Schriften*, Dietz ed. (Berlin, 1955), p. 128.

35. We use the text in E. K. Chambers, *William Shakespeare. A Study of Facts and Problems* (Oxford, 1930), II, 208f.

36. *Shakespeare in a Changing World*, ed. Arnold Kettle (London, 1964), p. 10.

ROBERT WEIMANN

POINT OF VIEW IN FICTION

The modern critic's growing interest in point of view, like the modern fiction on which it is largely based, reflects a changing and increasingly complex world in which the artist, in order to create, can no longer take wholeness for granted. In one of its important aspects, the history of modern literature can be described as a process in which the breadth of the object is supplanted by the precision of the subject, pattern by texture, the narrator's whole vision by the functional point of view of fictional characters. In the past, as long as the artist's position *vis-à-vis* his world positively corresponded to the character's imaginary reactions to the world of his fiction, the relationship of author and point of view was more direct and self-evident, and less self-conscious; the subjective experience of the writer was more obviously part of the objective social whole which he, as a writer, set out to explore and to tell tales about. Thus, for the early modern novelist, such as Cervantes and Fielding, as well as for Scott, Balzac and Tolstoi, the method of representation was more organically related to the means of evaluation; for the narrator's wide angle of selection corresponded to the freedom and (relative) security with which he evaluated in terms of character, incident and direct or stylized commentary. In the structure of the eighteenth and nineteenth century novel, incident and character themselves served more efficiently to define a way of looking at the world. Hence, the narrator's real world and the imaginary world of his creations, the actual and the fictitious points of view could be brought into a meaningful (if sometimes verbose or slipshod) correlation, and from this emerged, in the great novels of the past, a remarkable unity of objective representation and subjective evaluation.

But in a world of international class divisions, growing technical and educational specialization, and an ever increasing flow of information and communication, the modern writer's achievement of wholeness can no longer be that of Cervantes or Fielding. On the one hand, the comprehensiveness and the abstract nature of the social process is much less within his reach; accordingly, his subject-matter can no longer be approached in terms of the Hegelian concept of "totality" which Georg Lukacs has somewhat dogmatically used as a criterion

54

for realism. On the other hand, and precisely because the "total" world is out of reach, the writer's wholeness of perception will acquire an increased functional status within his narrative method. Here, clearly, a major social function of the novel is at stake, and it is one that a Marxist approach (which is hostile to the apology of alienation in whatever form it appears) will consider as a supreme criterion of value. As Goethe said, the true work of art will correspond to a human unity of thinking and feeling, the whole nature of man; and its understanding of the world is not merely of a logical or abstract nature, but—as Marx remarked—it amounts to a "practical-spiritual appropriation of this world" (*praktischgeistige Aneignung dieser Welt*).[1]

When, therefore, the novelist's comprehensive panorama of the whole of society has become difficult or even impossible to achieve, the novelist himself can still attain to a view of man and society from which a more functional kind of wholeness is within reach of his poetic perception and expression. If man, for so long a mere object of history, ever hopes to become its subject, he cannot—in the novel—relinquish the search for the *Kausalnexus* (Brecht) through which the structure of the social whole can be seen in its functions and movements. For the novelist, the narrative angle of vision may no longer be so wide as Tolstoi's but it can still achieve an element of integrity through the perspective linking of selection (or representation) and evaluation (or expression). If today "point of view" is to be more than the strategy of first or third person narration, it must involve the correlation of these two basic functions, and they are both part of the specific "practical-spiritual" achievement of art: *one* (representation) relates the novel to the objective nature of the world; the *other* (evaluation) to the subjective nature of the viewer and his view. Through this correlation of the world and the self, the narrative point of view functions as a connecting medium between representation and evaluation, and it is as a means of achieving their unity that point of view must be seen to be at the heart of the narrator's method.

Critique of a definition

From this approach one would wish to challenge some of the current and widely accepted definitions which appear in the literature on point of view. Admittedly, any approach to narrative method will feel

indebted to the important contributions from Percy Lubbock to Wayne
C. Booth. Also, it is easy to agree with such statements as that, in the
structure of point of view, we have before us "the central problem
of narrative method,"² or that, as Norman Friedman remarked, "the
choice of a point of view in the writing of fiction is at least as crucial
as the choice of a verse form in the composing of a poem."³ But as
soon as one begins to inquire into the underlying assumptions or even
into the meanings of the terms so used, one is struck by an element
of confusion and formalism, and sometimes impressionism, which is
in many ways a curious and unexpected phenomenon in one of the
most lively debated areas of recent English and American criticism.
As Wayne C. Booth, in summing up the discussion of almost half a
century, writes: Percy Lubbock "could hardly have predicted that
his converts would produce, in forty years of elaborate investigation
of point-of-view, so little help to the author or critic . . . we have been
given classifications and descriptions which leave us wondering why
we have bothered to classify and describe. . . ."⁴ In hinting at the merely
descriptive and typological approach, Mr. Booth stresses the frustrations of formalism, but he does not (although his *Rhetoric of Fiction*
goes some way in this direction) draw attention to the inherent contradictions within the theory of the concept itself.

There is an uncontrolled element of ambiguity which besets the
current definitions of "point of view," and lest our own use of the
same term appears to blur this over, it is important to look more closely
at some of the accepted formulas. Most of them, no doubt, derive from
Percy Lubbock's well-known phrase: "The whole intricate question
of method, in the craft of fiction, I take to be governed by the question of the point of view—the question of the relation in which the
narrator stands to the story."⁵ This has reached the textbooks and the
dictionaries long ago; to take only J. T. Shipley's *Dictionary of
World Literature: Criticism, Forms, Technique* (rev. ed. 1953) where
the echo of Lubbock's formula is quite distinct: There again, point of
view is "the relation in which the narrator stands to the story, considered by many critics to govern the method and character of the
work."

But who is the "narrator" in these definitions? In some of them
it is almost certainly not the author. Against the background of the
American New Criticism this should have been (and often was) clear
enough. However, Mark Schorer in his repeatedly anthologized essay

"Technique as Discovery" (still widely regarded as "the really significant advance in the theory of point of view which occurred in the
forties"[6]) considered point of view as a means of technique which he
defined as the *writer's* "only means . . . of discovering, exploring, developing his subject." Rejecting all "blunter terms than those which
one associates with poetry," Schorer could easily dispense with "such
relatively obvious matters as the arrangement of events to create plot;
or, within plot, of suspense and climax; or as the means of revealing
character motivation, relationship and development." But what then
had become of "the relation in which the narrator stands to *the story*"?
If Schorer's approach to point of view as "thematic definition" had
very little to do with plot, character, relationship and development, it
had also, as a matter of course, to belittle the concept of point of view
as a "narrowing or broadening of perspective upon the material"[7]—the
"material," that is, as something outside the autonomous status of the
art-work.

As most of the elements which might possibly infringe upon this
alleged autonomy were rejected or minimized, the new critical definition of the "relation in which the narrator stands to the story" left
no room for a relationship so grossly untechnical as that of the writer
to the society in which he, simply as a human being, lived as a character in history. In this sense, the term "narrator" would presumably
be thought of as a technical or imaginative medium, so that the "narrator's relation to the story," was, say, Zeitbloom's relation to the story
of *Doctor Faustus*. Or was it still Thomas Mann's attitude to his times
and materials as transmuted into the whole meaning of the novel? This
question hardly received a straightforward answer, but the full extent
of the underlying ambiguity emerged when, in Wellek's and Warren's
Theory of Literature, "the central problem of narrative method" was
defined as "the relation of the *author* to his work."[8] Here, "author"
must needs refer to a character in history; "his work" would—from
René Wellek's position—mean the work of art as "a stratified structure
of signs and meanings which is totally distinct from . . . the author."[9]
The resulting relationship, the suggested basis of point of view, involves a singular incongruity, from which the actual connection between the world and the viewer cannot be seen in any meaningful
correlation with that of the story and its medium.

This correlative function of point of view (which we hold to be
its perhaps most essential aspect) is equally ignored by the more recent

German *Stilkritik* although here, in the work of Wolfgang Kayser, there is at least a hint that narrative perspective is a two-dimensional phenomenon and that it exists in both the real world and the imaginative world of the art-work: The term "Perspektive" (although never sufficiently defined) is *either* used in the fictitious sense of an "optischen Standpunkt," *or* as a "Manifestation des Stilwillens,"[10] which would link it up with the historical background of the writer and his society. This twofold aspect is most clearly brought out in an American textbook which is more than ordinarily aware of the "two different connections" of narrative perspective. As Cleanth Brooks and R. P. Warren remark in *Understanding Fiction,* point of view

> is used in two different connections. First, it is used in connection with the basic attitude or idea of the author, and second, it is used in connection with the method of narration. In the first meaning, one refers, for instance, to the author's ironical point of view, or his detached point of view, or his sympathetic point of view, or the like. Or one might say that a certain piece of fiction embodies a Christian point of view. In the second meaning, one refers to the mind through which the material of the story is presented— first person, first-person observer, author-observer, and omniscient author. Confusion will be avoided if the use of the term *point of view* be restricted to the first meaning, and if the term Focus of Narration be used for the second meaning.[11]

The differentiation is extremely useful, but as a purely descriptive definition it seems to ignore the fact that these two aspects of narrative perspective, although distinct, also form some kind of unity and that criticism (if it is to see the wider context of history and aesthetics, development and value, genesis and structure) would find its most rewarding task in the discovery and interpretation of the very crossing-points and links between the two aspects. Again, if "the basic attitude . . . of the author" and "the method of narration" are anywhere related, criticism would have to examine the degree and the nature of this relationship in order to see the historical as well as the structural elements in any given narrative perspective. Not that their whole unity will be found always to be achieved, but in the completely integrated narrative work of art, the historical and the beautiful, origin and structure have become irretrievably fused, and the tensions and the correlations within this whole fusion form the dialectics of narrative method. From this approach, then, a recognition of the "two different connections" of narrative perspective can be helpful only if the differentiation of terms leaves room for both the contradiction and the unity of the historical and the structural aspects of point of view. In order to stress the possible degree of unity, one would wish to bracket the two aspects by one comprehensive term for which "narrative perspective" (*Erzählperspektive*) or simply "point of view" is perhaps best suited. This "narrative perespective" or comprehensive "point of view" (which we use in a wider sense than Brooks and Warren do) is understood to comprise both an author's actual and his ironic or technical points of view. The author's "actual point of view" or his achieved attitude to the actual world of history, may conveniently be called his standpoint; the author's "ironic" or "technical point of view" will simply indicate his (unreliable, omniscient, etc.) medium or focus of narration. Both aspects are approached as an infinitely variable synthesis, but the synthesis of this wider "narrative perspective" is extremely complex and never the result of any one determining factor. It is a relationship which cannot be deduced from any fixed formula, but can finally be studied only within the infinite particularity of each individual story or novel.

In order to illustrate the theoretical nature of this relationship, one might be tempted to compare (though not to identify!) the "two different connections" of narrative perspective with the interplay of form and content. Just as form and content constitute a reciprocal relationship (in which "content" is only meaningful as far as it is already achieved through "form," and *vice versa*), the author's standpoint and the focus of narration possess similar areas of interaction. The author's narrative standpoint is itself not simply a biographical category, which a clever writer, when interviewed, might sum up into a neat statement. The author's point of view, when transmuted into a work of art, cannot be deduced from his private or political opinions or from anything less than the writer's total amount of created *Weltanschauung* or sensibility. The artist's opinions, whether expressed privately or publicly, are relevant mainly in so far as they reflect or inspire his sensibility or his all-round apprehension and comprehension of things. This is a point that Arnold Kettle made when he remarked that if "we refer to a writer's point-of-view in the artistic sense we are referring to his sensibility rather than to his opinions or intentions."[12] Consequently, the *achieved* standpoint of an author is not simply identical with his declared position as, say, scholar, journalist or politician, but may by itself be the means of defining his *Weltanschauung* more conclusively.

If the narrator's standpoint makes sense only in so far as it is achieved through form, the technical point of view or focus of narration is meaningful only as long as it helps to create content. In the light of this functional approach, the technical focus of narration (that is, the assumed point of view) can never be entirely abstracted from the ultimate theme of the novel and what it symbolically, metaphorically or generally has to say about the world as it is. While constituting a reciprocal relationship, the factual and technical points of view will hardly ever be synchronized; there is room for all sorts of tension: ironical, satirical, humorous, etc., so that—on the surface of things—the imaginary point of view or medium (say, that of Moll Flanders, Jonathan Wild, or Felix Krull) will be worlds apart from the standpoint of the author. But this tension, between the imaginary positions of Flanders, Wild or Krull and the actual sensibilities of Defoe, Fielding, Mann, respectively, is the very stuff from which the method of narrative derives its form and pressure. To try to understand this method merely in terms of the author's relation to his *story* (and not also to the world from which the raw materials of his story are in the last instance taken) would be as one-sided as considering Jonathan Wild or Felix Krull without reference to the art-work's all-out comprehension of things against which the respective character's point of view (satirically, ironically, etc.) falls into place.

Thus the need for a more comprehensive historical-structural angle of reference becomes apparent. When the more comprehensive point of view (which we prefer to call "narrative perspective") is seen in its widest connections, it can comprise no less than the sum total of all the achieved attitudes to both the world (which includes the audience) *and* the story as a generalized image of what the novelist wishes to say about the world through his art.

Point of view and the rhetoric of narration

Although point of view is widely held to constitute a central problem of *narrative* method, the changing art-form of the living novel makes any generalization about the specifically narrative element in point of view rather hazardous. The impact of photography, film, psychology, etc., has definitely turned the novel into a mixed genre where there is plenty of room for dramatic and, perhaps to a lesser degree, lyrical conventions. Nevertheless it may be claimed that the rhetorical function of point of view is of much greater structural consequence in the epic or in the novel than it is in the drama or in lyrical poetry. Why this is so, is certainly worth pondering; but an answer to this question will have to go beyond Wayne C. Booth's important contribution and at least attempt to sketch some of the problems arising out of the special relationship between the teller, his tale and his audience.

Story-telling is an ancient convention which, in contrast to the even older art of miming, has a time structure and a convention of illusion distinctly its own. Although (let us repeat) the modern novel, so much influenced by drama and film, has largely dispensed with the traditional conventions of story-telling, the structure of the narrator's relation to time, and the non-dramatic character of narrative illusion, have a tradition which is relevant even today. The original process of telling a tale, or the *Ursituation* of all story-telling, involves a social act of communication. The object of communication is never in the present but is always a matter of the past. For the narrator, there is no point in telling about things which, in his presence, his listeners themselves are witnessing. Story-telling at its beginning, and much after, is the telling of things which needs have (or are said to have) already happened at the moment of their telling. To *relate* or to *report* something is never identical with that which is so related or reported. It is probably this aspect which Goethe and Schiller had in mind when in their correspondence they attempted to define "the great essential difference" between the epic poet and the dramatist: while the first renders an event which is "completely past" (*vollkommen vergangen*), the latter represents something which is "completely in the present" (*vollkommen gegenwärtig*).

Consequently, the respective elements of illusion in the two genres are quite different. While on the traditional proscenium stage the actors aim to re-present an imaginative world by pretending to be that world and thus ignoring the audience, the criterion of narrative illusion is, and was originally, the narrator's act of recollection and the convincing tone of his address to the audience. The dramatic assumption of the picture-frame stage (that a story or plot renders itself) is quite alien to the narrator whose recollection is the source of his reliability and who reviews the things which he thinks are worthwhile telling others about. To expect the narrator to render an event *telle qu'elle est*, is a contradiction in itself. As the narration is so obviously not identical with the subject which it is about, it contains an unashamed element of selection and evaluation. Without it, no narration is possible: How else could the narrator in real life hope to comprehend and arrange the multitudes of details which he—in summary or silence—thinks fit to condense or pass over? To achieve the necessary selection and evaluation is impossible without a point from which to select and to evaluate, and this view-point (whether consciously or unconsciously taken) is indeed the absolute prerequisite of all narrative activity.

Any *mimesis* or dramatic representation of reality is unthinkable without some such selective and partial view point, but in the narrative genre it assumes more of a structural function. In contrast to the dramatist, the narrator may incorporate the process of his evaluation (which means partiality) and his selection (which also means organization) into the work of art itself. While the traditional dramatist cannot very well articulate or stylize the *process* and the *rhetoric* of his perspectives, the novelist may transform the simplest prerequisite of ordinary story-telling into a highly effective convention of his art. Thus, as in Jean Paul or many first person narrations, the actual effort of the author's imagination and organization can—through irony, metaphor, symbol, or simply stylization—find a correlative in the work itself. In this way, it can be transmuted into the narrative attitude of a fictive medium, thereby helping to build the structure of the artwork. The process of this transmutation assumes myriad forms and many stages of distance and irony, but eventually it must achieve some meaning which, although quite different from the author and his world of history, sheds some new and generalized significance upon them.

When we suggest that point of view is at the core of this specifically narrative transmutation of reality, there is no need to ignore that (as we shall see) the author's omniscient and reliable angle of narration has—as a convention—been increasingly given over. But this tendency, which in Flaubert's concept of *impassibilité* is already quite explicit, is in itself a symptom of the novelist's increased need to come to grips with the changing forms of an achieved perspective. Obviously, the correlation of the historical and the technical points of view had become more difficult, when the naive and immediate solution of the omniscient narrator seemed no longer acceptable. But when the novelist, as does Dickens after his early novels, began to abandon the personal narrator, he gave up a stylized convention, not the real function of the narrator to select and evaluate. By abandoning the omniscient convention, the author surrendered his reliable correlative, but he certainly did not cease to exist. The relationship between the author's real and his technical (or ironic) points of view became more subtle and, as it were, invisible, but it was not simply cancelled or annihilated.

If the critics of the modern novel believed that it was, the fallacy of their dogma was partly due to an unquestioning (and largely unconscious) acceptance of the norms and appearances of "scenic" showing and naturalistic "objectivity." To approach point of view (as Norman Friedman and other American critics do) merely as a *"modus operandi* for distinguishing the possible degrees of authorial extinction in the narrative art,"[13] will *nolens volens* lead the critic to accept the bias of one type of fiction, preferably that of naturalism. If "the prime end of fiction is to produce as complete a story-illusion as possible" and if this is indeed "the basic assumption of those who are seriously concerned over technique," then a very questionable concept of 'illusion" is made a criterion of artistic truth. To quote in full: "If artistic 'truth' is a matter of compelling rendition, of creating the illusion of reality, then an author speaking in his own person about the lives and fortunes of others is placing an extra obstacle between his illusion and the reader by virtue of his very presence."[14]

This kind of argument—confounding reality with realism—seems to assume that the author's "presence" (or his actual point of view) is dispensed with as soon as he decides to suppress "his own personal voice in one way or another." True, as the influence of the dramatic or film scene on modern fiction is very powerful, there is some justification for using a basically dramatic concept of illusion as a touchstone for the "artistic 'truth' " of the novel. But to make this partially justified argument serve for an absolute maxim in the theory of the novel, to claim (in the words of Percy Lubbock) that "the art of fiction does not begin until the novelist thinks of his story as a matter to be *shown*,"[15] is to ignore or distort the very bases of the narrative element in fiction. The bias of naturalism is rationalized into a system of poetics which merely seeks to apologize for the novelist's increasing reluctance to face the rhetoric of his communication, and the responsibility for his own whole narrative perspective of society. This, of course, is entirely in line with the assumptions of the New Criticism (so dominant until recently) which, with some consistency, loaded the discussion of narrative method by considering point of view almost exclusively as an autonomous technical strategy inside the art-work.

Although recent American critics have gone some way towards redressing the distortions of the autonomous fallacy, the confusions of formalism are still wide-spread and influential. When, after some more general strictures on "Fiction and the Criticism of Fiction" (as by Philip Rahv in *The Kenyon Review*, Spring 1956, pp. 276-299), academic critics such as Mark Spilka felt the need for an alternative solution, they began to plead for a reconsideration of the author-narrator as the one basis from which the style of the novel could more fruitfully be interpreted. But "The Necessary Stylist"—designed expressly to repair the absence of the "author" in "new critical terminology"—was approached almost as a necessary evil ("If we can connect the author *formally* with his works, rather than historically . . ."[16]). It was still the cramped logic of *Stilkritik*. From this, even the most fundamental modern contribution to the theory of fiction is by no means free, although, here, as the title of Wayne C. Booth's *The Rhetoric of Fiction* indicates, the focus of interest is remarkably shifted and the problems of narrative communication no longer ignored. There is a new sense of "the implied author" as the comprehensive "core of norms and choices," a "choosing, evaluating person,"[17] and the most basic problems of method are shown to result from his attempt "consciously or unconsciously to impose his fictional world upon the reader." This is a far cry from the formalist ghost of the "affective fallacy"; and the dogma of the self-contained autonomy of the art-work as "a stratified structure of signs" is pretty much shattered when Booth, with no more than common sense acknowledges that, although the author can to some extent choose his disguises, "the author's judgment is always present." But the "author's judgment" (one would assume) is definitely affected by historical, social and psychological forces, and without reference to them, the nature and the functions of these judgments can hardly be subjected to criticism. In Mr. Booth's book, however, these "social and psychological forces that affect authors and readers" are *expressis verbis* dismissed in favour of "the narrower question of whether rhetoric is compatible with art."[18]

This question is not merely narrow, its assumptions are simply wrong. Apart from the fact that the author's relations to his readers cannot be subsumed solely under rhetorical categories, the whole way of posing this question makes wholesale concessions to the New Criticism. Perhaps Booth's concept of rhetoric reflects the climate of the early sixties (1961) when some caution might still have appeared advisable with which to smuggle the idea of the "Impurity of Great Literature"[19] into the discussion of the purists. With this kind of strategy, Booth did indeed score an immense success, but he had, ironically enough, to use not merely the terminology of, but get himself entangled in the contradictions of formalism. As if it were at all possible to narrate without rhetoric! To conceive of rhetoric as something "impure," makes (despite Booth's expressed intention) a vital concession to the old sterile opposition between 'mere' rhetorical telling and artful showing. Thus, there is an uneasy element of ambiguity in the irony of his protests against "cleaning out the rhetorical impurities from the house of fiction." Says Booth: "If the most admired literature is in fact radically contaminated with rhetoric, we must surely be led to ask whether the rhetoric itself may not have something to do with our admiration."[20]

The argument may point in the right direction, but this line of reasoning is unsatisfactory. If we are repeatedly told that "even the greatest literature depends on 'impurities' for its greatness," there is something wrong with this whole system of reference. The art of the novel is not (as the ambiguous phrase goes) *contaminated* with rhetoric, for rhetoric *is* a means of narrative *structure*. The (allegedly) "impure" world cannot be opposed to an (allegedly) "pure" structure, any more than the historical can finally be abstracted from the technical points of view. To the degree that these are both correlated in the larger historical-structural dimensions of perspective, the (social) purpose and material of narration and the (aesthetic) method of narrative interact. This interaction and this integration is achieved through point of view. The interaction and the integration themselves are a result of artistic creation, and as such are only meaningful in so far as they are correlated and thus objectified through the art of narrative perspective.

Point of view: origin and function

A historical-structural approach to point of view will have to be critical of any value judgments and generalizations based on the dramatic mode of perspective, but in its turn must refrain from any facile preference for this or that focus of narration, such as either impersonal showing or personal telling. Since the focus of narration is not determined by, but correlated to the narrator's standpoint, any evaluation of point of view will have to be functional, not sociological. In other words, the historical origins of any particular mode of focussing cannot possibly limit its concrete use in a given modern context. There it is always the twofold historical-technical aspect of point of view which will have to be considered in the achieved amount of its unity, which includes (as we have seen) all the infinite degrees of tension—ironical, satirical, comic, etc.

This does not mean, however, that the history or the origins of any one mode of perspective is meaningless in a theoretical approach to narrative method. Far from it; for any given structure, although it can survive the constellations that gave it birth, so reflects their social nature and particular dynamism that its deeper meaning can only be grasped in reference to them. If the criticism of point of view is to overcome the frustrations of forty years of formalism, the historical approach must be seen as a *conditio sine qua non*. But such a historical approach is absolutely dependent on the recognition of a more comprehensive narrative perspective as an ultimate correlation between the world and the whole work of art.

To illustrate the historical nature of this correlation more clearly, we propose to look at the origins of modern point of view. Although, again, space forbids more than a few and necessarily incomplete remarks (which—as above—run all the risks of oversimplification), even a tentative sketch may perhaps suggest the extent to which, in its early stages, narrative perspective constitutes itself through the interplay of social and technical points of viewing. This is probably most obvious in the changing angle from which the narrator implies or expresses his attitudes towards his audience as the—to him—most relevant section of society. It is here that the perspective of the epic poet differs most radically from that of the early novelist, and the degree of this difference can best be measured by the changing social and rhetorical functions of the narrator. The corresponding change in point of view (far from being anything "impure" or external to the artwork) manifests itself in tone and structure, and thereby helps to explain why, at the outset, the modern novel is so vastly different from both the heroic and the courtly epic.

As we see in *Beowulf* or the *Nibelungenlied*, the epic poet disposed of a frame of reference which was taken for granted by an audience with which he shared "some unity of sentiment, some common standard of appreciation."[21] In a society where the division of labor was undeveloped, the poet did not—in his individual point of view—radically dissent from that of the society to which he belonged. The opening lines of the epic stressed this community of perspective:

HWÆT, wē Gār-Dena   in gēardagum
thēodcyninga   thrym gefrūnon . . .

Uns ist in alten maeren wunders vil geseit . . .

von küener recken strîten muget ir nu wunder hoeren sagen.

The *wē* and the *uns* comprised the audience *and* the poet in their joint attitudes towards both the actual world and the imaginary world of the epic. The distinctive function of the poet was to remember and to relate the past world of the epic to the real world of his audience. As "the mediator, the messenger, the guide . . . the knower of the names,"[22] he knew best about the "prym" and the "wunder" of the past; but the degree of his individual excellence lay in his capacity for mediation, not invention. More than his audience, he had *heard* of the "alten maeren," and from this mediating and interpretative capacity alone, the point of view of his "I" was justified (as in the characteristic *ne hyrde ic* and similar first person phrases in *Beowulf*, 1.38, *et passim*).

Thus, the epic poet built up a narrative perspective which was—for his audience—valid, not relative; real, not fictitious. For Homer, the muses served as an unchallenged source of inspiration. For the audience who applauded, and the poet who cherished, such inspiration or *mania*, there was no need for an indirect medium of narration; the poet himself was already mediating, and an indirect narrator would have interfered with the direct nature and the helpful pathos of his inspiration. As the ancient epic poet was not self-conscious of any (particular) perspective, he was in no position to wish to stylize it. Accordingly, the modes and forms of point of view remained undeveloped. The narrator's focus of narration was wide enough to leave room for summary and scenes with dialogue, but as a rule the epic point of view was inseparable from the poet's actual function as "the mediator" and "the knower of the names." There was an indispensable correlation between the poet's actual attitude towards his society and audience and the imaginative perspective of his narration, and from the security and the stability of this correlation the epic point of view drew the strength of its peculiar restraint and dignity, but also its limitations.

Against the background of the epic, point of view in the novel may be seen more clearly in the historical nature of its origins and functions. Right from the beginning, from Cervantes onwards, narrative perspective presents itself as an individual problem of approach and attitude, for which the early novelist (who is remarkably aware of it) has to find a solution all by himself. Between novelist and reader the unity of comprehension, if not entirely broken up, can no longer be taken for granted; and the narrator must tap all the springs of his individual *humor* (in the sense of ancient physiology) and his good humor in order to make his own temper consonant with the multiple taste and pleasure of his readers. Cervantes, Defoe and Fielding no longer address any homogeneous audience but the individual reader, to whom they expound their own (equally individual) point of view. In doing so, they take up this kind of attitude:

> Pero yo, que, aunque parezco padre, soy padrastro de D. Quijote, no quiero irme con la corriente del uso, ni suplicarte casi con las lágrimas en los ojos, como otros hacen, lector carísimo, que perdones ó disimules las faltas que en este mi hijo vieres; y, peus ni eres su pariente ni su amigo, y tienes tu alma en tu cuerpo y tu libre albedrío como el más pintado, y estás en tu casa, donde eres señor de ella, como el rey de sus alcabalas. . . .

> but I, who, though seemingly the parent, am in truth only the step-father of Don Quixote, will not yield to this prevailing infirmity; nor will I—as others would do—beseech thee, kind reader, almost with tears in my eyes, to pardon or conceal the faults thou mayest discover in this brat of mine. Besides thou art neither its kinsman nor friend; thou art in possession of thine own soul, and of a will as free and absolute as the best; and art, moreover, in thine own house, being as much the lord and master of it as is the monarch of his revenue; . . .

> The world is so taken up of late with novels and romances, that it will be hard for a private history to be taken for genuine, where

the names and other circumstances of the person are concealed; and on this account we must be content to leave the reader to pass his own opinion upon the ensuing sheets, and take it just as he pleases.

An author ought to consider himself, not as a gentleman who gives a private or eleemosynary treat, but rather as one who keeps a public ordinary, at which all persons are welcome for their money. . . . Men, who pay for what they eat, will insist on gratifying their palates, however nice and whimsical these may prove; and, if every thing is not agreeable to their taste, will challenge a right to censure, to abuse, and to d-n their dinner without control.[23]

This reflects a different kind of society, and it is a different kind of rhetoric. The society is that of "free competition" where the individual, as Marx says, is outside the older "natural bonds" and no longer "part of a definite, limited human conglomeration" (*Zubehör eines bestimmten, begrenzten menschlichen Konglomerats*). The structure of this new society is reflected in the nature of the narrator's address to his audience. It is an address which—although obviously made to the real world of history—is of profound consequences to the structure of the rhetorical and technical focus of narration and—beyond that—to the composition of plot and character. There is a sense of the individual as being apart from the community, and the consciousness of the "I"—which stimulates the interest in a person's "own history" (Defoe)—leads to a new freedom of perspective. As Cervantes shows, the narrator no longer thinks of the reader as his "relative"; for he, too, has a "mind of his own" and a "free will," and he is master of his own "house" (and property) no less than the sovereign monarch over his revenues. The *bourgeois* element in the structure of this rhetoric could hardly be more emphatic. From this, Defoe's appeal to the reader's "own opinion" as the final and legitimate verdict on his work, is very much in line with Fielding's respect for the reader's "right to censure" and the gratification of their "palates, however nice and whimsical these may prove." The narrator's attitudes (no less than the reader's) reflect the structure of a society where "the different forms of social union confront the individual as a mere means to his private ends, as an outward necessity."[24]

But it is not merely the reader who is seen as using the novel (like all art) as a "means to his private ends"; and it is not simply the narrator's personality which—as a biographical fact—is now much more outside the social nexus. More than that, it is the narrator's work itself which now, as it were, is considered as his own product or even his own property, so that Fielding, in his characteristic simile, can liken his attitude to that of an inn-keeper or host "who keeps a public ordinary." As a kind of entertainer who is free to sell his fare, he may quite deliberately approach his narration as the product of his own comprehension of things: *como hijo del entendimiento* (Cervantes)— the "offspring of my brain" (Charles Jarvis), which Tobias Smollett in *his* translation more literally renders as "the child of my understanding."

This phrase reveals more than the sociological and rhetorical context in which the novelist now communicates with his readers: The work itself is seen as the intimate product and the immediate result of the individual artist's apprehension of the world. The modern novel is born in the consciousness of its narrative perspective. It is the perspective of the individual artist who knows his work to be the direct product of his own personal sensibility and understanding. In the words of Goethe, the novel emerges as a "subjective epic, in which the author asks for the freedom (*Erlaubnis*) to treat the world according to his own manner (*Weise*). The point, therefore, is whether he have such a manner. . . ."[25] Since the early modern novelist can no longer fall back on some common standard of evaluation, this indeed is the first and foremost problem of his narrative method: To have some distinctive "manner" or angle of comprehension from which to approach, and hence to impose some unity upon, the myriad details of the world as his material.

Goethe's idea of the "world" is of course (in new critical terminology) a highly "impure" concept; but the point is that in the last instance it is the social structure of this world which allows or demands the new personal "manner" of viewing. What is more, the historical and social foundations of this new "manner" are connected with the changing structure of the technical focus of narration. At this stage, the correlation between the novelist's social and technical perspectives is still pretty obvious, but this is not primarily (as Wayne C. Booth seems to suggest) a question of communication or rhetoric. Here to abstract from the analysis of concrete works of art is dangerous, but at the risk of oversimplifying one would suggest that, basically, the freedom and instability of the novelist's subjective view of the world are correlated to the increasing diversity of his narrative focus which, right from the beginning, is more freely flexible, more subtle, more 'relative,' and more easily subject to stylization. Hence results the growing breadth of variation among the three obvious forms of narration (the omniscient, the impersonal and the "I"-medium) as well as the conventional use of the memoir and criminal or picaresque biography. Apart from having to maneuver in the face of puritan suspicion of fiction, the early novelist like Defoe, who himself is tossed on the waves of free speculation, enterprise, journalism, and a multitude of projects, has obvious difficulties in imposing some pattern or fictional unity upon his world through the "manner" of his own personality. Unlike Cervantes and Fielding, the lesser personalities, in a situation like this, are powerfully attracted by the conventions of the picaresque tradition: There, a minimum pattern is established by the point of view of one adventurous individual who, chameleon-like, can reflect all the light and shadow of his ever changing surroundings. To this, the author's own standpoint could roughly be reconciled if, what Defoe calls "the life of the person," the "story" or "fable," or simply "the wicked part," is at least partly seen in perspective by "the moral" or "the end of the writer." To pose as editor and to pretend (as in *Moll Flanders*) "that the original of this story is put into new words and the style . . . is a little altered," must have liberated the narrator's vast talent for empirical observation and largely freed him from the frustration of having throughout to sustain his own personal "manner." For similar reasons, the convention of the epistolary novel must have been very attractive (although again, the *bourgeois* nature of puritan psychology mattered largely). Still, the international success of Richardson's works, just as the vogue of the Spanish picaresque novel, could partly be explained in terms of the new needs, possibilities and frustrations of the early modern narrative perspective.

From a historical-structural approach, then, the emergence of the three obvious modes of presentation (omniscient, impersonal, "I") is indicative of a larger change of narrative perspective which, like every fundamental change in style, reflects, in the last instance, a change in the lives of the stylists. If the three well-known modes of focussing are seen in the wider context of a more comprehensive narrative perspective, their rise and subsequent variations will appear more meaningful than their merely descriptive classification has sometimes allowed. In that case it is, paradoxically enough, the historical approach which alone can bring out their larger structural context and functioning. Merely to sketch the lines of such an approach one would wish to suggest three or four aspects.

First, the novelist's relation to his subject-matter. The epic poet as the mediator of a traditional *matière*, achieves the larger perspective of his community (which includes his own view-point) through interpretation and accentuation. The novelist, at the outset, has to create a structural correlative of his individual perspective by himself, through the original invention of fable or plot. The traditional *matière* or the epic *Stoffkreise* are too remote from the reality of his society and they seem so discredited and (in their margin of structural variations) so rigid, that after Malory no new version or adaptation will ever—as a generalized image—leave room enough for the new narrator's different apprehension and comprehension of the world. The more objective *mimesis* (or mirroring) of the contemporary world as well as the more subjective expression of his own sensibility, demand the finding of a subject-matter and a new set of original images and motifs which the novelist, by means of his own creative point of view, will have to integrate on the cross-roads of self and society, subjective and social experience.

Second, the new and wider perspective of interpretation and evaluation. The nature of the epic perspective could admit of only a limited range of variation; the pathos and the personal restraint of the narrator encouraged the use of fixed formulas and certain paratactic syntax patterns (such as Malory's "And then. . . . Then. . . . And then . . . And then . . .": "And then the king let search all the towns. . . . Then much people drew unto King Arthur. And then they said that Sir Mordred warred upon King Arthur with wrong. And then . . . ; and there was. . . . Then Sir Mordred . . . etc. etc., Book XXI, chap. iii). This by itself left little room for, and reflected the absence of, the endeavour empirically, causally, morally to understand, connect and evaluate. But the novelist who can no longer fall back on accepted images and formulas of interpretation is almost everywhere called upon to suggest motives, connections and values. Faced with an original plot largely of his own making, he is at every turn of the story confronted with an unprecedented need for selection, interconnection and appraisal. As the range of his objective materials is so much wider and the potential of his subjective reactions so much more subtle and stratified, his point of view, in its supreme correlative function, must ever be alert in its structural, atmospheric and stylistic dimensions. And although the early novelist still has a public sense of significance and accepted norms of evaluation, such as Fielding's concept of "charity" (*Joseph Andrews*, III, xiii; *Tom Jones*, II, v) or Dr. Johnson's "Truth indeed is always truth, and reason is always reason" (*Lives*, ed. G. B. Hill, i, 46), the empirical, exploratory and critical nature of the modern novel will soon have to develop a wider and less secure perspective of reference and value.

Third, the increased variability of perspective. The social, spatial and temporal structure of point of view in the novel is much less fixed by tradition or convention than the narrative perspective of the epic. In bourgeois society, the more "accidental nature of the conditions of life for the individual" is indirectly reflected in the greater imaginative capacity for shifting the narrator's view-point; in the novel (as in contrast to neoclassical tragedy) this is not inhibited by *decorum* or any conservative code of poetics. The greater variability of perspective opens for inspection a wider horizon of society, and at the same time it assumes new spatial as well as temporal dimensions; the telescope can easily be exchanged with the microscope, and neither distance nor introspection is a problem. The new mobility of the narrative medium is closely linked with a more conscious control of the tempo of movement. The author, as Fielding remarks in *Tom Jones* (II, i), can leave a scene for a long period of time "totally unobserved," but he can also "open it at large to our reader." The more variable relationship between the time of the telling and the time of the tale can assume a conscious function of structure, and it usually serves as a means of emphasis and evaluation. The corresponding alternation of summary and scene with its respective modes of focussing, marks an essential process of narrative method in which the actual sensibility of the author (as a character in history) is transmuted into the purely fictional focussing of the work of art.

Finally, the ironic use of perspective as a means of distancing or disapproval. The greater freedom and responsibility in the choice of subject-matter (1), the wider range in interpretation and evaluation (2), and the increased spatial and temporal variability of perspective (3) all contribute to the more subtle use of point of view as a deliberate means of stylization. But the process in which the author's true meaning can increasingly dissociate itself from the view-point of his medium, is in the last instance based on the growing separateness and relativity of the individual consciousness as opposed to that of the whole of society. As the freedom and independence of the bourgeois individual are eventually linked with the subjective relativity of his norms and standards, the author finds it increasingly difficult to create a medium which is neither "relative" in comparison with, nor isolated from, the norms and relations of society. The emergence of the ironic or irresponsible focus of narration reflects this, but at the same time, it can be turned into a source of strength: The author can dramatize an attitude which he, even while revealing its fullest details and consequences, can morally disavow through the irony of his whole perspective. The stylized use of perspective as a use of moral distancing greatly enlarges the novelist's capacity for social criticism. Thus, the artist *vis-à-vis* his society is not simply confronted with an increased relativity of standards; he can avail himself of a critical position which is no longer part of, but more or less opposed to, the ruling norms of society. In this unique position, he can repudiate the excesses of individualism without himself surrendering the achievement of the consciousness of man as an individual. Consequently, the new variable and "accidental" nature of perspective, its increased instability and flexibility, do not rule out a more profound insight into the empirical and causal mechanism of the individual's relation to society. On the contrary, the increased particularity of point of view can help achieve a greater amount of realism. This, perhaps, is the distinction of the eighteenth and nineteenth century novel as a "prosaic" image of the world: the individual, more particular character of the narrative perspective does not preclude a more general insight into the objective world as it really is. Through the supreme correlative function of point of view, the subjectivity and variability of the narrator and his medium are perfectly congruent with the greater objectivity of the novel's image of reality.

REFERENCES

1. Cf. *Goethes Sämtliche Werke* (Jubiläums-Ausgabe"), XXXIII, 175; Karl Marx, *Zur Kritik der politischen Ökonomie*, in: Marx/Engels, *Werke* (Dietz Verlag, Berlin), XIII, 633.
2. René Wellek and Austin Warren, *Theory of Literature*, (London 1955), p. 231.

3. Norman Friedman, "Point of View in Fiction: The Development of a Critical Concept," *PMLA*, LXX (1955), p. 1180.
4. Wayne C. Booth, "Distance and Point-of-View: An Essay in Classification," *Essays in Criticism*, XI (1961), p. 60.
5. Percy Lubbock, *The Craft of Fiction*, (New York, 1957), p. 73.
6. Friedman, *op. cit.* p. 1167.
7. Mark Schorer, "Technique as Discovery," in: *Critiques and Essays on Modern Fiction: 1920-1951*, ed. J. W. Aldridge, (New York, 1952), p. 67 ff.
8. Wellek and Warren, *op. cit.*, p. 231.
9. René Wellek, *Concepts of Criticism*, ed. S. G. Nichols, (New Haven and London, 1963), p. 293.
10. Wolfgang Kayser, *Das sprachliche Kunstwerk*, (Bern, 1951), p. 209 ff.
11. Cleanth Brooks and R. P. Warren, *Understanding Fiction* (New York, 1943), p. 607.
12. Arnold Kettle, "Dickens and the Popular Tradition," *Zeitschrift für Anglistik und Amerikanistik*, IX (1961), p. 230.
13. Friedman, *op. cit.*, p. 1163.
14. *Ibid.*, p. 1164.
15. Lubbock, *op. cit.*, p. 62.
16. Mark Spilka, "The Necessary Stylist: A New Critical Revision," *Modern Fiction Studies*, VI (1960-61), p. 285.
17. Wayne C. Booth, *The Rhetoric of Fiction*, (Chicago, 1961), p. 74.
18. *Ibid.*, Preface.
19. *Ibid.*, pp. 98-109.
20. *Ibid.*, pp. 98 ff.
21. W. P. Ker, *Epic and Romance. Essays on Medieval Literature* (London, 1908), p. 21.
22. T. Greene, "The Norms of Epic," *Comparative Literature*, VIII (1961), p. 206.
23. *El Ingenioso Hidalgo Don Quijote de la Mancha*, ed. Clemente Cortejón, Madrid 1905, I, 16; Engl. translation by Charles Jarvis (ed. London 1892, p. iii). Daniel Defoe, *The Fortunes and Misfortunes of the Famous Moll Flanders*, Everyman ed., (London, 1930), p. 1. Henry Fielding, *The History of Tom Jones*, Tauchnitz ed. (Leipzig, 1844), p. 11.
24. Karl Marx, *A Contribution to the Critique of Political Economy*, transl. N. J. Stone, (Chicago, 1904), p. 267.
25. *Goethes Sämtliche Werke*, p. 255.

N. K. Gay

TRUTH IN ART AND TRUTH IN LIFE

Existing definitions of artistic truth are often unsatisfactory because they do not reflect the complex dynamic totality of the features of a work, a totality apart from which the creative idea remains unrealized. Authors writing on this theme usually do not see the complexity of the question and attempt to define artistic value not as an integral quality of a work but only as the sum of various characteristics. The result is a mechanical stringing together of different characteristics and at the same time an incomplete enumeration, since other characteristics, important in one respect or another, can always be added. In connection with artistic value they usually talk about the truth of life, about ideational content, about the folk or popular character, about the quality of partisanship, about fidelity to the actual or the contemporary, about typical characters, the positive hero, the breadth and depth of penetration into reality, the revelation at one and the same time of both surface and essential qualities, about the unity of the general and the particular, the rational and the emotional content of the image, about the clarity of the pictures, simplicity, plasticity, and vividness of the language, etc., etc. As is well known, at various historical stages normative aesthetics has sometimes made mutually exclusive demands.

Equally unproductive is the opposite extreme—the finding of artistic value in a "pure state" by a process of exclusion. According to this view, artistic value is what remains in a work after ideology, national character, the typical, etc., have been subtracted.

The nature of artistic value cannot be explained as a sum of isolated qualities, and there is even less ground for reducing it to a problem of the writer's skill, understood as the ability to find the most successful artistic form for a content already in the artist's mind.

At the same time it would not be correct to set forth criteria of artistic value on the basis of peerless models of art and to judge a given work by that standard. Nor is it possible to explain the secret of artistic value by finding something common to all significant works of art. Such an abstraction from phenomena that are endlessly various and intrinsically heterogeneous would give rise only to empty scholastic categories.

The task is to find in the very nature of art itself a general criterion for determining artistic value. With this aim in view, it is necessary for us to determine the fundamental principle of the phenomenon under study and then to examine the historical movement of the given phenomenon and find its inner logic. The basis of scholarly definition thus becomes the attempt to understand what the concept was and what it has become.

Content and Form

In classical art the main criterion for determining artistic value was unity of content and form.

This became the central position of Hegel's aesthetics and then was materialistically reinterpreted by Russian revolutionary democrats. In Plekhanov's, Lunacharski's, and Gorky's outlook on art, this position became the basis for solving the question of the chief function of artistic ideas, of the meaning of the truth of ideas for the correct, deep, truthful and graphic mastery of reality.

The drive to say something necessarily calls forth one or another kind of artistic form. The richer the content, the more developed is the artistic form in which it is realized. In this connection the statement of L. Tolstoy in *Anna Karenina* is significant: "The more experienced and skillful painter-technician would not be able to paint anything with his mechanical skill alone if the outlines of the content did not first become apparent to him."

Contemporary foreign critics often object to establishing a definite role for content in art. The critic John Aldridge, for example, in his critique of the book *Fiction of the Fifties*, by Herbert Gold, wrote about the prose of modern writers: ". . . What the stories are about could not matter less, since their subjects seem almost uniformly less important than the author's struggle to endow them with importance. It is as if we were at last seeing fulfilled on every side the ambition Flaubert once had: to write a beautiful piece of fiction about absolutely nothing."[1]

But in reality "pure" form does not exist, just as content does not exist apart from the form of conceptual or artistic thought.

And although alchemists did not succeed in finding in art that "philosophical," or, more truly, "aesthetic stone" which would turn anything into a beautiful idea, theorists are very busy trying to satisfy this demand. Setting out from Kant, they have gone farther and created a so-called theory of "values" (Charles Morris, Herbert Read, Roger Fry) in accordance with which the artist is the originator or the creator of form, while the artistic work is a specially organized structure possessing an independent aesthetic value. Hence it follows that the best artistic works are those which have the best form.

The unity of content and form is a principal law of image-creating thought, the source of its artistic essence. However, this correct position frequently leads to a conclusion about the "primacy of the criterion of content in comparison with the criterion of form" for determining the artistic merits of a work. At first sight the erroneousness of the formulation is not apparent. What is more, it would seem that only thus, indeed, can the question be posed by anyone who argues against the well-known Schiller position: "In a truly beautiful work of art everything must depend on form, and nothing on content. . . ." Or even more decisively: "The real secret of the master's skill consists in annihilating content by form." Good intentions guide the authors of the thesis about the primacy of the criterion of content—they aspire to develop a position more correct than that of formalistic idealism, in accordance with which "only form distinguishes an artistic work from an inartistic one."

Nevertheless, the contention of the primacy of the isolated criterion of content only seems to refute the formalistic principle in accordance with which form has an absolute value in art while content has a relative one (as Paul Valéry held in part).

As a matter of fact, to acknowledge the autonomous existence of idea content and of artistic value is unconsciously to take a position that has much in common with that of the formalists.

Setting the criterion of content apart from the criterion of form sanctions, as it were, the presence of two different types of artistic value. One inevitably assumes that there are writers who are masters of thought and writers who are masters of form, method, style. If we take such a position, we should have to agree that in case the features we have named fail to coincide, two possibilities arise: an art of ideational importance without aesthetic value, and on the other hand an art of aesthetic value without significant content.

Whenever we speak separately of the criterion of content, we inevitably separate content from form—and consequently affirm the independence of form. It is on this base that there arises a polar, but equally false, dualism of outlook on the essence of art; on the one hand, theorists see art as illustration of content that has already taken shape; on the other hand, they advocate a "pure" art in which the criterion of content is irrelevant.

The extremes meet: content, existing apart from form is just as much a fiction as form without significant content.

This is why it is impossible to understand art without understanding form. Every time this is forgotten, the critic attributes to a book a content which is not and cannot be in it.

A genuinely artistic work arises when there takes place not a reconciliation, but a dialectical Aufhebung of vital content and graphic form. But once we acknowledge the unity of content and form, we exclude the possibility of employing two corresponding criteria.

The attainment of high levels of artistic value demands the creation of a beautiful work in an interesting artistic form. An image having artistic value cannot be the embodiment of a completed idea—it is the very being of the idea.

To acknowledge the unity of content and form does not mean to regard them as dialectically indivisible, as if—and this is what Benedetto Croce held—the work were a monistic totality and it was senseless to divide it into form and content because form is the content of art while content in itself represents nothing except aesthetic fact (or, in other words, form again) outside which there is nothing in art.

The "scholastic division of a work into content and form" was subjected to attack from quite other positions by certain RAPP theorists. If formalists brought content as a victim to form, then vulgar sociologists, instead of the unity of content and form, brought forward as an "objective sign of artistic value" the demand for some sociological equivalent of life. Examination of the problem of the relation of content and form from positions of their indivisibility was regarded as aesthetic idealism.

Another way to avoid the reproach of traditional dualism is to transform a work into an indivisible structural whole and to subtract from it all content except that of form. The reduction of content to form is characteristic for contemporary formalism and structuralism. René Wellek and Austin Warren[2] take matter and structure as the initial components of a work and attribute to the first an unaesthetic quality and to the second whatever gives aesthetic meaning to the material.

Nevertheless we must go beyond the content-form duality. This twofold unity will not enable us to form valid judgments concerning artistic worth. We must examine a further quality, namely, the truth of art.

Truth of Art versus Truth of Life

There is good reason to talk about a threefold unity, or more exactly about the unity of form and content in genuine art as the source of a new quality, namely, artistic truth. It does exist, this third quality, the specific object of the present study, something that heretofore has been thought of as a synthetic quality in art.

Both materialist and idealist aesthetics make use of the concept of artistic truth, but the meanings associated with the concept are different.

Often the term is used in order to contrast art with life. Artistic truth is taken to mean precisely what does not correspond with the truth of life. This view of things had its origin with Plato and his followers. They held that the very essence of art could be nothing other than an illusion—a shadow of shadows, for the whole real world, in consonance with this philosophical system, is a pale reflection of another world of ideas. The followers of Plato advanced a thought that has become widespread: art is what the artist adds to nature. Such a premise even leads to the assertion: artistic value is everything over and above the real, it is what makes art more beautiful than life or unlike it. Art becomes the creative transformation of reality. Whereas the scholar must remain within the bounds of logic and necessity, according to this view of the matter, the artist possesses unlimited freedom—he creates according to his own will.

The opposite extreme from this view would be the contention that artistic truth and the truth of life are identical. But in fact things are much more complex than that. The tendency to identify artistic truth and truth of fact leads invariably to a tyranny of fact over artistic meaning, as in naturalism.

The artist introduces and cannot but introduce a creative principle into the representation of life and thereby the truth of art is distinguished from the truth of life, is not equal to it. Art does not copy and does not duplicate the object portrayed. Yet at the same time artistic truth which is contrary to real truth is inconceivable.

The fact is then that art cannot be a mere copy of life, nor can it be absolutely unrelated to life, and it is right here that the whole complexity of the problem opens up.

As part of his thesis concerning the relationship between art and reality, Aristotle spoke of the necessary or inevitable as a feature of art. He held that tragedy must include as many necessary and plausible facts as are required for understanding what is taking place. The spectator must not only believe, but must also understand the whole chain of events and the inner logic owing to which, for example, a happy man is transformed into an unhappy one. Art has not to do with some definite person who actually lived and with the facts of his life as they really were, but with what might have happened under certain circumstances. Not by chance did Aristotle consider literature more philosophical and serious than history, for poetry tells about the general, whereas history tells about the particular.

Starting out from the theory of imitation, Lessing, Diderot, Belinski, and Chernyshevski created a conception of the artistic reproduction of life according to the laws of probability.

The Marxist theory of reflection also does not reduce the artistic image to simply "taking a copy" of an object, although "taking a copy" in essence is not a simple matter of passive mirroring but a complex and contradictory process that may include the flight of imagination away from the realm of fact. Actually, as a matter of fact, fantasy has its role even in the strictest scholarship. In art it performs a special creative function. Comprehension of life through literature cannot dispense with imagination and invention, whether in the fantastic panorama of Dante's Hell or in the mundane narratives of Emile Zola. Even in a work based upon historical events or in a portrait sketch, the artist thinks about his subject, discovers a meaning in it, and develops a creative conception of what is to be portrayed.

In fact, if we assume that artistic truth and the truth of life are synonymous phenomena, equal to each other, what will become of the greatest works of art like *The Iliad* and *The Odyssey* or *The Divine Comedy?* Transmission of uncoordinated factual information about the life, manners and morals, and customs of a distant past? Of course,

the Homeric poems place at the disposal of historians of culture, ar-
chaeologists, and ethnographers much unique and valuable material. But
this is hardly what makes the Homeric poems important for us. Was
the maker inspired by such a purpose? The artistic works of the past
—be it *The Iliad* or *The Lay of Igor's Host*, a tragedy of Aeschylus
or of Shakespeare—continue to live a special aesthetic life because the
pulse of life beats in them and a living world of artistic truth reveals
itself.

Artistic fantasy enables the writer to penetrate into the meaning
of life, to reveal its essential characteristics—the whole of world literature testifies to this, realistic literature included. If realism comprehends reality by exploring typical characters in typical circumstances, this implies no diminishing of the role of creative invention.

Sometimes artistic truth is taken to mean exclusively the product
of fantasy. Of course, Pushkin's "Brazen Horseman," the St. Petersburg
stories of Gogol, Lermontov's "Demon," Goethe's *Faust*, Heine's
lyrics, Saltikov-Shchedrin's satires, and the plays of Mayakovsky and
Brecht provide sufficient illustration for the flight of fantasy as opposed to verisimilitude, but even in these works truth of life is a significant component. Conversely, in Gogol's *Old World Landowners*,
Madame Bovary, Furmanov's *Chapayev*, and Fadeyev's *The Young
Guard* not only is material of life reflected in each case, but there is
also created a finished image of reality, a conception charged with
imaginative, emotional and aesthetic content; truth of life has been
transformed into artistic truth.

The Forsyte Saga

Let us clarify the basic thought with an example from John Galsworthy. The writer makes one of the heroes of *The Forsyte Saga*,
young Jolyon, retell nearly the whole content of the first three novels
of the Forsyte cycle. Involuntarily the supposition suggests itself: in
introducing Jolyon's extensive letter to his son, in which *the already
known* is repeated, does not the author act uneconomically? Is this
not an artistic error? Is the cursory repetition of facts from the life
of Soames, Irene, and Bosney necessary since all this is not only already
known but has indeed been fully experienced by the reader?

Let us turn to the letter. "The man your mother married . . .," it
says, "once at night forced his marital rights on her. On the following

day she met her lover and told him about it. Whether he committed suicide or in his depressed state accidentally fell under an omnibus, we never found out; but thus or otherwise—he perished. Think what your mother lived through when that evening she heard about his death. I happened to see her then. Your grandfather had sent me to help her, if possible. I caught only a glimpse of her—her husband slammed the door in my face."

Here we have the brief retelling of events linked with one of the basic plot lines of the *Saga*. It not only adds nothing, but does not compare with the pages where what happens is directly conveyed.

Let us recall the staggering scene of the last minutes of Irene's stay in the house of the man who has destroyed her life. She sits quietly in the corner of a divan, not moving and not answering a word to Soames' questions: "Now he looked closely at her face—as pale and frozen as if the blood had stopped in her veins; her large, frightened eyes, like the eyes of an owl, seemed enormous.

"In a gray fur coat, shrinking into a corner of the divan, she somehow called to mind an owl, a clump of gray feathers pressed to the wires of a cage. Her body, as though wretched, lost its flexibility and shapeliness, as if that for which it was worth while being beautiful, flexible, and shapely had disappeared."

Later comes a comparison with a fatally wounded animal which returns to its lair, not understanding what it is doing, not knowing where to get to now. The image of a gray, wounded bird pressed to the wires of a cage not only conveys Irene's state, but even gives a definite emotional tone to the scene, calls out a corresponding reaction in the reader, and explains the conduct of Soames. Seeing that his wife has come back to his house as if into a cage, Soames wants to drive her out and at the same time he holds her there. A struggle is going on inside him. He loves his wife, suffers for her, pities himself, knows that his situation is hopeless—and bursts out sobbing. The unexpected arrival of young Jolyon with a request to see Irene transforms Soames once more—instead of an unhappy man, before us is once more the man of property: "Soames squeezed by him, blocking the entrance. 'She is not receiving anyone,' he said again. Young Jolyon suddenly looked past him into the hall, and Soames turned. There in the living room door stood Irene: in her eyes there was a feverish fire, her half open lips were trembling, she was stretching out her arms. Seeing them both, the light on her face died; her arms fell powerless; she stopped, as if turned to stone.

"Soames turned sharply, caught his visitor's glance, and a sound like a growl burst from his throat. Something like a smile opened his lips. 'This is my house,' he said, "I will not let anyone mix into my business. I have already told you, and I repeat it again, we are not receiving.' And he slammed the door in young Jolyon's face."

To comment on these excerpts, to reveal the meaning of what stands behind all this, would take many pages. Every stroke is not simply a detail of the story, one more touch in the striking picture, but also it conveys the character of the people in the novel, the story of their mutual relations, the sum of what has been lived through and the motivation of what follows. "She is not receiving anyone," changed to a tell-tale "we" when Irene has rushed to meet Jolyon, creates the whole dramatic tangle out of which arises the entire *Saga*. The fragments cited are indeed not so very great in volume, they are fully commensurable with the corresponding citations from the letter, but how much more is told in them about life and people!

And now, perhaps, we can return to the question about the advisability—more than that, the artistic necessity—of parallel epistolary and directly told events. Galsworthy was solving a definite creative problem. We see how difficult it is for the father and mother to make what they have experienced the property of their son. What the letter tells remains for Jon an "alien experience," an "alien" life, incomprehensible and somehow irrelevant to him, notwithstanding his tremendous love for his parents. The letter merely states, names facts, but this is insufficient to make them "speak." And the reader sees very well the barriers between the parents and Jon from the lack of understanding which has arisen between them, they see that the experience of their life is not to be conveyed in words even to a person close to them. And once this is realized by the reader (and this is indeed so), it turns out that the "alien experience" of Irene and Jolyon is alien to Jon, while not at all so to the reader. As a result of magic art, the life of the heroes becomes *his own* experience to the reader. The truth of the fact about which the letter tells and the truth of life in the work, which has become artistic truth, turn out far from equal in artistic meaning.

Neither in the content of the letter nor in its style is there anything poetical. Yet even in the fragments cited there is that which forces us without hesitation to judge *The Forsyte Saga* a work "poetical in itself" (Hegel). Where did this poeticality, this aesthetic quality, come from? Apparently not simply from the description of the soul-harrowing scene between Jolyon, Soames, and Irene. Otherwise the "poetical-ness of the content" would have left itself be known even in the letter with a simple statement of facts. It would be precipitate to see the source of the poetical in special artistic details, for example in the comparison of the woman with a big gray bird sitting motionless in a cage, although the detailed comparison does indeed give the scene a special emotional tone and helps us to understand much in the work.

The truth of a fact harrowing to the soul is in the letter; as regards the direct artistic reproduction of events, they possess much more meaningful content when one approaches them thematically, than do the fragments cited. Before us arises an aesthetic antithesis of the beau-tiful and the ugly, of the natural, the human, and of an egotistical civilization, and all this serves as the point of departure both for the recreation of life and for affirmation of the aesthetic ideal. The artistic value thus finally appears to be nothing else but the truth of life, ob-jectified under the impact of the great tasks facings mankind and under the influence of great aesthetic ideals which this work of art serves. Only when these conditions have been met does it make sense to talk about artistic truth.

The Voice of Life and the Voice of the Artist

Defining artistic truth as the truth of life realized in art and by means of art (the reflection never equal to the thing reflected), we really have to do with a phenomenon complex and contradictory.

Augustine said that a quality of illusion in art becomes a means to the truth. The outer illusion, so to speak, becomes a condition for truthful portrayal. It may also be true that the aesthetic illusion will create a deceptive world. Fantasy is a powerful means toward the ar-tistic analysis of life, but it may be a source also of aesthetic mys-tification.

Aesthetic illusion having this character has many of the marks of art, but in the end it lacks truthfulness. In such works the best that can be said by the artist is—that is the way the world looks to me. So you have modernist works in which truth to life is lacking and in consequence artistic truth is lacking also. Genuine art has always been impaired by aesthetic illusions of this kind, particularly such as we get in Robinsoniads large and small, in Proust's isolated man, or in Camus' "Millions of Lone Persons."

Contemporary foreign art criticism justifies aesthetic illusion of whatever kind and defends the absolute freedom of the artist's imagination. Idealist aesthetics does not require that art reflect objective reality and denies or minimizes its cognitive function. (". . . if art were a means of cognition, it would be much lower than geometry," says J. Maritain.)

We can speak of artistic truth, however, only when the artist's imagination does not break with the actual facts of reality but penetrates into them. This is why poetry cannot be defined, with Shelley, as an "expression of the imagination," although here indeed the role of the imagination, its necessity, is underscored. It would be more exact to say that it is not an "expression of the imagination" but an expression *by* the imagination. Fantasy is not the content of poetry, but only a means of reproducing the truth of life.

The imagination, fantasy, is capable of giving birth to senseless images and phantasmagorias, but it is indeed a necessary principle in the creation of an artistic image, even a graphically factual one (the imagination is necessary even in mathematics!). If a medicine in a certain dosage is dangerous to life, this does not call in question its curative virtues. Subjective fantasy created the most sordid images of contemporary modernism, but nevertheless it was fantasy that brought forth the Venus of Milo, it called to life the symphonies of Beethoven and the immense worlds of Goethe's *Faust*, Tolstoy's *War and Peace*, and Gorky's *Life of Klim Samgin*. Here the fantasy does not work arbitrarily, however, but in accordance with measure and retaining communication with objective fact.

What is called for is the boldest kind of invention, so long as the imagination does not lead the artist astray, does not obscure, but helps to comprehend life in all its hidden possibilities. There are many well-known examples of fantasy leading apparently far from the truth of life, yet in the end being directed not away from reality but toward its comprehension.

To banish the imagination from artistic creation, to substitute truth of fact for the truth of life, would be like death for art.

Those who insist only on the truth of fact support the one-sidedness of naturalism and sociological positivism. They identify the aesthetic ideal with idealism, and artistic fancy with poetical falsehood, and on this basis banish them beyond the barriers of art. But now the artistic content of the work evaporates. Robbed of the ideal, of the power of generalization, of aesthetic content, it is transformed into a citation from the social sciences.

Much has been said in the Soviet Union lately about the error of seeing in realism the tyranny of fact and in poetry only the artist's self-expression. In a genuine work of art the voice of life and the voice of the artist necessarily sound like an original duet. Just try to separate the epoch and the writer in the works of Homer or Shakespeare. The epoch spoke through their mouth, and their creations became the epoch in art.

Artistic truth cannot be understood apart from the complex dialectics of the objective and the subjective. It would be useless to seek the dosage of each of these principles. The practice of art admits immense possibilities for the flight of imagination from the truth of fact and forms countless correlations between the objective and the subjective, always balancing this mobile unity by artistically adjusted harmony, so that one can sense a deep and vital content in the most fantastic image.

The truth of art comprehends the objective world in its aesthetic interpretation. It brings us closer to knowledge of reality by special means. The imagined in art is that poetical magnifying glass which makes accessible the hidden meaning of phenomena, reveals the general and aesthetic meaning of the object, allows us to understand the link between reality and the ideal, checks ideals by life, and appraises life from positions of the ideal.

Some of the complexities in the problem of artistic truth were dealt with by Aristotle when he wrote of the insoluble antinomy between an impossibility that creates artistic truth and the possible that proves artistically false. For Aristotle the impossible that seemed to be true was to be preferred to the possible when artistically unbelievable.

These extremes mentioned by Aristotle may be defined as the limits of artistic truth. Within them the truth of life finds its expression in art, and by them are defined the bounds of genuine art. Inclining toward a preference for the "probable impossible," Aristotle exhibited the "metaphysical" method in philosophy. It is for this reason that he contrasts two extremes as something uncorrelated and mutually exclusive, and gives preference to one of them at the expense of the other.

With a dialectical approach, the link between the extremes reveals itself. The points mentioned are present, not in isolation, but as living contrasts which are the source of the projection of the artistic image. Impossible reality—in a literal sense it is absurd, but as a feature in the dialectics of artistic truth it is a real fact.

If the artistic image is convincing, if it possesses artistic truth, then, no matter how far-fetched it be, it has "scooped up" and carries within itself something of the truth of life.

In this sense the artistic image is not a copy of fact but its special recreation, an aesthetic analogy of reality, which, subject to the specific laws of art, recreates or "refashions" the truth of life.

The artistic image develops out of dialectical interchange between the ideal and the actual, the real and the potential. Artistic truth will remain unrealized if idealization does detriment to the truth of life, if it fails to reveal the essential in what is typified. The genuine artistic image is truer than reality itself, more alive than the phenomenon or character we run into daily. This is because the truth of an image is adjusted not only by correspondence to the truth of life, but also by the quality of the ideal content included in it.

The real and the imagined will differ much in their comparative weight, as is obvious from everything said above. The truth of art is the truth of the image. Even Dante's *Divine Comedy* is not a hypothesis about the existence of life after death, but a bold search for the meaning of human life and happiness.

If we turn to Milton's *Paradise Lost*, Shelley's "Prometheus Unbound," or Lermontov's "Demon," we would scarcely think that each of these artists strove to convince the reader of the reality of the other world. However, how trustworthy and how impressively written are the fanciful scenes! In fact, when Hoffman's door opens and the devil comes in, you "believe," whereas in another instance you sometimes do not believe even when he who comes in is simply Ivan Ivanovitch Ivanov.

Nowadays one meets more and more evidence that a fact trustworthy as a document can turn out to be completely unconvincing in art, whereas the most fantastic inventions are capable of communicating a sense of truth.

Truth in Art — Changing Criteria

Having come to the conclusion that the truth of art is related to the truth of life—that it concerns a special means of understanding and aesthetic evaluation of the truth of life—we see that the criterion for determining truth in art has an objective content. Some will agree with this position and some will disagree, as does idealist aesthetics. But in any case there will be difficulties.

We must not think that the truthful portrayal of life is something immutable, given once for all time. The fact is that the truthful portrayal of life, artistic truth, is vastly different in the Homeric epics and in Tolstoy. If we do not take account of these historical changes, we might easily go along with the bourgeois assertion that there has been no real progress in art since Homer.

In a word, the content of the notion of artistic truth has gone through great changes in literary history. In defense of truth in art, Boileau condemned burlesque literature, Hugo in his turn attacked the classical writers, and later Zola attacked Hugo. Each age, we see, has its own conception of what artistic truth requires.

The historic transformation of the concept of artistic truth explains the changes in the rules for evaluating literary work, as set forth for example by Aristotle, by Horace, by Boileau, and in the aesthetics of romanticism and then in realism and socialist realism.

The criteria of appraisal at first find expression in practical rules about what a work must be like. In Aristotle's *Poetics* a whole string of concrete differences is set forth between "good" and "bad" tragedies, and the poetic tracts of Horace and Boileau set up rules of the same kind. Many of the "rules" had a temporary, conditional, relative character. They were dismissed by the subsequent development of art. Thus, for example, romanticism affirmed itself in the struggle against classicism.

V. Djirmunski proposes that we divide the early history of art into stages conforming with the way the fairy tale gives way to the heroic and the heroic in its turn is superseded by poetic idealization. The latter is characteristic of the Renaissance and is linked with the rise of realism in that period, when the image of man takes the form of an individual harmoniously developed and rich in possibility. We have the triumph of the human principle in art, and this constitutes the triumph of artistic value, marked as it is by a true depiction of reality and a deeply poetic affirmation of the beautiful. Along with the emancipation of the personality, the Renaissance liberates artistic fantasy and puts it in the service of man. Creative imagination becomes an important instrument in the service of artistic truth. The liberation of the fantasy in the Renaissance went hand in hand with a deepening of realistic motivation. Fantasy no longer claims to give access to reality independently but it makes possible a true, vivid and impressive comprehension of reality. In contrast to this, the fantasy of romanticism—especially of that tendency in romanticism marked by a reaction against the epoch of the Enlightenment—acquires an independent force and becomes a demiurge of reality and demands acknowledgement of its fruits as in themselves the highest reality.

In the age of classicism, the imitation of elegant nature became one of the laws of art. In contrast to the Renaissance, strict rules of art were established, and for this reason the principle of imitation took on more and more a taint of artificiality. The demand for the three unities came to hamper the effort to achieve artistic truth. Yet the "rules," which in fact tie the artistic imagination to a Procrustean bed, were intended to promote maximum conviction and a complete illusion of reality. The classicist tried to attain verisimilitude by synchronizing the stage time with real time, by confining the action to one place, and by unification of the plot.

In contradistinction to the Renaissance, where the creative fantasy associated the ideal with man in the present, the romantics strove to affirm or recreate an ideal word order unlike the present, and thus established a new role for the imagination. Henceforth, if we set aside the claim of intuition or the imagination to penetrate the mystical and other-worldly experience, we see that the unique function of fantasy is to penetrate to those essential aspects of reality which are inaccessible to direct observation, to contribute to the comprehension of the ideal and the possible.

Romanticism was not a flight from life, but only from life as it is, especially in its outward appearance. Romanticism strove toward the affirmation of an idealized past or an idealized future. In each instance it was often enough relevant to the problems of the present and to political struggle. If at times romanticism diverges from probability in its portrayal of life, it shows a heightened sensitivity to the real needs and demands of life. Shelley's Prometheus is significant, not because of the moral or physical torments of the Titan but because of the deep and energetic expression of the artistic idea of struggle against tyranny in the name of freedom. The same can be said of much of the poetry of Byron or of Lermontov's "Demon," where artistic truth appears as the truth of an idea that is strikingly expressed in a symbolic protagonist.

Truth of the ideal was expressed in romanticism also in the depiction of a hero to be emulated in contrast to the petty aspects of everyday life, as also in the handling of local color themes and in the representation of a way of life close to the people.

Romanticism continued the liberation of fantasy that had been begun during the Renaissance. The artistic imagination, long restrained by the dogmas of classicism, proclaimed its complete freedom in the manifestoes of the romantics. This development had its own logic, but at the same time there arose a new contradiction. While the subjective treatment was accompanied up to a point with an increased penetration into the truth of the idea and the truth of life, at the same time romantic subjectivity eventually came into collision with the necessity of showing human character and social history in their development.

In the novels of Walter Scott, whose work marks the transition from romanticism to realism, the historical method acquires a new base. Where romanticism had put reality to the test of the ideal, now realism puts the ideal to the test of reality. The modern novel, one recalls, had originated with Cervantes' *Don Quixote* where, in the characters of a poor but noble hidalgo and his squire, the problems of the ideal and the real were presented in a new way.

Realist writers tend to be concerned with the mastery of time and the movement of history. They try to define the link between the truth of existing reality and truth of the idea. This is a creative method that as a whole gravitates toward the portrayal of man in his actual behavior. The creative imagination here becomes a means of comprehending and depicting the truth of life in its concrete reality. The typical character becomes the chief object and the principal aesthetic category of literature. The breadth and scope of the writer's command of the world, the epoch, the personality and inner experience all contribute to the creation of the typical character. It was the ability to create the typical character that enabled Pushkin to furnish an "encyclopedia of Russian life" and that enabled Balzac and Zola to exhibit a panorama of French society. Each separate novel of *The Human Comedy* and the "Rougon-Macquart" cycle represents a section of French society, within the boundaries of the real, with the separate social layers distinguished from one another. In these novels, however, Balzac and Zola did not undertake a consecutive narrative; instead they devoted their attention to separate points in the movement of history.

Tolstoy's *War and Peace* shows the link between society and historical movement in a different way. The course of time is realized in the novel through the development of single characters whose lives are fused with the development of history. This Tolstoyan synthesis made possible the monumental canvasses of Romain Rolland and Galsworthy.

With the transition to socialist realism, where the movement of time always has a positive significance, we note a change of no small importance. The ideal of a reasonably ordered society had once been associated with far-off lands, the golden Eldorado, the Island of Utopia, or the City of the Sun. But as the blank areas disappear from the map, utopias come to be associated not with the geographical discovery of some traveller but with the future. The ideal society and the "new" man are localized now not in an unknown land but in an unknown future. But then with socialist realism a qualitatively new feature enters in and makes possible a deeper penetration by the artist into the very essence of the progressive development of human experience; this is the transformation of the time factor into the actual condition for practical realization of human and aesthetical ideals.

This may be seen in the handling of time in Gorky's *Klim Samgin* as opposed to Galsworthy's *Forsyte Saga*. In Gorky's novel time has a positive content; leading toward the realization of great socialist ideals, it moves past the shadowy protagonist, who turns out to be a mere onlooker in relation to the events of his age. The handling of time here is in striking contrast to that of Galsworthy, where time is felt to be moving in the direction of a society quite hostile to beauty, love, and generous human feelings. The difference between Gorky and Galsworthy is all the more noteworthy in that the two novelists, both concerned with the changes in their characters during the course of a decade, have much in common as regards plot and structural conception.

These comments will serve to point up some of the changing considerations bearing upon the concept of artistic truth in different historical periods.

REFERENCES

1. *New York Times*, December 6, 1959.
2. *Theory of Literature* (New York, 1956), p. 128.

LATE CAPITALISM AND THE HUMANIST IMAGE

INTRODUCTION

The last decades of the 19th century were a turning point. Two new trends were initiated then: a new development in art associated with the perspectives of a revolutionary movement guided by Marxist theory; and a literary trend associated with ruling-class culture and marked by consciousness in some ways stultified and by symptoms of artistic decline. The purpose of what follows is to indicate some elements of a Marxist approach to this latter trend, for which the term modernism has been used (not the happiest of terms, but what substitute is there?). A principal challenge in taking up this material is to form a judgment concerning conflicting kinds of significance within modernism and in accordance with this to determine the right tone and approach for the critic or teacher.

A main secret of the phenomena of disintegration in modern society and art lies in Marx's theory concerning capitalist alienation. Marx describes alienation as a condition in which man comes to be ruled over by that which he himself has created (his material society with its institutions and dominant ideas) as if by an independent and foreign force. It is a situation in which worth and potency become attached to a world of objects and processes outside of man, while man himself becomes increasingly impoverished. Alienation in our time is the mark primarily of a society in which production becomes increasingly socialized but ownership continues in private hands. Marx discloses the operation of this society when he analyzes its simplest component, the commodity. In the analysis he makes clear how relationships between people come to be thought of as products not of people but of things. If we understood clearly that we are confronted with the consequences of relationships between people and not things, we would have little difficulty in assuming control of the situation and making the necessary changes. But when we confront what appears to be the behavior of impersonal forces, we come to feel that the course of events is beyond human control. Relationships created by man come to be thought of as constituting objective powers pitted against him. These powers eventually extend far beyond the commodity; they embrace the totality of existing society, its technology, its division of labor, its science, its institutions. What Marx discovered, in a word, is that the source of alienation lies in the capitalist system of exploitation. For those who have not learned of Marx's analysis, the source is hidden. The secret of alienation is a mystery. (It is important to insist that the source of alienation lies in the private ownership of the means of production rather than in an industrialized economy as such. If the source lay in industrialism, we would find ourselves once more helpless, since no one seriously wants to go back to a pre-industrial society; we would then have to regard alienation as an inescapable condition of modern man.)

Capitalist alienation comes to affect all members of society, but it affects different classes in different ways. Those only are in part exempted who understand the roots of the phenomenon and engage in struggle to bring about the kind of change in the structure of society that will start the process of disalienation.

In the later stages of capitalism, the condition of alienation is intensified by the increasingly monolithic ruling-class domination of the media. The seemingly anonymous power of capital has at its disposal the almost limitless capacities of modern technology, pervasive bureaucratic institutions, and a vast apparatus for cultural manipulation. The peculiar paralysis of will associated with an alienated society comes to seem inescapable. The existing situation is thought of as the only conceivable one, or at any rate better than whatever alternatives might be tried.

If one were to give a systematic account of appearances associated with an advanced stage of capitalist alienation, it would be necessary to distinguish between trends manifested in actual behavior on the one hand and the reflection of these trends in literature and the arts on the other. It would be useful to distinguish also between trends that grow almost inevitably out of the condition of intensified alienation and those that have their source in deliberate manipulation, though these two factors are so closely interrelated that a distinction would generally be difficult. We would want to keep in mind the shift from the more or less progressive stage of capitalist society to the period in which the system becomes increasingly obsolescent. In the progressive stage, during the struggle against feudalism, the capitalist class represented the interests to some extent of all oppressed classes. It was then able to produce culture and art that speak for humanity as a whole, though it is also true that early in the progressive stage of capitalism contradictions between the interests of the bourgeoisie and those of the proletariat set in. Capitalism was both a progressive and alienating force from the beginning. In the declining phase, the continuation of the system stands in the way of every advance for humanity as a whole. In this period the most constructive art the dominant class can produce will be critical of the existing society (critical realism).

A leading feature of modernist literature is inability to penetrate to the causal nexus of society. The kind of symbolism that deals with abstract or timeless values is an example; so also is the naturalism that attempts to get at the secret of social reality through mere accumulation of surface detail. Inability to penetrate to the causal nexus has a further consequence, as becomes apparent when one thinks of the Marxist conception of personality as the ensemble of social relations. Failure to grasp the social relations leads to a diminished capacity to create character. Modernist literature is marked also by a debased image of man. Man is no longer presented, as in the tradition of humanism, as ready to accept responsibility for the social enterprise or as sustained by feelings of solidarity with others. Instead he thinks of himself more and more as a prisoner condemned to solitary confinement. Confidence gives way to a temper marked by pessimism and resignation.

In his study of two main trends in contemporary drama, the psychological play and the absurdist theater, Mittenzwei gives special emphasis to the writer's inability to penetrate to the causal nexus. The root trouble, he argues, is a faulty understanding of the condition of alienation in modern society. The dramatists under examination see man as necessarily victimized by incomprehensible forces—or forces that, even if they can be understood, cannot be opposed. Only a materialist dialectic would be able to disclose the true cause of capitalist estrangement and thus enable the dramatist to connect individual motivation in his characters with an understanding of social causation.

This short-circuiting of the capacity to understand the essential forces in modern society results in a breakdown in the ability to create character. Dramatic characters tend to become ciphers, not individuals; Mittenzwei speaks of the "static picture of reified man" in Beckett and of the emptiness and spiritual poverty in Ionesco. In the psychological play, he notes a tendency to move from psychology to neurosis, and to preoccupation with sex, especially with sexual abnormality. Mittenzwei traces the beginning of this tendency in Strindberg, and cites

Tennessee Williams as a contemporary example. He notes that even in *The Glass Menagerie* the social is present only in a perfunctory way.

What has happened, then, in both the psychological and the absurdist play, is that individual motivation has become separated from an understanding of social causation. The dramatist loses the capacity to portray the individual through the social and vice versa.

In her study of *Ulysses*, Zhantieva calls attention also to the failure to grasp the fundamental movement of society. Joyce takes as universal what is in fact temporally conditioned. In its detailed account of the class character of the "vision of reality" in *Ulysses*, and in the attention given to formal features of the work, the Zhantieva essay illustrates the depth and comprehensive character of Marxist criticism at its best.

While dealing with a particular time and place, Zhantieva argues, Joyce believed himself to be confronting the condition of man. Joyce's Dublin is representative of bourgeois society but Joyce takes it to be representative of human society generally. Stephen Dedalus, like Joyce, is filled with revulsion when he confronts a society where market values have become predominant, but the revulsion he feels is transformed into an indictment of all humanity.

Both Bloom and Marion belong to a stage in cultural history (they represent the attitudes and behavior of petty bourgeois society) but are set forth as universals. Marion—"all-accepting, infinitely unfastidious, low, animal," at the opposite extreme from Penelope and from Goethe's "eternal feminine"—is intended by Joyce to represent not woman of a specific time and place, but universal woman.

Nighttown represents in fact terrible and monstrous qualities of bourgeois society. Both the strength and the weakness of Joyce are seen at their most characteristic here, Zhantieva says. The strength is manifested in the literary power of the scene, the weakness in the sick view of man and the repugnance to humanity that results from it. The sick view comes from modernist philosophy and from the Catholic notion of original sin which strengthens Joyce's inclination to attribute the evils of a given state of society to human nature. In Nighttown what is in fact "the incarnation of the capitalist world" becomes for Joyce "the night of mankind." Bloom's fantasies of being elected lord mayor, etc., are in fact a clever satire on the poverty of content in bourgeois culture, but Joyce negates the effect of the satire by representing Bloomism as a universal malady.

The result of Joyce's equation between bourgeois society and the condition of man is that the hostility and despair aroused by the society he knew was transformed into a terrible indictment of human nature as such. The philosophic error fettered Joyce's creative power. He was able to capture the visible reality of his world with extraordinary effect, and yet he did not try to discover and render that which was specific of time and place, for he did not regard this as important. He did not attempt "a realistic re-creation of reality."

The author's sense of life as chaos appears everywhere in the novel. Zhantieva makes a special point of Stephen's interpretation of Shakespeare. Admittedly, the tone is ambiguous; Stephen does not necessarily believe his own theories, and Haines is made to remark that "Shakespeare is the happy hunting ground of all minds that have lost their balance." Still, in Shakespeare Joyce finds confirmation of his own thoughts concerning the depravity of man. History is a chain of crimes. Shakespeare serves to focus Joyce's perceptions concerning the baseness of man's nature—those thoughts which had been "formed under the influence of modernist philosophy in crisis" and intensified by the Catholic view of original sin.

The note of the novel as a whole is one of "unbelief and nihilism, born of despair." The "all in each" theme—the assumption that all lives are somehow to be discovered in each single life—reenforced Joyce's pessimistic outlook. The main philosophic prop of the novel was the view of history as endless and meaningless repetition. Joyce's consciousness came to be "traumatized by the notion of life as a senseless cyclic recurrence" and by the idea of "the ruin of civilization." Both Stephen and Bloom "perceive life as a senseless, ever renewing cycle in which birth and death take turns." The union of Stephen and Bloom at the end of the novel accomplishes nothing. They achieve no closeness, nor are they liberated from the closed cycle of life. Nothing is resolved, the cycle continues, each is as lonely as before.

One result of Joyce's pseudo-philosophy is that the protagonists of *Ulysses* are creatures of singular passivity. Stephen "may be regarded as the prototype of many central characters in contemporary modernist literature" in that he does not oppose his environment. He regards the struggle to liberate Ireland as a snare he must avoid. As artist, he is determined to isolate himself from a hateful reality. Bloom, likewise, with all his revulsion from the society that he confronts, cannot agree that this should be opposed with force. Here he speaks for the author, embodying Joyce's conviction of "the uselessness of struggle."

The nihilism in Joyce's novel and the passivity of the characters are features that one could not expect a Marxist critic to pass over, since in his view the great task of man in our time is to free himself from the destructive influence of the kind of world view represented here, so that, within a framework provided by the perspectives of socialism, he can continue the struggle for human emancipation and fulfillment that began in the Renaissance, was advanced in the period of Enlightenment and romanticism and then was interrupted in the late 19th century when the epoch of capitalist crisis began.

Zhantieva keeps the reader aware of Joyce's unrivalled literary powers, his extraordinary gift of phrase, and his preeminence as a satirist. She calls attention to the warmth and humanity of which Joyce was capable. But she is at pains to point out also that Joyce's failure to understand the structure and movement of society inevitably results in a certain impoverishment. Joyce's characters become depersonalized; individuality is lost and the psyche becomes merely a receptacle for sensations. If Joyce offers a naturalistic depiction of man in place of true characterization, this is at bottom an expression of the disgust he felt for his own creations and his world. After him, depiction of the ugly, the monstrous and the revolting becomes a standard feature of modernist art.

Zhantieva believes that Joyce's technical innovations, influential as they were, did not yield profound insight. She distinguishes between Joyce's stream of consciousness and the inner monologue Tolstoy used, pointing out that the difference has its source in a different attitude toward life. Her conclusion is that while free association "is inherent in human consciousness," yet when it is employed as a principal means for depicting spiritual life, it becomes "a fruitless and tiresome thing." It is an illusion to think that the stream of consciousness technique enabled Joyce and the modernist writers who came after him to probe deeply into psychology. This is precisely what they do not do, Zhantieva says.

Toward the end of the novel, Joyce spent more and more time on far-fetched experiments in technique in which in the end the form contributed little to content, or even became an impediment. Examples are the imitation of literary styles in the Oxen of Helios episode, the parodies illustrative of "gigantism" in the Cyclops episode, and the questions and answers suggestive of a catechism or arithmetic text in the Ithaca episode. A further example of unproductive formal experimentation in *Ulysses* is the system of references, analogies and correspondences, involving parts of the body, aspects of knowledge, colors, etc. Harry Levin and others have claimed that Joyce's system of correspondences makes for unity and universality, but Zhantieva views them as pedantic and formal. She feels too that the construction of prose on the analogy of music was an unproductive experiment. The fugal construction of the Sirens episode is an experiment that fails, she believes.

She adds that after we have taken account of Joyce's great skill with words, we have to concede that in the end words cease to be expressive and language comes to veil meaning. In all this Zhantieva is describing an element of formalism, in that form becomes an end in itself and also in the sense that the functions of form and content are reversed; form becomes a barrier to meaning instead of an outlet for it. The relationship between writer and reader breaks down. Joyce, and the modernists who follow him, write more and more for an elite.

Zhantieva believes that Joyce's literary powers did not reach fruition in *Ulysses*. Although he believed he had sacrificed everything to his art, he was in fact unfaithful to the aims of art.

The Marxist approach to modernism will become more clear if we contrast it to leading bourgeois interpretations. Here are four:

(1) The change is seen as the breakdown not of a ruling class but a civilization; it signalizes the decline of the West. Those who represent this point of view are not able to discern any possible source for the renewal of humanism.[1]

(2) Others see the shift toward modernism not as a sign of incipient collapse but as an advance toward a clear-sighted and up-to-date existentialist sensibility. We see something of this point of view in the work of William Madden, Morse Peckham, Martin Esslin, and William Barrett.[2] The existentialist outlook in our time itself embodies bourgeois perspectives, and the same may be said for the notion that a change in temper pointing in the direction of existentialism is to be thought of as an advance toward clear-sightedness.

(3) Modernism is looked upon primarily as a consequence of the breakdown of traditional religious faith. The Victorians themselves often thought of the matter this way. Both Tennyson and Browning, for example, shielded themselves against the assault of modernism by

reaffirming traditional belief—belief in spite of the evidence, as it often seems, especially with Tennyson. Robert Penn Warren takes at face value the Victorians' own understanding of the situation and writes as if the collapse of religious faith were sufficient explanation for the onset of modernism.[3] In *The Disappearance of God in the Nineteenth Century*, Hillis Miller likewise assumes that the modernist sensibility was brought about primarily by the collapse of religious faith. But one can think of other periods in which skepticism concerning religion has been associated with a confident world view; also those Victorians who abandoned traditional belief but at the same time looked forward to the possibility of social advance were not affected by the modernist temper. While the religious crisis often precipitated modernist attitudes, it cannot be thought of as the primary cause. The effect of ascribing the transition to modernism to the breakdown of religious belief is to make it appear that the change was inevitable and that no alternative can be expected.

(4) Sometimes the interpretation is so eclectic as to yield no significant meaning for our time. Eclecticism generally functions in such a way as to obscure significant meaning; it does so by making it appear that any one kind of interpretation for a given problem will be canceled out by others that must also be considered.

All four interpretations blind us to the fact that the new temper has its source in the changed perspectives of the dominant class in the epoch of transition in social systems. In so doing they deny us an understanding of past and present that might equip us to solve the problems of today. We have an example here of how in current establishment scholarship a class-oriented view of the present leads to a class-oriented interpretation of the past, and then how the latter comes back to corroborate the former. We are confronted, in other words, with a class view of both past and present in which each confirms the other. (The same may be said, of course, of the Marxist interpretation of the emergence of modernism; here also a class view of the present helps to make clear the nature of the historical crisis just behind us, and then this view of the past serves to reenforce our understanding of today. The difference between establishment and Marxist scholarship, then, boils down in a sense to a difference in class position. But we do not have to leave the matter there, for we then confront the question whether one class view is more in accord with objective reality than the other.)

What tone should the teacher or critic adopt when he deals with the literature of modernism? It is sometimes assumed that a literature that describes the disintegration of capitalist society must have an inherent humanist function, so that the teacher's role need be only to help the student understand what the literature says and how it says it. Further, it may be felt that we cannot very well take a critical position in regard to modernist literature because it has many positive features.

To form a judgment on the question of the appropriate tone, we should look more closely at the leading characteristics of modernist literature. First, what are some of its positive features? It commonly embodies an intense revulsion from bourgeois values, as with Wilde, Yeats, and Joyce; we have a recent example of a similar response in beatnik and hippie culture. Again, this is a literature marked by outstanding candor in expression. It often embodies spectacular release from psycho-sexual-social inhibition, and is in consequence able to draw from deep sources in instinctual life. In its affirmation of the whole self and its reliance on spontaneous impulse, it has something in common with romanticism. The release from repression, making possible a new awareness of the depths of the self, brought a new continent into the sphere of art; it made new materials available for artistic expression. We can add, too, that much of the ground won in this enlargement of the scope of art will continue to be available for a literature whose over-all purpose is at the other extreme from modernism. Again, modernist literature has been marked by much technical innovation, as with the interior monologue, departure from traditional ways of handling time, and experiments in points of view. Many of the gains made in the period of experimentation are now available for a literature having a different character and purpose.

On the other hand, in modernist literature a view of man having its source in the period of capitalist disintegration is universalized. The sickness that belongs in fact to a given class in a given stage in the breakdown of a social system comes to be interpreted as representative of the human condition. Some elements of the sickness can be listed: man comes to be thought of as powerless to alter his condition; he is presented as victim of history (we see the beginnings of this in the period of Edward Fitzgerald, Housman, and Hardy in England, and Henry Adams and Mark Twain in America). Society is felt to be chaotic and incomprehensible. One reacts to it with a sense of bewilderment and is overcome by feelings of futility. The experience of helplessness may lead also to insensitivity and apathy. (Both may be at times combined with a high degree of awareness and concern in certain areas; in other words, the changed sensibility may affect some portions of one's life, not others, as was seen in the death-camp officials in the Nazi period who performed Mozart quartets in their leisure time.) Again, in modernist literature the individual is represented as isolated from those around him; he is condemned, as was said, to the prison of the self. In this literature scorn for man often takes the place of feelings associated with the humanist tradition. The picture of man in modernist literature is fragmented in other ways. Brutalization may take the place of the sense of community and the moral awareness we associate with the humanist tradition. The sources of this may lie in the need to deaden consciousness of what is felt to be man's plight, or the effort to achieve identity at a time when this can hardly be accomplished on the "higher levels." Brutalization also is to some extent an inevitable product of the increasing inhumanity brought about by a dominant class that can find no other response to the increasing vulnerability of its position except genocidal aggression. Along with its picture of a brutalized human nature, modernist literature may stress the abnormal and perverse, something to be explained in part perhaps in terms of a quest for meaning through sensationalism at a time when other kinds of meaning appear unavailable.

After considering the contradictory characteristics of modernist literature, one is likely to come to the conclusion that the teacher has an obligation to establish a critical attitude toward it. If he does not do so, this literature is almost certain to function as an apologetic for the society it describes. The estranged and morally deteriorating world of capitalism will appear as the only one available to us. What then can the teacher do? While he will certainly feel free to point out the merits of modernist literature, some of which have been indicated above, he might perhaps do certain other things also.

He might, for example, show how the trends in modernism are generated within the process of disintegration in a given kind of society. One would want to explore their roots in the condition of alienation and to show also more specific causation in changed class perspectives accompanying the period of transition. At the same time one would want to make it clear that we are dealing with a transitory condition and in so doing to spell out in some detail the nature of the process through which changes in society can be brought about. One would want to give some conception of the prolonged struggle that will be required; no one should be encouraged to imagine that changes of this dimension can take place in the period of a generation or two. Still, it would be desirable at the same time to indicate just what tasks in the present constitute a first step.

It might be helpful also to describe modernist trends in literature as constituting one of the two alternatives that Lukacs poses for the modern writer, namely to portray the destruction of man without comment or to represent the struggle against it. "One can take the destruction of man—which is the result of capitalism—as a basic subject; or one can portray the struggle against such destruction, the beauty and nobility of the human forces which are destroyed but which, with greater or lesser success, rebel." This is a struggle, Lukacs adds, in which the individual cannot rely on himself alone; he can survive only by adhering to those popular forces which economically, politically, socially and culturally guarantee the final victory of humanism. Lukacs speaks of Gorky as "a leading writer of world literature . . . because his works are a supreme artistic expression of this truth." The horror of life in capitalist society is revealed in the most somber colors, but at the same time Gorky depicts "the organic tendency toward harmony and the development of rich, suppressed, distorted, disoriented faculties, even in the poorest examples of the human species." Furthermore, he does all this in "an artistically concrete fashion," that is, "he shows how the revolutionary workers' movement, the people's resistance, arouses and develops the individual, leads to a flowering of his inner life, gives him awareness, strength and tenderness."[5]

REFERENCES

1. In *The Soviet Impact on the Western World* (New York, 1947) E. H. Carr describes the epoch from the Renaissance to the period we are discussing as a hiatus between two totalitarianisms, that of the Middle Ages and that of the 20th century. Similarly, Barbara Ward describes the mid-19th century as a lull before the emergence of "an inhuman order of society," a "social order . . . alien to human personality and human freedom." "The Illusion of Power," *Atlantic Monthly*, December, 1952.
2. William A. Madden, "The Victorian Sensibility," *Victorian Studies*, September, 1963. Morse Peckham, *Beyond the Tragic Vision: The Quest for Identity in*

the 19th Century, New York, 1962. Martin Esslin, *The Theater of the Absurd*, New York, 1961. William Barrett, *Irrational Man: A Study in Existential Philosophy*, New York, 1962.

3. See Robert Penn Warren's essay on Hemingway in Morton D. Zabel, ed., *Literary Opinion in America*, New York, 1951.

4. This kind of eclectic treatment of the Victorian period is to be seen in Jerome Buckley's *The Victorian Temper*, Cambridge, Mass., 1951, and *The Triumph of Time*, Cambridge, Mass., 1966.

5. Georg Lukacs, "Das Ideal des harmonischen Menschen in der buergerlichen Aesthetik," *Essays ueber Realismus*, Berlin, 1948, pp. 5-23.

WERNER MITTENZWEI

CONTEMPORARY DRAMA IN THE WEST

Dialectics of the Individual and the Social

The French literary critic Camille Bourniquel, quoting Aragon's words, "There is no such thing as the history of one man and the history of the world, there is only the inseparable history of both,"[1] writes that this sentence could serve as a motto for our century. Bourniquel, who in general makes much of Joyce and Camus, uses it to support the contention that man in our time, whether he wants it or not, must be aware of history. But Aragon's sentence goes much farther; it answers a basic literary question; to what extent can a work of art represent great social events through the experience of an individual?

This question has always occupied writers. However, the solutions they found have been varied. Each individual life is different, each has its own events, which are not interchangeable. Each event, even though experienced by many individuals, is lived differently by each one; each experience remains unique. Thornton Wilder writes of the innumerable varieties of individual experience, then goes on to point out that they all have nevertheless something in common. The question then, Wilder goes on to say, is which is the more important truth, that of the individual in its uniqueness or the common element. "Which truth is more worth telling?" Wilder is at a loss for an answer; he admits only that, "Every age differs in this."[2]

As early as the 1920s, Brecht was looking at this question dialectically. He writes in his notes:

Man flying	Man jealous
Man building bridges	Man ambitious
Man waging war	Man in conflicts of conscience
Man exploiting	Man unselfish[3]

In this way, the social and individual elements oppose each other. However, Brecht is far from proposing a mechanistic separation. For

105

him the undialectical either-or which torments Wilder does not exist.
He stresses expressly that the categories at left and right of the page
have to be mixed. The problem for Brecht is not an either-or but the
variable influence that each side exerts on the reality. It seemed to him
that from these facts certain consequences should be drawn when the
playwright constructs a character. "In reality," writes Brecht, "man,
that is to say the complete, warm-blooded, living man, is much more
determined by the categories on the left in the list above. As to the
categories on the right, they have not disappeared, they have not ceased
to differentiate a particular individual; he is in fact characterized by
a great many of these categories." Yet Brecht recognizes the primary
significance of the social categories in life and his concern is to make
them visible in the drama. If the type of Napoleon, for example, were
formed only of the category ambition, it would be, in his opinion,
very poor dramatic art. He mentions the work of the great bourgeois
realists whose effectiveness derives from their taking into account social
as well as individual categories and he sees no reason why we cannot
do as well.[4]

These considerations of Brecht mark his going over to the Marxist
position. But late bourgeois literature has not solved the dilemma described by Thornton Wilder, and it is at this point that literary theory
now breaks away from classical aesthetics, as is discussed by the West
German critic Wilhelm Emrich in his book on Kafka. He explains
the break by stating that in the clasical works of art "what was truly
general was verifiable by human reason and was thus capable of being
given an artistic form."[5] But in the 20th century, when man is exposed
to increasing alienation, what is general can no longer be expressed in
what is individual, or vice versa. The break between the general and
the individual is obvious, according to Emrich, in all modern forms of
art. This is not the place to discuss his theory, which he seeks to prove
in the particular instance of Franz Kafka. What matters is to show
that the mechanistic split between individual and general, even though
with different demonstrations, has become a characteristic basic trait
of late bourgeois literature and aesthetics.

The literary historian W. A. Berendsohn, whose book "The Humanist Front" is to be regarded as an anti-fascist literary work, mentions two great literary currents: in one, the fate of an individual is
in the foreground; in the other, to which belong mostly writers with
strong "social imagination," the "mass destiny" takes precedence.[6] This

mechanistic split is even more pronounced in Walter Hinck's book on Brecht. To the individual-centered drama he opposes the society-centered drama.[7]

Of course, the principle of division worked out by W. A. Berend-sohn and W. Hinck does not come out of thin air. In the last 40 years this split in the development of the drama cannot be overlooked. The late bourgeois dramatic authors succeeded less and less in making one of the sides visible through the other one. Let us only consider a number of famous characters. We shall mention only a few of those who have become typical of the different directions the modern drama of the West has been taking.

The most exemplary case is that of Beckett. The two bums Estragon and Vladimir in "Waiting for Godot" are barely sketched. Aside from their symbolic value in the play, their actions are limited to removing their shoes, buttoning their pants, taking off their hats, contemplating them, then putting them on again, spitting, embracing each other, looking into the distance, occasionally asking about Godot, and then waiting again. Nikolaus Gessner, in his dissertation on Beckett, counts no less than 45 such situations in which the characters in his opinion lose their human dignity.[8] Beckett's characters represent a radical break from previous aesthetics, since they can no longer be grasped as men, they are only ciphers in a given situation. Although we don't have here to go into the dialectics of the individual and the social, it is evident that in the creation of such characters, dialectics is completely eradicated.

Tennessee Williams builds his characters quite differently. In "A Streetcar Named Desire," his sensitive, neurotic Blanche withdraws into a dream world all the more intensively as she sinks into a prosaic petty-bourgeois way of life which, as the daughter of a wealthy Southern plantation owner, she can no longer stand. She becomes a victim of her own morbid imaginings. Williams finds the elements to construct his characters in the realm of psychology, in the individual. Although his creations are totally different from Beckett's, there is as little dialectics in them as in those of the Irish author. Thornton Wilder's play "Our Town" rests completely on individual categories. In this play, the author shows the simple life of two families, the Webbs and the Gibbs in Grover's Corner, a small town in New Hampshire: the wedding, the birth of a child and the death of Emily Webb who had become Mrs. Gibbs. Here we have no great passions, no psychic pecu-

liarity which cannot be overcome, as in Tennessee Williams. Wilder
is much more concerned with daily events and their countless repetitions. He wants to show what fills the lives of millions of people: the
little cottage, the baby carriage, the Sunday ride in the Ford, the first
rheumatism, the grand-children, the second attack of rheumatism, and
finally the death bed, the reading aloud of the will. In certain scenes
he has successfully endowed daily life with poetic charm. However,
Wilder's intention was not only to represent the individual life, but
he was trying to depict a generalized truth. He thought the best way
was to show the eternal return of the daily cares. But the dialectic of
life cannot be discovered by this method either.

A character like Johan Wilhelm Möbius, Dürrenmatt's physicist,
is conceived much more dialectically. Möbius has discovered "a system
of all possible inventions." He also knows that what the physicists discover has consequences. He feels himself responsible for the consequences of his thoughts and will prevent his work from falling into
the hands of other men. He chooses to play the fool, pretending that
King Solomon appears to him, ending up by staying in an insane
asylum, the only exit which his reason showed him. Dürrenmatt has
built his protagonist in a way which is far superior to that of the other
playwrights mentioned above, although he has recourse to the predominantly idealistic dialectics of the social versus the individual. But
man is conceived by Dürrenmatt as a social individual who sees disorder in the society where he lives. That's why we find at the center
of his plays a courageous human being. Dürrenmatt goes farther than
most bourgeois playwrights. But he too sees man as a victim. The writer
is not yet aware of the force contained in the social element and its
contradictions.

As a matter of fact, to be conscious of this force means to have
already crossed over to the working class. It is from this new socialist
position that Sean O'Casey writes; the characters he creates, the way
he constructs them, are totally different from those of Dürrenmatt. In
"Red Roses for Me," O'Casey shows through the life and death of
Ayamon Breydon that man assumes new basic human traits in the
measure in which he becomes aware of capitalist alienation and struggles
to overcome it. Breydon's story—his yearning for the beauty without
which he cannot live, his death in the strike—this is a page in the history
of man in the sense Aragon meant it, in which we are concerned with
the movement and development of mankind.

Contemporary bourgeois writers construct their characters in different ways, and often in opposite ways, if one judges from the outside. However, if these figures are analyzed from the point of view of their relationship to life, to society, their attitude is basically the same. The late bourgeois playwrights represent man as a being alienated from himself and from the surrounding world, who does not determine his destiny but is led by foreign, unknown powers, who is denied insight into the phenomena which rule him. Whatever he sets out to do turns out in the end to his disadvantage. Whatever he tries to puzzle out remains enigmatic, ominous, opaque and impossible to influence. In whatever way the bourgeois writers attack the problem of alienation, they find no solution. Alienation is for them a permanent condition which cannot be overcome.

Here we must pause to make a few remarks concerning the problem of alienation, since it has come to the fore in literary discussions since World War II among bourgeois as well as Marxist writers. The talk about alienation is not to be dismissed as a mere literary fad. Many writers discuss the theory of alienation from a philosophical point of view, but most of them have also confronted it in everyday reality through the circumstances of capitalist society. Hence its central place in contemporary bourgeois literature.

As we know, the concept of alienation plays an important role in Marx's early writings.[9] Later, when Marx and Engels worked out the basic features of historical materialism, they used it relatively seldom. But they never discarded it. Marx used it in *Capital*. The Marxist concept is very inclusive, involving not only the alienation of work on the primitive level but also the relationship of the individual to his world—to his society, to social classes, to the State—as well as the problem of the individual's insight into the social process and other points. The term alienation is one of great conceptual generalization. This is what makes it attractive as well as ambiguous. Its misuse by bourgeois theoreticians is not new; Marx already had to mention the "alienation twaddle" of his opponents.

What does alienation mean? In the course of his history, man reaches the degree of universality which makes possible his specific individuality. At this point of his development, man also reaches the condition when he sees himself in an alien, reified world. In capitalist industry and competition, he sees his part in the production as something foreign, non-personal. Out of the cooperation of men grows a de-

pendence on circumstances which exist independently. Since under the
conditions of commodity production man does not control the product but is controlled by it, these relationships in the minds of men become relationships of things. As Marx says, man becomes aware of the
objective world with "false consciousness." His personal abilities, the
degree of his universality and individuality appear to him as depend-
ing objectively on capital. The individuality which has grown out of
capitalist society is shackled again immediately by the process of
alienation inherent in capitalist production. Individuality as a product
of social development is objectively present but it is alienated and deprived of any vital force.

About Marx's concept of alienation, I. S. Narski writes: "Marx
showed that the alienation of work is a result of the split character of
the dialectical contradiction of work itself, thus pointing to the way
to answer the question: What role does alienation play as a category
within the Marxist philosophy? Alienation is one of the specific forms
of the dialectical contradiction."[10] Narski proposes then the following
definition of the Marxist concept of alienation: "Alienation is a process consisting of two phases; in the first, man's forces, his abilities and
generally the product of his social activity are separated from him as
a member of a social collective; in the second, the products become
independent, escape man's control and become a force dominating the
social classes, groups, etc., thus influencing retroactively the social
classes or groups in a way which is not only unexpected but often
destructive."[11]

The bourgeois theoreticians interpret the concept of alienation in
their own way. They detach it from its social context and subordinate
it to an anthropological principle, taking it as a starting point that man
disposes of his own being when he disposes of the product he has
made. Thus they grasp one of the aspects of man's work, but not the
essence of alienation. This aspect supplies the bourgeois ideologists with
a justification for making alienation an eternal, almost cosmic category
from which man cannot escape.

But the process of man's expressing his essential force in the product is not what necessarily brings about alienation and all its consequences; it is only at a certain stage of social development, only under
the conditions of private ownership of the means of production and
especially under monopoly capitalism that the object made by the
worker, his own product, appears to him "as an alien object, as a force

independent of the producer."[12] The devaluing of man increases in the same proportion as the valuing of the world of objects, reaching its highest point under imperialism. The more men produce, the greater is the loss of their essential human powers, and the greater the domination of the product, of capital, according to Marx's formulation in the *Economic and Philosophical Manuscripts*. "All these consequences," he writes, "are contained in the fact that the worker relates to the *product of his own work* as to an *alien* object. It is clear that the more the worker produces, the greater the power of this strange world of objects which he himself creates, the poorer he becomes, the less is his inner world his own."[13] The classic Marxist authors stressed already in their early works that alienation is determined objectively by the capitalist relationship of production. These are the causes, means and reasons of the process of alienation. With the dissolution of private capitalist productive relationships under socialism, alienation loses its base, has no objective roots any longer and its influence disappears gradually, although some elements of alienation may survive a long time.

An important aspect of the capitalist alienation process is the estrangement of the "species life" of men. Man stands before man as before a stranger. The cooperation of men takes place, as Marx says, in a continuous process of "reciprocal separation." This process is a consequence of capitalist private property and associated with alienated labor. "An immediate consequence of the fact that man is estranged from the product of his labor, from his life activity, from his species being," Marx says in the *Economic and Philosophical Manuscripts*, "is the estrangement of man from man."

It is not primarily a concern for estranged work which repeatedly induces the late bourgeois writer to deal with man's alienation. It is rather two phenomena which terrify and paralyze him and which lie at the roots of his pessimism: One is the increasing alienation of man from man, his progressive loss of contact and separation. The individual who is estranged from his own essential nature, sees in another only the reflection of his own deformation. For him all forms of social life are an unbearable strait jacket. Jean Paul Sartre expresses it in his play, "No Exit": "Hell is—other people."[14] The second cause of the pessimistic outlook of many contemporary bourgeois writers is to be traced back to the fact that under capitalism the individual is oppressed by the force of things, a condition that appears to him inscrutable and ineluctable. One of the most fatal conclusions derived by the late bourgeois writers from the capitalist estrangement process is that man is unable to comprehend social development, that he is bound to be confronted by dark and incomprehensible forces. Their poetic creativity, the construction of plot and characters in their works inevitably suffer.

Such a concept of man originates necessarily from the fact that estrangement is conceived not as a historical, passing phenomenon but as an anthropological condition. The late bourgeois dramatists are themselves so deeply caught in estrangement that its mechanism and causes remain inaccessible to them. The reification of everything human taking place under capitalism through alienated work brings it about, as Marx says, that what is animal becomes human and vice versa.[15] Late bourgeois authors have tried in different ways to represent this process in their plays. Beckett and Ionesco stress again and again the animal in man. But these are only surface phenomena of the process of estrangement. Although these writers show the real deformity of man under capitalism, their image of man remains superficial because they are unaware that the predominance of the animal is not to be interpreted as part of the "nature of man" but results from a mode of production in which the estrangement of the true human qualities of the individual makes these qualities appear to be reified, foreign. However, man is able to change this condition, although the change cannot come from the individual alone and not at any time. But social cooperation creates the preconditions for getting rid of the appropriation by private capitalism of the means of production and thus makes it possible for man to regain his essential nature. The late bourgeois authors are not aware of this dialectical process which will do away with estrangement and, as a consequence of this, the characters they create remain static. The writers are unable to show through their characters the dialectics of the individual and society.

Of course it is true that in many of their best known plays, Beckett and Ionesco were not attempting to create character in the usual sense —quite the contrary. But it would be too simple to say that these playwrights were not successful in creating character simply because they did not choose to try. A more significant comment would be, rather, that they did not choose to try to create character in part at least because, having no understanding of the dialectical relationship between the individual and the social, they lacked the capacity to put living people on the stage.

In Beckett's works, the problem of alienation is conceived in such a radical way that the bourgeois conventional concept of destiny in its most extreme form results paradoxically in an Aufhebung of all traditional elements of the theater. For Beckett the character as an aesthetic category does not exist any longer, therefore it doesn't make sense to blame him for not creating characters. His notion of alienation renders him unable to see man in the process of developing. All he can do is again and again to evoke the same image of totally alienated man. Any differentiation proves unfeasible. His plays and his characters are all alike. They are always static studies on the theme of reified man. Such monotony eventually destroys the author's talent.

Alienation as the ineluctable fate of man—this is the implicit theme of the late bourgeois playwrights. No matter how varied the art of the individual writer, whether he belongs to the theater of the absurd or writes psychological plays, this concept of man and human destiny is the same for all. They all take it as self-evident that estrangement lies in the nature of man and this dogma levels down their talent. Even the progressive bourgeois writers who still hope for the man of courage do not see any real possibility that the chains of estrangement can be broken.

The Psychological Play and the Theater of the Absurd

What differentiates late bourgeois writers from one another is the position each takes concerning the fate of estranged man, the way the condition of estrangement is handled. After World War II, two tendencies appear, the absurd and the psychological. On the surface there is a strong contrast between these two tendencies; on one hand man is represented only in his naked, animal-like functions, having lost all contact with others; on the other the individual is analyzed with the most minute psychological refinement. Whereas in the first case what is sought is to represent the absolute reification of all that is human, in the other there is an attempt to escape from the reification by retreating into the "inner life" of man. The more this inner view of man is pursued, the closer do the absurd and the psychological tendencies draw together. These two apparent extremes come together in the poetic expression of the plays.

It will be easier to understand these present tendencies and their representatives if we go back to the precursors of the modern bourgeois theater, to the ancestors of both the psychological and the absurd play. Here we have above all August Strindberg for the former and Maurice Maeterlinck and Alfred Jarry for the latter.

Strindberg can be called the father of the psychological play. In his creation of characters, what is individual begins to separate itself from what is social. With the increasing development of capitalism in the second half of the 19th century, especially under imperialism, the action of reified, foreign forces on the individual becomes very strong. Strindberg reacts by retreating in many of his plays into the "inner life," but there too he encounters the phenomenon of estrangement. He is one of the first playwrights who see only the individual "in himself," no longer a social individual. Strindberg shows the separation of the individual from the social first of all in the estrangement of man in his species being. The natural and necessary species relationship is evidenced in the relationship of man and woman. The central motive in Strindberg's work is the bitter struggle of the sexes. It may be that his own personality played an important role, but it would be a mistake to explain the characteristics of his art by his own temperament. What he presents in his dramas, his love-hate toward women, the impossibility of an harmonious living together, this is basically a reflection of the relationships between man and man in general. Strindberg's struggle of the sexes is only the artistic expression of the absolute estrangement of the individual. He tears the soul apart obsessively in his search for the causes of man's separation and reciprocal repulsion. The individual estranged from his own essence sees in another one only his own distorted, reified image, that is to say the "alien," the "other one." When Strindberg sees woman as foreign, satanic, as the incarnation of evil, it means primarily that the individual stands before society without being able to enter it. In the measure that he considers his own essential force as something foreign, society also appears to him as an alien, threatening power. Since Strindberg is unable to recognize the objective social relationships, the social becomes more and more detached from the individual in his characters.

Even in his historical dramas, where the vision of the alienated individual is not so prevalent, he is unable to see his creations at the point where individual and social intersect. Once, as Brecht was stressing the essential difference between the early and the late bourgeois dramatists, he proposed a comparison between Shakespeare's historical plays and those of Strindberg. The latter's heroes in "Eric XIV" (1899) and

"Gustav Vasa" (1899) have the miserable appearance of plebeians; they are also alienated men. Here the influence of alienation is attenuated only by the historical presentation. Prince Eric's behavior (in "Gustav Vasa") is that of a disobedient dissolute young man of the middle class. The great clash between Eric and the king in the third act reminds us painfully of the argument of a petty bourgeois father when his son hurts the good reputation of the family.

In Shakespeare one can always see the social concerns behind the individual traits and utterances of his characters. Like all the other Elizabethan dramatists, he could give an extreme form to individual peculiarities since for him the individual and the social were not differentiated. Thus his characters remain always real. This is something that we miss in Strindberg. Even in important moments his people never escape from mediocrity, from the average. In the play "Gustav Vasa," Magister Olaus says: "If I were to say in one word what is reprehensible in the great king, then it is—lack of reverence!"[16] Upon which the king answers that this is the worst he has heard. We often have in Strindberg dialogues of this kind; they are typical of the subjectivistic development in the bourgeois drama at the beginning of the 20th century. Strindberg becomes more and more the prey of mysticism. In his plays certain twists of the plot do not evolve according to any rational logic as in Shakespeare—but are brought about in a mystifying way. The petty bourgeois figures are unable to fill up the historical costumes which are put on them.

At the end of his life, Strindberg declared himself to be a disciple of Maeterlinck. The "inner" vision with which he tried to grasp poetically the individual becomes as a result mystical. This psychologizing construction of characters ends up in a mystical symbolism. For the later development of the modern bourgeois drama, it has programmatic significance that the creative principles of both authors are so close. Maeterlinck, who is bound in many ways to the psychological drama, must likewise be regarded as one of the ancestors of the theater of the absurd. The contrasts and similarities of the psychologizing and absurd drama, both resulting from an alienated vision of man, are spiritually related to their precursors, Strindberg and Maeterlinck.

As a matter of fact, only one of Maeterlinck's works, "The Blind," had a decisive influence on the theater of the absurd. The representatives of this group are tied to Maeterlinck by two elements: first, the symbolic, model-like situation which for him replaces the plot; then,

the loss of contact between men which for the first time found a strong
expression in "The Blind." As in the later plays of the theater of the
absurd, Maeterlinck gives us no development, only a basic situation.
Blind men and women have been taken out for a walk, by a priest,
but the latter has died, unnoticed by them. They go on waiting for
their leader, the priest. They don't know what to do, and wait, wait
and wait for somebody to come. It is easy to see the similarity between
this story and Beckett's "Waiting for Godot," the latter being basically
the radicalization of Maeterlinck's model situation. Maeterlinck explains
the loss of contact of his characters by their blindness. But that very
blindness is already symbolic. One of them says: "We have never seen
each other. We ask and we reply; we live together, we are always
together, but we know not what we are! . . . Years and years we have
been together, and we have never seen each other! You would say
we were forever alone."[17] Beckett portrays this solitude and this loss of
contact, giving it the greatest possible generalization. Maeterlinck's
blindness has become a general deformity of man. The comparison
between "The Blind" and "Waiting for Godot" is interesting and
revealing: it shows us to what a frightening degree the estrangement
of the individual in capitalist society has increased in the last century;
also it becomes clear—and this is symptomatic for the late bourgeois
literature—that Beckett, after more than sixty years, has nothing more
to say on alienation than did Maeterlinck.

Alfred Jarry has given us with "Ubu Roi," the most marked counterpart to the psychologizing drama. For him puppets become the symbol of estranged, reified man. The wooden rigidity of the puppets
appeared to him as the proper artistic mode of expression to represent
human relationships. Jarry's drama has not had the same wide influence
on bourgeois literature as Strindberg and Maeterlinck. Although he has
been important in some literary circles, his play does not appear often
on the stage. It was only after World War II, as the theater of the
absurd was establishing itself, that Jarry's dramatic work became well-
known. He was remembered as one of the great precursors of this
school.

This attempt to sketch the different tendencies of late bourgeois
drama is not intended to be exhaustive; it is only a working tool to
enable us to represent a complicated and extremely contradictory
situation. Among other things, the situation is complicated by the fact
that bourgeois playwrights—conditioned by a conception of man which

is in principle the same—often exhibit both tendencies. Moreover, the two currents are often combined in the same work.

The psychologizing theater and the theater of the absurd, which seem to oppose each other, represent the main dramatic currents of the late bourgeois drama. Their influence has varied according to countries. In America, the former has played the dominant role. These two tendencies must be described as "dogmatic," since, as was said above, their vision derives from the same dogma of the eternal, fatal alienation of man. Both consider alienation as an immutable natural process. Whereas the precursors of these tendencies, Strindberg, Maeterlinck and Jarry, looked upon the phenomenon of alienation with deep, helpless horror, trying to find an answer to it and not succeeding because of their class position, the present representatives of the abstract and psychologizing schools go on working with the old dogma that man's estrangement is determined in human nature. The cry of protest and of despair has given way more and more to acceptance of the condition of estrangement.

The theater of the absurd gained prominence especially after World War II. From then on, the bourgeois literary theoreticians have often attempted to trace a continuous tradition which goes from Alfred Jarry, Antonin Artaud, Guillaume Apollinaire, Gertrude Stein down to Eugene Ionesco and Samuel Beckett. Today, as this current, which is apparently subsiding, is subject to marked transformations, it becomes obvious that its influence was enhanced by political considerations, and we can now see what was a mere literary fad or what was a true literary movement.

Like most literary schools, the theater of the absurd does not have a homogeneous character. It is made up of personalities with quite different political and literary views, and within this direction there are various subdivisions, such as the poetic or autonomous theater, etc. However, it is very difficult to define these subdivisions so as to differentiate their specific significance. This school reached its highest degree of influence in France, centered around Eugene Ionesco, Arthur Adamov and Samuel Beckett, the latter Irish although writing in French. They were joined by George Schehadé and the Spaniard Fernando Arrabal, who writes also in French. Jean Tardieu with his Théâtre de Chambre and Armand Gatti became also well-known. In America, where the psychologizing tendency was uppermost, only Edward Albee came to the fore. The most famous West German abstractionists Wolfgang Hildesheimer and Günter Grass remained in the shade of the French avantgarde whose technique they took over but without being able to add original contributions in the field of the theater.

The theater of the absurd suffered its first shock in 1957 when Arthur Adamov with his play "Paolo Paoli" turned his back to the absurdists. In it Adamov tried to discover the causes of alienation. The fascination exerted by Brecht's plays had a corrosive action on the theater of the absurd. The second shock was hardly noticeable at the time and can be felt only in retrospect. It took place in 1958 when Eugene Ionesco brought out "Rhinoceros," a play which is quite different from his one-acters or his anti-plays, having a concrete and clear plot and constructed characters. The playwright, following in the same direction, next published "Apprendre á marcher" and "Exit the King." Other representatives of the theater of the absurd at the beginning of the 60s gave up their theatrical provocations, which no longer aroused fear or indignation. They either took positions as critics of society or became reconciled to the conventional theater.

Speaking of the psychologizing tendency, we must stress the fact that our criticism of it is not to be understood as calling into question the use of psychology in the creation of characters. A playwright who wants to create real, living people will never be able to do without a psychological structure. It is only the absolute use of it, the use of an anthropological, psychologizing interpretation of objective processes which makes a playwright representative of this tendency. The psychologizing school is even more heterogeneous than the school of the absurd. Very often the dominant psychologizing style is mixed up with naturalistic or absurdist elements. For example, in the plays of John Osborne, the psychologizing tendency which determines his dramatic creation is full of naturalistic elements. Osborne, however, who is one of the so-called Angry Young Men, is unable from his point of view and with his technical means to make any significant social statement.

The French author Jacques Audiberti mixes in many of his plays the psychologizing vision with absurdist elements. He is able to follow these two diverging directions only because for him the psychological is reduced to the sexual. Strictly speaking only the psychologizing drama of American literature has really formed a school and become prominent. Following Eugene O'Neill, most of the American playwrights have evolved in this direction. The most important are Tennessee Williams, William Saroyan, Maxwell Anderson, Elmer Rice and William Inge.

Strindberg with his theme of the battle of the sexes had already staked the ground on which this tendency later developed. Jean Giraudoux, although he was very far from the destructive obsession of Strindberg and avoided the latter's naturalistic form, entered that ground after World War I. With him the theme of the war of the sexes becomes a witty philosophical excursion, verbally fascinating. However, man's potentialities are judged even more pessimistically. In his play "Sodom and Gomorrha" he uses the old motif of the search for a good man in a way that betrays immediately the psychologizing point of view. For him men's crimes which bring about their ruin originate in the "awareness of their own sex." He says in the play: "God has allowed himself to enter combat with an angel, and the devil appeared. Man has allowed himself to enter combat with a woman, and Woman appeared."[18] Giraudoux eliminates almost completely the social aspect which the old tale gives about the flourishing cities going to their destruction. As the author excludes the social significance and withdraws to the "inner self," his concept of mankind becomes entangled in a deadend pessimism. Lia, one of the main characters of the play, rejects relentlessly any illusion of salvation offered by a hopeful angel. "Isn't it touching, an angel who expects a miracle from men! And when he has lost all hope about me, when he has understood that man and woman do not know each other any longer, that they insult and despise each other, then he will raise his arm, utter his great cry and everything will be over."[19] Almost all of Giraudoux's characters —Lia, Judith, Isabelle, Electra, Alkmène—suffer from the destructive "knowledge of one's own sex." The author cheats himself of the possibility to see them in a wider relationship.

Human estrangement, becoming unbearable in the age of capitalism, is also the cause of Giraudoux's pessimism. All his works express a lament for the present condition of society. But as long as the cause of this estrangement remains unrecognized, the rejection of this inhuman condition often takes an odd, almost grotesque form. The antagonism related to the process of alienation is not understood by the bourgeois dramatists as class-conditioned but as simply deriving from human relationships. Giraudoux expresses it in the eternal irreconcilable confrontation of man and woman. It is from that bitter strife that Giraudoux creates the field of tension of most of his plays. This position makes it impossible for him to understand events as historic, hence capable of change. It is entirely lacking in historical sense. The author expresses it clearly when his Judith—in the play of the same name—says: "There is no history of peoples, there is only the history of God chasing poor half-intelligent men and poor half-pretty women."[20] The world torn by class struggles is mirrored by Giraudoux in the general hostility of men to which he gives poetic expression in the tragic dualism of man and woman. Since he seeks its cause outside of society, he cannot find any solution within society; this explains his grotesque statement concerning man's solitude, the tragic consequence of which he well knows. As his anthropological position prevents him from seeing how alienation can be eradicated, the painful lament of the author about man estranged from himself and others gives rise to the demand that all aspects of community be done away with, even that between man and woman. In "Ondine," the knight Hans von Wittenstein makes the following demand: "What do I want? What any servant, any maid wants! I demand the right for men to be a little alone with themselves on earth. What God has granted them is not much, these six feet between heaven and hell! . . . This human life is not too exciting, with hands that have to be washed, stopped-up noses that have to be cleaned, with hair that falls!"[21] The motif of the struggle of the sexes becomes with Giraudoux a poetic synonym for the increasing isolation and separateness of man. The human "inner space" is for him, even more than for Strindberg, the real playing field of the drama. It has become so narrow that a dialectic of individual and society is hardly possible any more.

In the 40s and 50s, the theme of the struggle of the sexes was increasingly reduced to the domain of neurosis and sexuality; the psychological is reduced to the neurotic, neurosis becomes sexuality and the latter turns to homosexuality. For many late bourgeois writers, the question of how to live in our time is exclusively a psychologizing problem. Tennessee Williams has reduced to its lowest denominator the vision of the representatives of the psychologizing school, in the United States especially. In "Period of Adjustment" a character says: "The whole world's a big hospital, a big neurological ward."[22] Increasingly degenerate forms of sexual life, such as homosexuality and incest, become the focus of interest. In his book on Frisch and Dürrenmatt, Hans Bänziger writes that incest draws attention in modern bourgeois literature primarily because it throws light on the social crisis better than conjugal problems could do.[23] It is hard to see why marriage problems are less conducive than incest to lay bare inconsistencies in the social order. True, it makes it possible to show the decaying tendencies of a given society. "The Chosen One" by Thomas Mann, "The Man without Characteristics" by Robert Musil, Max Frisch's "Homo Faber" are all instances of it, within certain limitations. However, the plays of the psychologizing school lack all social concern. The strong drive toward the "inner self" leaves no room for this concern. Although the consequences of this reduction to the "inner space" vary according to the different plays, in most cases the dialectic of the individual and the social is excluded.

The American playwright Tennessee Williams has created a whole group of characters whose individuality is to be understood in terms of neuroses and sexual psychology. With them the unusual takes the form of the abnormal. They are not human beings in their aliveness, their universality, their fullness but in their illnesses, their instinctual drives, in their solitude and their flickering indecisions. The social element has been driven out of most of them. Even in "The Glass Menagerie" where the author, contrary to his habit, speaks directly of the great socio-political events, the social element is not incorporated in the play, it remains a "marginal remark" addressed by the narrator to the public. This is the way this narrator refers to 30 years which in America were a period of bitter class struggle: "In Spain there was revolution. Here there was only shouting and confusion. In Spain there was Guernica. Here there were disturbances of labor, sometimes pretty violent, in otherwise peaceful cities such as Chicago, Cleveland, Saint Louis. . . . This is the social background of the play." It could be argued whether this period in reality appeared as peaceful as the narrator presents it to his public. But that is not the point. What matters is that this background has no significance for the development of the characters, who are almost completely seen psychologically. Not only the timid, sensitive Laura but also her mother wrapped up in the world of her memories as well as the more vital figures of Tom and Jim O'Connor and the visitor, they are all seen beyond any social relationships. It is true that an author has the right to show figures that have turned away from social life. Such figures do not necessarily stand outside of the dialectic of the social and the individual, the playwright can reveal what social causes have driven them to this condition. But the behavior of Williams' characters is only explained one-sidedly by

psychic, often neurotic reactions. They are varieties of psychic behavior such as are to be found in text books on psychology. With
great skill Williams has transported them in dramatic creation.

Beside these two trends, the psychologizing and the absurd, there
are in the late bourgeois theater a few groups which also have a dogmatic point of departure but have not become wide and influential
literary currents. Let us repeat once more that we have here no rigid
limits but a continuous overlapping. We shall mention briefly two of
these groups, the traditionalist play and the modern Christian mystery
play.

The traditionalist drama is the refuge of the prosaic capitalist present, with its undersized people. These authors are as conscious of man's
alienation as the representatives of other schools. They too observe
that in the process of constant reification the individual is levelled
down, that more and more whatever could make him great is taken
away from him. They think they can escape from such an image of
man by turning to the great historical subjects of the past, using for
the most part a technique which can be described as classicist, although
it is mixed up with modern elements. However, it is an illusion to
believe that it is possible to escape from alienation with the help of
the great figures of the past. No matter what the traditionalist authors
have done with their historical heroes, these remain alienated men
whose small stature is all the more noticeable in that the historical
costumes they wear are too large for them. The classicist construction
of characters clashes with the content and makes of the alienated reified
individual in Renaissance clothes a downright grotesque creature. This
is why most of them strike us as artificial, false, not true to life. At
best they are good theatrical roles.

The main representatives of this group are Henry de Montherlant,
Christopher Fry, and, in a larger sense, Maxwell Anderson, whose
traditionalism is of another kind, since the American theater does not
have a well-marked tradition.

Between the traditionalist drama and the modern Christian mystery
play there is no well-defined border. Because of their beliefs the Christian authors are strongly attracted to the form of the traditionalist
drama. But they have also attempted to put modern formal elements
at the service of their religious purposes, as Paul Claudel did in "Christopher Columbus." . . . Next to the mystery play which they try to
revive, the Christian authors have not neglected the society play. T. S.

Eliot wrote both "Murder in the Cathedral," a mystery play, and "The Private Secretary" and "The Cocktail Party," society plays. For most representatives of this trend, alienation is a "cosmic category." They interpret the alienated, reified condition of man as estrangement from God, as an everlasting and immutable state in which man fell through his "sins" and from which he can only be redeemed by death. Here too there is no possibility of a dialectical construction of characters.

Between the two main dogmatic groups, the theater of the absurd and the psychologizing theater, we find a few playwrights who show traits of a variety of schools but who attempt, with a relative degree of success, not to remain caught in their dogmatism. The following beliefs determine their character: man's daily struggle and the heroism he shows in day-to-day life give to human existence, in spite of the alienation of the individual, a certain positive value. Of course, it is hard to maintain such a position in capitalist society where the individual is constantly threatened. Therefore, we find great fluctuations as well as eclectic traits in the playwrights of this group. Next to a taste for Christian redemption—as in Thornton Wilder, for example— there are also pessimistic tendencies—as in Jean Anouilh—which relate these writers to the theater of the absurd. They are characterized by a search for the significance of practical life, but they do not take a progressive position.

Thornton Wilder betrays very clearly the great difficulties confronting playwrights who do not have access to the dialectical understanding of how a literary character is constructed. The American author does not exhibit his people in terms of psychoanalysis or sexual psychology to make them "interesting" or "unusual," as Tennessee Williams does. In his play, "Our Town," we hear about floor polishing and Grandma Wentworth's cold buffet, about the church organist Stimson who drinks too much, about rain on a wedding day, or raising chickens according to the Philo method, baseball games, etc. Everything is juxtaposed in the same order of importance. The whole play is like a mosaic made up of daily details. The social relevance is brought into play when the narrator calls upon the newspaper editor, Mr. Webb, to describe the political and social configuration of the small town. Mr. Webb does it as follows: "I don't have to tell you that we're run here by a Board of Selectmen. All males vote at the age of 21. Women vote indirect. We're lower middle-class, sprinkling of professional men . . . 10% illiterate laborers. Politically, we're 86% Republicans,

6% Democrats; 4% Socialists; rest, indifferent. Religiously, we're 85% Protestants; 12% Catholics; rest, indifferent."[25] Undeniably this political and social characterization of the town is relevant, the Gibbs and Webb families fit perfectly into this picture. The social background of Wilder's characters is much more definite than in Tennessee Williams' "The Glass Menagerie." But it is still only a collection of social facts, while the true driving forces, the causal connections are not apprehended; the play, therefore, remains static. Social forces in Grover's Corner cannot be incorporated in the individual way of life of the characters. It is true, Wilder knows how to weave together the single, often insignificant episodes, which are often shaped in a naturalistic way. But this technical montage which discloses a sense of poetic refinement is devoid of any dialectical element. It doesn't throw any light on social relationships as happens in the plays of socialist authors who give the impression of using the same technique. Wilder uses it mainly to stress the recurrence of the same. This method is applied to an even greater extent in his one-act play, "The Long Christmas Dinner."

Thornton Wilder deplores the state of human estrangement but manages to reach a compromise by avoiding a climactic showdown. However, even such a brilliant artist and technician is unable to maintain his position for any length of time. It is no coincidence that he has written mostly very short plays and only a few ones of any significance, in fact only "Our Town" and "The Skin of our Teeth."[26]

The position of the American Arthur Miller is to be traced back to the influence of the great depression of 1929. It was thanks to the depression that Miller and many others became aware of the social contradictions. The recognition that the individual is not master of things but is mastered by them did not impel Miller to withdraw to the "inner self." As a very critical observer of social relationships, he is beginning to uncover the inadequacies of the system. In his play "Death of a Salesman," he questions the validity of the capitalist way of life in which Willy Loman can support his family only with the insurance money his death will bring. For Miller alienation is no longer a generalized destiny; for him it has a face and a name. Although he is not yet able to see the possibility of a change from capitalist relationships, he is already attempting to create characters through whom the social processes can be understood historically.

Political Function of the Theater of the Absurd

Now that the theater of the absurd has become a literary school of the past, it is easier to see it with clarity and objectivity than it was a few years ago. Earlier, Marxist critics did not judge it with sufficient discrimination. They found fault with representatives of the school primarily for the pleasure in man's abject condition expressed in the plays. This criticism is not without justification. But the absurdists point out that they want to show the terrifying extent of man's alienation of which he is not conscious enough in his comfortable day-to-day life, and that one shouldn't blame the mirror if it reflects a grimace, as Gorky once said. Wolfgang Hildesheimer holds reality itself as absurd, thus posing the question of the relationship of the writer to reality.[27] Many of the absurdists have a very fine feeling for the contradictions of the world they live in. They see with terror to what extent the individual is exposed to the increasing alienation of his whole personality, how oppressed he is by the reified world, and for them there is no hope for mankind any longer.

Some of the bourgeois critics who reject the theater of the absurd but not capitalist society attempt to minimize man's alienation under capitalism. Things are not as bad as all that, they say. However, criticism must come from a different direction. As has already been said, the absurdists are to be criticized not because they portray alienated man but because they do not see historically the causes of his deformation, because they don't look for these causes in the system of capitalist production. To them alienation appears as the eternal fate of man, no longer imposed by God, simply absurd, immutable, senseless and cruel. According to Hildesheimer, a theater critic from West Germany, this reality is so absurd that no lesson can be derived from it. In this senseless world, the author has no message any more for his public; he can only describe the absurd as absurd. This literary school thus fuses two different points: the logical revelation of alienated man and the everlasting character of this condition. Precisely this fusion made the theater of the absurd welcome in certain political circles of capitalist society, where an effort was made to put it at the service of political goals. The theater of the absurd became a literary fashion. For the discontented minds in capitalist countries who were vaguely aware of the abnormality of social conditions, it contained that mixture of relentless criticism and impudent excuse which proved politically expedient. The consistent exposé of alienated man is again cancelled by the fact that the process of alienation is detached from social life and given an anthropological or cosmic interpretation.

The theater of the absurd is the logical consequence of the bankruptcy of bourgeois ideology which became notorious especially at the end of World War II. To disappointed, disillusioned and despairing minds, the current articles of faith had proved useless. Bourgeois society was no longer capable of setting goals that would have validity for at least a part of the intellectuals. The absurdists elevated purposelessness to the rank of profound meaning. Ionesco wrote: "Absurd is that which is devoid of purpose. . . . Cut off from his religious, metaphysical or transcendental roots, man is lost; all his actions become senseless, absurd, useless."[28] The more, however, despair, disillusion and Angst are declared to belong to the spiritual attitude through which the world is to be understood in its terrifying absurdity and which at the same time permit one to exist within the world with dignity, the more does the absurd become a new myth, a sort of substitute for religion. In their attitude toward the religious or metaphysical sense of the absurd, the representatives of the theater of the absurd—who like to call themselves "outsiders"—are back in the ranks of bourgeois society and reconciled to its ideology. Martin Esslin, a theoretician of the absurd, assails those critics who call the theater of the absurd grotesque, frivolous and irreverent; it is rather "a return to the original, religious function of the theater, the confrontation of man with the spheres of myth and religious reality."[29] In this way despair and disillusion lose their rebellious meaning; they are incorporated into an ideological attitude which, however paradoxically, is utilized by the very society which caused their appearance. Transformed by the theater of the absurd, they are used objectively to reconcile man with his alienated world. The individual finds it possible to "adjust": he feels his estrangement no longer painful but instead pleasurable. Martin Esslin has described it with fine apologetic candor: "But by facing up to anxiety and despair and the absence of divinely revealed alternatives, anxiety and despair can be overcome. The sense of loss at the disintegration of facile solutions and the disappearance of cherished illusions retains its sting only while the mind still clings to the illusions concerned. Once they are given up, we have to readjust ourselves to the new situation and face reality itself. And because the illusions we suffered from made it more difficult for us to deal with reality, their loss will ultimately be felt as exhilarating."[30] From these considerations it is easy to discern clearly the political commitment of the theater of the absurd. With a certain measure of success it has served indirectly to support the capitalist system, and, now that the school has found its political role, it arouses strong suspicion even among its followers.

We have shown above the close ties between the psychologizing and the absurdist theater. Exploration of the "inner space" of man as a dramatic goal leads with consistent logic to the theater of the absurd. At a certain point, the "flickering, cloudy, hard to grasp" inwardness which we find in Tennessee Williams turns into the abstraction of the absurd. Here the subjectivism becomes complete. The absurdist makes of certain moments of life, which he holds as typical functions of depersonalized man, the symbols of his "inner self." According to Ionesco, "The play is a picture of my inner universe projected onto the stage. The resistances and contradictions of an inner world drawn with lines of abstract force—a dynamic drawing."[31] However, the authors of absurd plays aim in no way at showing the psychic world of one individual. Their purpose is rather to show the universal in the individual. Thus Ionesco adds: "But this individual world contains the universal being within it."[32] Here is the beginning of the error. What is individual points to something wider only when it is conceived in dialectical relationship with the social of which it is a part. It is precisely through society that man becomes a *particular* individual; he is, as Marx says, an "individual member of the collectivity." The "inner self" cannot be transported mechanically into a wider context. Ionesco oversimplifies greatly when he says: "The innermost truth of each one is universal."[33] He believes that when the writer succeeds in detaching the "inner world" from man, it turns out that it is made in the image of the universe. Of course, when the writer under the pressure of alienation, withdraws to the "inner space" of the individual, this is an expression of the outer world. Ionesco's "inner world" reveals what alienation makes of man. But he is unable to communicate a really universal vision of the phenomenon and of its objective base, because for him only the individual "in himself" exists. The particular individual is always "an individual member of the collectivity," whether he wants it or not. The more Ionesco stresses the "inner universality" as the starting point of his outlook on life, the better he reveals to us his alienated consciousness. He understands man only from the ideological viewpoint of his class.

Such is the philosophical position which conditions the construction of Ionesco's characters. In spite of his effort to go beyond the individual, the accidental, his characters remain isolated illustrations of an estranged world; the essence of this estranged world, the causes of the estrangement, also what is truly "universal" remain outside of his creation. Such a creation can only result from a materialist dialectical point of view which alone enables the writer to conceive his characters in the dialectic of the individual and the social. Ionesco on the contrary destroys and eliminates any dialectical relationship.

The point of view of the other playwrights of the theater of the absurd is not essentially different from Ionesco's. They, too, search for the universal in the "inner self" since they see in alienation an eternal human condition. It is not possible for us to analyze here more than a few typical representatives of this school, Samuel Beckett, Eugene Ionesco, Fernando Arrabal and Georges Schehadé.

Giraudoux's demand for man to have "the right to be alone with himself on this earth" has been presented with the greatest consistency by the Irish dramatist Samuel Beckett, who has put on the stage what Giraudoux had only postulated. Beckett's characters are free of any social connections; they live in complete isolation, without contact, and their physical condition enables them to have only few vital functions. The difference between things and men has become insignificant, the passage from life to death almost imperceptible. Beckett shows human life as being finally remaindered. The titles of many of his plays indicate this: "Endgame," "Krapp's Last Tape." Marianne Kesting observes in her sketch of the author that Samuel Beckett "is the most remote and most exemplary of the modern dramatists."[34] We can only agree with her. But the exemplary character, his "monomanic consistency," becomes also the measure of his talent. Of all the representatives of the theater of the absurd, Beckett has the most dogmatic vision of man. For him alienation is fatally predetermined and assumes for the individual the necessity and the tangibility of a natural event. His dogmatism makes everything rigid. The author is no longer able to develop human characters. Any differentiation proves unfeasible. His plays and his characters are all alike. They are always static studies on the theme of reified man.

Because of the individual's isolation, many of Beckett's plays are in fact monodramas; either there is only one character (as in "Krapp's

Last Tape") or only one has a function, the others having only walk-on parts. This is the logical consequence of Beckett's "monomanic consistency." He wants to show the loss of contact of the individual, the impossibility of inter-personal relationships. The dramatic construction of characters requires a steady interplay of reciprocal influences. Beckett's idealistic concept of alienated man forces him to negate all forms of character construction, not only the traditional ones. In his play "Krapp's Last Tape," the author demonstrates the extent to which the individual is estranged not only from the others but also from himself. Shut up in his shabby room, Krapp plays the tapes recording the various, often insignificant events of his life. He is now confronted with his past selves which appear to him completely alien. Krapp dictates again: "Just been listening to that stupid bastard I took myself for 30 years ago, hard to believe I was ever as bad as that. Thank God, that's all done with anyway."[35] The way in which Krapp, by technical means, summons up his life, has something eerie about it. He finds no access to himself. His life is more alien to him than that of a stranger. With great lyricism Beckett plays on the theme of an almost forgotten memory of "one dark young beauty. . . . all white and starch, incomparable bosom."[36] Even in the most intimate union of the sexes, Beckett expresses the wish of man for absolute solitude. Krapp does not yearn for the truly human moments of his life; for him they are part of ". . . the old muckball, all the light and dark, and famine and feasting of . . . (hesitates) the ages! (In a shout) Yes!"[37] The light and dark of life —Krapp doesn't want it any longer. We witness here the most extensive and radical form of the "repudiation" of the human, as advocated by Adrian Leverkühn in Thomas Mann's *Doctor Faustus*. Leverkühn wanted to repudiate the Ninth Symphony, a synonym for all that is good and beautiful. Krapp's rejection goes much farther; it includes life in its total social essence. This rejection is not only postulated, as by Jean Giraudoux and Paul Valéry, but already put into practice. With Giraudoux's knight Hans von Wittenstein ("Ondine") and Valéry's Faust ("My Faust"), this rejection grows out of a deep tragic schism, as with Adrian Leverkühn, and the writer invokes it in full consciousness. Such is not the case with Beckett, who is more concerned to vulgarize Adrian Leverkühn's gesture. For him man's alienation is an inevitable natural process against which it is senseless to protest and to rebel, just as senseless as was Voltaire's protest against a natural catastrophe such as the Lisbon earthquake of 1755.

It goes without saying that Beckett's title "Happy Days" is meant ironically. The writer here uses the motif of Philemon and Baucis. At the beginning of the play, the old couple Winnie and Willie are almost completely defunct. Their vital functions are just about dead. However, they feel happy. In order to stress the insanity of their happiness, Beckett introduces an extremely grotesque, although formal, effect of alienation. While the life of the old people is ebbing away, Winnie sings blissfully the old sentimental melody from Lehar's "The Merry Widow," "Lips are silent, violins murmur, do love me!" Beckett wants to show that men feel comfortable in their increasing estrangement. It may be that the author meant it in a critical sense and felt it as painful, but this criticism is not at all evident in the play. Beckett's fatalistic, cosmic view of alienation excludes any critical stance. In this play he represents the same dogmatic concepts as in "Krapp's Last Tape," but here he exhibits them in a different mode of behavior. Whereas Krapp calls "muck" what to men is happiness, Winnie is "happy" even in the ebbing away of all her vital force. Krapp becomes aware of the power of alienation in his ties with others; Winnie is not even conscious of it as she is being deprived of her vital functions.

The Beckett character lacks not only the dialectical linking between the individual and the social but even any mechanical bond. To the degree that the author concentrates his creative gift in doing away with all interpersonal connections of his characters, sometimes through the use of irony, the individual and social elements fall apart. Since he understands the process of alienation only in its superficial mechanism and not in its essence, the social is no longer comprehensible to him. Beckett's thinking itself is so strongly marked by the domination of object relationships on men that he is completely unaware of how these relationships affect us. The capitalistic mode of production does not only create the power of the product over the producer; it also brings about conditions which make this power relationship anachronistic and capable of change. But this remains outside of Beckett's vision. In his characters, instead of the social relevance, we encounter the destructive power of alienation. He understands the social only as a relationship of things; the temporary, the surface covering which can be ripped off by revolution, is for him the eternal.

Beckett's "Waiting for Godot" is an image of the "eternal condition" of man. This play has become world-famous maybe because with great poetic force, it expresses two contradictory postures of the bourgeois mind: man's alienation as an eternal condition and waiting. Estragon and Vladimir are waiting for something; they do not know exactly what they are waiting for and, as a matter of fact, they wait without confidence. This paradox may be what constitutes the attraction of the play for a certain group of intellectuals who have only a mystical notion of the process of alienation. Like Estragon and Vladimir, they, too, are waiting for—nothing, but they are waiting.

Shortly before his death, Brecht expressed the intention of "adapting" this play. What interested him in it was the alternative. He intended in his adaptation to carry ad absurdum Beckett's position. He meant to divide the play into several short parts. With the insertion of film sequences and pantomimes describing the great social upheavals while Beckett's heroes are still waiting, he wanted to expose to the audience's laughter Beckett's dogmatic extreme; in the presence of people who had through their revolution broken the chains of alienation, the tragic pose of the "eternally" alienated man would have been exploded as a lie and even as an intentional lie. Beckett—Brecht, one can hardly imagine a greater contrast in modern literature, Beckett who, with maniacal consistency describes human alienation as an eternal state, and Brecht whose work aims at changing social conditions and at widening man's potential.

Today it is impossible to speak of Eugene Ionesco without stressing the two different stages of his development as a playwright. Until 1957 he wrote almost exclusively one-act plays, like "The Bald Soprano," anti-plays, as he called them himself. From 1958 on, with "Rhinoceros" and even before with "The Killer," a change appears. A play like "Exit the King" is described by its author with the straightforward conventional term "drama." Since 1957 we have a series of plays where Bérenger reappears as the "hero," first as the man who alone resists the metamorphosis into a rhinoceros, then as the king. The difference in point of view in these two plays is slight and not clear-cut. But the rejection of the absurdist line is an important symptom of the inability of the theater of the absurd to establish itself for any length of time and to develop consistently in the art of the drama.

Like Beckett, Ionesco in his first plays was concerned to show the complete loss of contact of men, the magnitude of the alienation from oneself and from the others. At that time Ionesco, in the construction of his characters, was exclusively aware of the liquidation of all interpersonal relationships and used a whole series of different means to portray this. For Ionesco's characters there is no point of contact any more; even when they converse about trivialities well-known to all, they don't hear each other. The English couple in "The Bald Soprano" use imitation English in a conversational talk. During the talk completely contradictory and senseless statements are made, without anybody being aware of it. The same character states opposite opinions. Here is an example of the dialogue between Mr. and Mrs. Smith:

> Mrs. Smith: How sad for her to be left a widow so young!
> Mr. Smith: Fortunately they had no children . . .
> Mrs. Smith: But who would take care of the children? You know very well that they have a boy and a girl. What are their names?
> Mr. Smith: Bobby and Bobby like their parents.[38]

The same technique of juxtaposing contradictory statements is also to be found in the tragic farce "The Chairs." Ionesco uses these contradictions not to bring out real opposition but in order to reveal the emptiness and loss of contact in the alienated individual. The characters exchange only senseless words; human communication through language has become impossible. "The world appears to me as empty of ideas and the real as unreal. This feeling of unreality, this search for an essential, forgotten, unnamed reality, separate from which I don't believe I am, this is what I wanted to express through my characters who wander in chaos and can name nothing their own except their anxiety, their remorse, their failure, the emptiness of their lives."[39] Often Ionesco gives expression to this "feeling of unreality" by letting a conversation on a situation that is normal at the start degenerate step by step into senselessness and complete absurdity, as for instance the story of the serpent and the fox in "The Bald Soprano." Here the most diverse bits of conversation are patched together and several levels of talk run into each other. The climax of one of Ionesco's dialogues often consists in dissolving the concreteness of the single word. At the close of "The Chairs," the orator only stammers: "He, mme, mm, m, Ju, gou, hou, hou. Heu, heu, gu, gou, gueue."[40] Instead of the great climactic finale typical of the classical drama, Ionesco gives us a series of senseless mumblings. Like the orator of that play, the author has no message to the world. In an interview, Ionesco once made the malicious remark that it was not his style to deliver messages, that he was not a mailman like Brecht with his political communications.[41]

In the alienated man of capitalist society, Ionesco discovers only its emptiness, only the stifling power of the reified relationships—nothing more. The real causes, the essence of the mechanism of alienation remain hidden to him. And so our author reaches the false conclusion: "How could I, to whom the world is incomprehensible—how could I understand my own play? I am waiting to have it explained to me."[42]

The bourgeois literary critics often point out that the loss of contact between individuals brought about by alienation is to be found already in Chekhov's dramas. According to them, he was the first to let his characters talk without really addressing each other, with conversations that become progressively emptier to end up as mere conventions. "The dialogue marks the disappearance of comprehension,"[43] Marianne Kesting writes of Chekhov's plays. As an example there is the famous talk between Andrei and the half-deaf Ferapont in "Three Sisters," in which Andrei says that he talks with Ferapont only because the latter is hard of hearing. It is assumed that the playwrights of the theater of the absurd have continued to use this technique of "talking into a void." As a matter of fact, Chekhov has developed an original technique thanks to which the spectators would recognize that in certain social circles people no longer communicate their ideas but only talk at each other. But Chekhov uses his technical means in a very different way. The critical realist Chekhov uses them to reveal a social condition, whereas Ionesco aims only at giving expression to the "nature" of alienated man. The characters of the Russian author are "superfluous men" who are unable to have a significant activity in a society turned parasitic and who look desperately for the meaning of life. In "Three Sisters" Tusenbach says that throughout his life he has never worked. He is moved by a vague, romantic yearning for work. All these characters sense that such a life cannot go on. The heroine of one of Chekhov's short stories exclaims: "Oh, if only it would come soon, this new clear life when one looks straight and boldly at one's destiny, knows one's rights and feels gay and free! Such a life should start sooner or later."[44]

Chekhov's heroes are as unaware as their author of the way to this new society. Chekhov himself saw only the effect of alienation, not its causes; its complicated mechanism escapes him. But, contrary to Ionesco and Beckett, he sees this condition as a *historical* phenomenon. He is certain that a new time will come, bringing a new human type. Chekhov uses the "talk into the void" to criticize a society in which the forms of social living have become so unbearable that each one tries to escape them in his own way. But because their class position prevents them from recognizing a common solution, their efforts become increasingly subjective, and their alienation is deepened by their disgust at the old way of life. Chekhov uses his technical means to show that the social conditions are inhuman, obsolete and due for a change. The social criticism is inescapable in his works.

Ionesco, on the contrary, is intent to prove the "eternal" subjection of estranged man to an absurd world. In his dogmatic vision, alienation takes an extra-social character which resists change. For the playwright and the figures he creates, the result is that the social no longer assumes concrete form but remains a distorted abstraction. The individual and the social no longer touch each other; man exists no more as an "individual member of the collectivity." Since the individual "in himself" is non-sense, the characters of the play can only exhibit abstract, absurd traits. The liquidation of the social can only lead to "grimacing man," as Thomas Mann said. Chekhov, on the other hand, was able to show in his characters the dialectic of the social and the individual, although this dialectic had to remain idealistic because of his cognitive limitations.

In his second creative period, Ionesco wrote "Exit the King," largely abandoning his absurdist technique. Estranged man's solitude and emptiness are no longer made obvious through a montage of contradictory fragments of conversation. In this play the spectator gets acquainted with a Ionesco whose dramatic idiom is of great poetic beauty. But Ionesco's "metamorphosis" is not as radical as Arthur Adamov's. For him, the individual's alienation is still an extra-social phenomenon, a fate which man cannot control and with which he has to put up. For a drama, the base of ideas and plot in "Exit the King" is much too narrow. It is really a long lyric-elegiac dialogue on the subject of death. The author had in mind, as he says himself, to remind us of a truth "of which we do not think, and which is simple and infinitely banal: I die, you die, he dies."[45] Ionesco shows us the different phases of Bérenger I's death, how Bérenger pretends to strength and influence which he no longer possesses. He then wishes to put to death everybody if he could thus save his own life. Later he starts to complain, which means that he begins to accept. Bérenger then clings to his posthumous fame: his portrait must hang everywhere and future generations must learn to read by spelling his name. Finally he asks the dead to help him over the threshold that separates them from the living: "Help me to go over the threshold which you have passed. Come back for a while to this side in order to help me! Help me! You who have been afraid and reluctant! How was it? Where did you find the strength? What has torn you away? Have you been scared to the very end? And you who have been strong and courageous, you who have been indifferent and even willing to die, teach me your indifference, your joy or your poise."[46]

To represent death has always been one of the great literary themes. It has been treated in famous examples as a sort of taking stock of life. Whether it is Ivan Ilyich in the story "The Death of Ivan Ilyich" by Tolstoy, or Yegor Bulichev by Gorky—they all wonder whether they have lived "on the right street." The approaching end calls up a painful questioning about life with other men. For them, death is not only a natural event but also the occasion to reflect on social life; the society in which one has lived becomes visible. But not for Ionesco, who sees death as a "cosmic" occurrence. For Bérenger as for Ionesco, it is "the whole world" who dies with the individual.[47] If the truth of the individual is universal, Ionesco says, then his death is also the world's death. Through his strong drive to abstraction, the author raises Bérenger's death to the level of the "universal," that is, the mystical, the "cosmic." Death is celebrated as a great act of nature; the king's physician comments as follows on the events in nature which take place while the king is dying: "On the North Pole of the sun, snow is falling. The Milky Way seems to have shrunk together. The comet is exhausted; like a dying dog it has rolled itself in its tail."[48] And later: "Until last night it was spring here. Now spring has left us two and a half hours ago. Now we are in November. On the other side of the border, the grass is sprouting. Over there new leaves are opening. . . . Here the leaves are drying up and falling. The trees are moaning and dying."[49] In this dialogue Ionesco detaches consciously the king's end from the social context, in order to make of it a great "cosmic" symbol. He is not interested in the world which the individual Bérenger is leaving. For him it is only a backstage which enables him to translate the decay of the individual into the "universal." But the playwright, by developing a technique to eliminate the social, closes to himself access to a larger dramatic base. His characters lack space to develop as individuals. They are the spokesmen of a lyric confession. The intended "universality" becomes spiritual poverty.

The crisis and the decadence of the school of the absurd was brought about less by the evolution of its spokesmen than by dramatists like Schehadé and Arrabal. They brought social problems on the stage of the theater of the absurd and, although they did not really come to grips with them, in the eyes of the public they carried to extremes, ad absurdum, the program of this school. To the degree that the playwrights handled the great, vital questions of our times, for instance destruction of the world by thermonuclear means, it became increasingly impossible to represent only the absurd destiny of estranged man and to throw light on his "inner self" only. Recently representatives of this trend have turned even more to themes critical of society. To what measure they will go beyond the theater of the absurd and adopt a new point of view depends not so much on the intensity of the class conflicts in their countries as on the depth of their commitment to these conflicts. The period of the absurd is over, although there are still some absurdists who, like King Bérenger I, go on tormenting themselves and revolt against their end.

REFERENCES

1. C. Bourniquel, "Frankreichs Literatur des Linken," in *Literatur zwischen links und rechts, Deutschland-Frankreich-USA* (Munich, 1962), p. 106.
2. Thornton Wilder, "Auf der Suche nach neuen Wegen," in H. Frenz, *Amerkanische Dramaturgie* (Hamburg, 1962), p. 120.
3. Bertolt Brecht, *Schriften zum Theater* (Berlin und Weimar, 1964), Bd. I, S. 195.
4. *Ibid.*, p. 197.
5. W. Emrich, *Franz Kafka—Das Baugesetz seiner Dichtung* (Bonn-Frankfurt a.M., 1960), p. 23.
6. See W. A. Berendsohn, *Die humanistische Front*, 1.Teil (Zurich, 1946), p. 136 ff.
7. See W. Hinck, *Probleme der Dramaturgie und Spielweise in Bert Brechts "epischen Theater."* Dissertation. (Göttingen, 1956), p. 238.
8. N. Gessner, *Die Unzulänglichkeit der Sprache* (Zurich, 1957), p. 37.
9. Karl Marx, *The Economic and Philosophic Manuscripts of 1844.* Edited with an introduction by Dirk J. Struik. (New York, 1964).
10. I. C. Narski, Ob istoriko-filosofskom razviti poniatia "otchudenie," in *Filosofskie nauki*, 1963.
11. *Ibid.*, p. 105, ff.
12. Marx/Engels, *Kleine ökonomische Schriften*, p. 102.
13. *Ibid.*, p. 99.
14. J. P. Sartre, *No Exit* (New York, 1955), p. 47.
15. Marx/Engels, *Kleine ökonomische Schriften*, p. 102.
16. A. Strindberg, *The Vasa Trilogy* (Seattle, 1959), p. 224.

17. M. Maeterlinck, *The Blind.*
18. J. Giraudoux, *Sodom and Gomorrha.*
19. *Ibid.*
20. J. Giraudoux, *Judith.*
21. J. Giraudoux, *Ondine.*
22. T. Williams, *Period of Adjustment* (New York, 1960), p. 118.
23. H. Bänziger, *Frisch und Dürrenmatt* (Berne and Munich, 1960), p. 16.
24. T. Williams, *The Glass Menagerie.*
25. Thornton Wilder, *Our Town* (New York, 1938), p. 29.
26. Ebenhard Brüning judges Thornton Wilder very severely in his thorough and extensive work (*Haupttendenzen des amerikanischen Dramas der dreissiger Jahre, ein Beitrag zur Literaturgeschichte der Vereinigten Staaten unter Berücksichtigung des Einflusses amerikanischer Dramatik auf die Spielplangestaltung deutscher Bühnen nach dem 2. Weltkrieg.* Leipzig, 1961) We can agree with Brüning in his analysis of Wilder's class position but he is unfair to him when he stresses primarily his "anti-humanistic, inhuman attitude." This evaluation, which lacks literary and political discrimination, does not do justice to Wilder's position within the international late bourgeois literature of the drama.
27. W. Hildesheimer, "Die Realität selbst ist absurd," in *Theater heute*, 1/1962, p. 8.
28. M. Esslin, The Theater of the Absurd (New York, 1961), p. xix.
29. *Ibid.*, p. 293.
30. *Ibid.*, p. 314.
31. E. Ionesco, "Aus Interviews," in S. Melchinger, *Dramen zwischen Shaw und Brecht* (Bremen, 1957), S. 99.
32. *Ibid.*
33. *Ibid.*
34. M. Kesting, *Panorama des zeitgenössischen Theaters* (Munich, 1962), p. 146.
35. S. Beckett, *Krapp's Last Tape* (New York, 1958), p. 24.
36. *Ibid.*, p. 19.
37. *Ibid.*, p. 24.
38. E. Ionesco
39. E. Ionesco
40. E. Ionesco
41. E. Ionesco, "Brecht ist ein Briefträger," in *Theater heute*, 2/1962, p.l.
42. E. Ionesco
43. M. Kesting, *op. cit.*, p. 148
44. A. Chekhov
45. E. Ionesco
46. E. Ionesco
47. E. Ionesco
48. E. Ionesco
49. E. Ionesco

B. G. ZHANTIEVA

JOYCE'S *ULYSSES*

Ulysses (1922) was written in the years 1914-1921. This was a period marked by stormy events. When the First World War was in full swing, there flared up in Joyce's homeland the Easter Uprising of 1916. The great October socialist revolution gave rise to an upsurge of revolutionary movements in the countries of Europe and to national liberation struggles in the colonies. In Ireland the years 1919-1921 were marked by partisan warfare against British imperialism; in 1921-1923 there was civil war. All these events served to sharpen Joyce's critical attitude toward bourgeois society, yet the basis of his world outlook was a pessimism characteristic of many Western intellectuals in that period. He saw the First World War as an explosion of animal instincts inherent in human nature; according to his beliefs, the development of technology, which was being turned more and more to destructive ends, must inevitably bring humanity to ruin. To him the contemporary world appeared as an evil, senseless chaos, in which man is solitary and helpless. All these thoughts found reflection in *Ulysses*.

The novel, which was seven years in the making, is not a single organic whole; in it are reflected various and often contradictory tendencies. The action of the novel takes place in Dublin during the course of one day—the 16th of June, 1904. Out of its pages rises the actual Dublin of the beginning of the twentieth century with all its peculiar characteristics. But this portrayal takes in something bigger. In sketching Dublin, the author shows all bourgeois society. Hostility toward this society, joined with hostility toward the whole world, and the despair that seized the author find an outlet in a secondary or symbolic plan of the novel, in which is concentrated all that is hidden behind the portrayal of the daily life of Dublin. As a basis for the second plan, the author used Homer's *Odyssey*.

As the biographers of Joyce testify, the image of Odysseus had a special meaning for him from his adolescent years on. According to the words of G. Borach, who in 1954 published a record of his talks with the author, Joyce considered the theme of the *Odyssey* to be beautiful and all-embracing, greater and more humane than the theme of *Hamlet, Don Quixote, The Divine Comedy*, and *Faust*. Judging from

138

Borach's notes, this talk took place in August 1917. Joyce was considering the *Odyssey* in the light of the events of the World War. He said that the Trojan War was needed by the Greek traders, who were looking for new markets—and that Odysseus knew this. He noted the wisdom and love of Odysseus, who did not want to take part in the war and began to plow and pretend madness in order to deceive those who came to call him to the expedition.

It was only not to destroy his young son, whom they laid in the path of his plow, that he acknowledged his deception. Joyce went on to speak of the noble motifs of the *Odyssey*, both in regard to Homer's treatment of Odysseus, the only man in Hellas who was against the war, and in the feeling with which the father-son relationship is portrayed.

In his next talk with Borach, Joyce spoke of the contemporary governments, which had filled the world with blood. "And the return, how profoundly human! Don't forget the trait of generosity at the interview with Ajax in the nether world, and many other beautiful touches. I am almost afraid to treat such a theme; it's overwhelming."[1]

As is evident from such expressions, when he began working on *Ulysses*, Joyce pictured to himself the image of Odysseus, who with his humaneness is a contrast to the evil of the world.

Through the consciousness of the principal heroes of the novel —the poet Stephen Dedalus and Leopold Bloom, a Dublin Jew, canvasser of newspaper advertisements—Joyce shows the characteristic features of the society in which they live.

The beginning of the novel is devoted to Stephen Dedalus, hero of Joyce's foregoing novel *A Portrait of the Artist as a Young Man*. We learn about the events of his life which precede the action in *Ulysses*. They correspond in many respects with the facts of Joyce's biography. Having left Ireland to gain experience as a writer in Paris —a Mecca for proponents of new aesthetic movements—Stephen Dedalus soon had to return home, summoned to his dying mother's side. Now, a poet by calling, he is obliged to teach history in a private school. He is tormented by memories of how in revolt against religion he did not fulfill his mother's last request—that he kneel and pray by her bedside; he is depressed by the way his life has turned out. He compares his fate with the destiny of Daedalus' son Icarus, who, having flown to the sky, fell into the sea because the wax on his wings melted in the sun. Long estranged from his family, after the death of his mother Stephen broke with his father, left home, and is living with his friend Buck Mulligan, a medical student, in a suburb of Dublin, in one of the watchtowers—now for rent—built by the English government in the period of the Napoleonic wars. In the tower has also settled an acquaintance of Mulligan's, the newly arrived Englishman Haines—a philologist who is studying Gaelic languages.

Stuart Gilbert, an investigator of Joyce's work and a man who knew the writer well, makes clear in his book about Joyce that each of the eighteen episodes in *Ulysses* corresponds with one or another episode of the *Odyssey*. Leopold Bloom, who roams the town from morning to night carrying out his newspaper commissions, is identified with Odysseus, Stephen Dedalus with Telemachus.

The episodes in Ulysses are set in the following order: 1. "Telemachus." Stephen Dedalus feels himself superfluous in the tower which serves him for home—the Englishman Haines has established himself there; in the symbolic plan the image of Stephen corresponds with Telemachus, who endures the insults of the suitors who have settled down in the house of his mother. 2. "Nestor." Stephen Dedalus gives a history lesson at the school, then has a talk with the director of the school, Mr. Deasy, who ironically corresponds to wise old Nestor, King of Pylos. 3. "Proteus." Stephen Dedalus wanders along Sandymount strand. In the title of the episode is contained the idea of the changeability of the sea and the instability of the shapes of things on the shore. 4. "Calypso." Morning in the home of Bloom and his wife Marion. 5. "Lotus-Eaters." Bloom, coming out of his house in the morning, goes in the direction of the city baths. The window of a firm that sells tea arouses in his imagination pictures of the Orient, a notion of the people who fall into oblivion as they lie in the sun. The bath has a similar effect on Bloom. 6. "Hades." Bloom attends the funeral of one of the inhabitants of Dublin—Patrick Dignam. 7. "Aeolus." The editorial office of the newspaper *Freeman's Journal*—Bloom's place of work. 8. "Laestrygonians." Bloom in a pub during the lunch hour. 9. "Scylla and Charybdis." A scene in the National Library, where a discussion about Shakespeare takes place between Stephen Dedalus and certain visitors at the library. 10. "Wandering Rocks." Dublin at the liveliest time of day, commotion in the streets, each of the heroes meets many acquaintances. 11. "Sirens." Bloom, going into a barroom, hears the singing of girls behind the bar. 12. "Cyclops." Collision in a pub between Bloom and a powerful-looking guest who proves to be a Sinn Feiner. 13. "Nausicaa." Bloom, resting on the beach, is captivated by the sight of young Gerty MacDowell. 14. "Oxen of Helios" (symbol of fertility). Bloom goes into a maternity hospital in order to ask about Mrs. Purefoy. 15. "Circe." Dublin at night. The red light district, where Bloom for the first time speaks to Stephen. 16. "Eumaeus." Refuge of night cabbies, where Bloom, on his way home, drops in with Stephen, who has suffered in an encounter with British soldiers. 17. "Ithaca." Bloom-Odysseus returns home and brings Stephen-Telemachus with him. 18. "Penelope." Inner monologue of sleepy Marion.

The action of the whole novel, numbering about 800 pages, is from eight o'clock in the morning to two o'clock at night.

For the characterization of Stephen Dedalus the episodes "Telemachus," "Nestor," "Proteus," and "Scylla and Charybdis" have the greatest meaning. In them are shown different facets of Stephen's spiritual world, which in turn reflects the cast of mind and the disposition of Joyce himself. In "Telemachus" is revealed the sensing of the dual yoke which was so heavy for him—national and religious. "I am the servant of two masters," he tells Haines with bitter irony. His masters are "the imperial British state and the holy Roman catholic and apostolic church." In Stephen's perception, his rejection of the power of the church unites with his refusal to fulfill the last plea of his mother. But, having renounced religion, he nevertheless feels its power, while Haines' presence hourly reminds him of British rule over Ireland. The author shows what thoughts are called out in Stephen by the very sight of Haines, by his manners, his smile: "Horns of a bull, hoof of a horse, smile of a Saxon."

"Eyes, pale as the sea . . . firm and prudent. The seas' ruler." "They wash and tub and scrub," thinks Stephen, looking at the clean Haines. "Agenbite of inwit. Conscience. Yet here's a spot." A sentence of Haines' sticks in his brain: "We feel in England that we have treated you rather unfairly. It seems history is to blame"—and again and again he returns to it: "The seas' ruler. His seacold eyes looked on the empty bay: history is to blame. . . ." And farther on: "We feel in England. . . ."

Stephen leaves the tower in the morning with the thought of not going back any more. His departure has a symbolic meaning: he is homeless in his own land, "strangers" are in his home. The theme of Ireland—so painful for Joyce—and his dual attitude toward his homeland are here incarnated in symbolic form with a force filled with deep meaning and permeated with emotion. The old milkwoman who brings milk to the inhabitants of the tower is at the same time "the poor old woman," an image out of folklore, personifying Ireland. The scene in which Haines, the newly arrived Englishman, a snob who shows off his learning, addresses the milkwoman in the Irish tongue contains a monstrous paradox: the old Irishwoman, who doesn't know her native tongue, thinks he is speaking French.

The whole complexity of Stephen-Joyce's attitude toward the native land with which he has broken, toward the problem of Ireland plunged in darkness, is expressed in his thoughts: "A wandering crone, lowly form of an immortal serving her betrayer, their common cuckquean, a messenger from the secret morning. To serve or to upbraid, whether he could not tell: but scorned to beg her favor."

The main thing in the next episode is the attitude of Stephen Dedalus toward the world, toward mankind and its history. The hero is depressed by the thought that he lives in a society where the law of buy and sell reigns. In the school, looking at his pupils—sons of substantial citizens—he thinks: "For them too history was a tale like any other too often heard, their land a pawnshop." In the money which is paid him at the school, he sees "symbols soiled by greed and misery."

Stephen rejects conciliation and the banal worldly wisdom of the loyal Mr. Deasy, director of the school, who stresses that his ancestors voted for the union of Ireland and Great Britain and is convinced that all history moves toward one great goal willed by God. "That is God," says Stephen, jerking his thumb toward the window, through which at that moment are heard the exclamations of schoolboys who have made a goal. "A shout in the street." The bombastic accusatory speech of Mr. Deasy against the Jews forces Stephen to turn his thoughts to the calamities which this people has suffered over the ages. Inclined, like the author, to indict all humanity, Stephen says, "History . . . is a nightmare from which I am trying to awake."

How Stephen understands the meaning of the artist is made clear in the episode "Proteus." Wandering along Sandymount strand, he thinks that he must read the signs of everything he sees around him. He returns to the thought of his enslaved land, but he perceives the long national liberation struggle in Ireland, torn by internal contradictions, as violence, which he hates. At the same time, he is vaguely oppressed by not taking part in the struggle personally. In his imagination arises the tower where the "stranger" has established himself. And then arises the thought: "Take all, keep all. My soul walks with me, form of forms." Here is sketched the cast of mind of the artist who has isolated himself from hateful reality, who has gone off to the citadel of his art. Just as in the Aristotelian thesis of Stephen's aesthetic program in *A Portrait of the Artist as a Young Man*, the intellectual spirit—the form of forms—appears of its own accord only when he is remote from everything.

In the episode "Scylla and Charybdis" we become better acquainted with the "intellectual spirit" of the artist, with his consciousness weighed down by gloomy notions of the world and by a load of dead knowledge and false theories. Discussions about Aristotle and Plato take place in the National Library between Stephen and those active in the Irish renaissance—John Eglinton and George Russell. They argue also about the work of Shakespeare.

About Shakespeare's meaning for Joyce we can judge from the numerous references to his work, images, metaphors, hidden quotations. It is noteworthy in particular that in the episode "Proteus" Stephen identifies himself with Hamlet when he makes the decision not to return to the tower. Walking along the seashore, he repeats to himself, "So in the moon's midwatches I pace the path above the rocks, in sable silvered, hearing Elsinore's tempting flood." Here the thought of Hamlet rises in Stephen in connection with the fact that his rights have been usurped, but possibly his "Hamlet" moods have also a broader base, being rooted in the consciousness that "the times are out of joint." However, actually the image of Stephen, which dooms itself to passivity, gives no grounds for parallels with Hamlet, who is sharply aware of the necessity of struggle in an evil world.

With his interest in universal themes, Joyce was drawn to Shakespeare as to Homer. Like Homer's *Odyssey*, the work of Shakespeare was for him an element from which he drew inspiration, ground for reflection, a base for parallels. Stephen agrees with Eglinton when the latter says that "after God, Shakespeare has created most" and is able to incarnate himself in his heroes: "Shakespeare is the spirit of both the father and the prince. He is all in all." However, thought about the universal character of Shakespeare's work ("he is all in all") acquires a special character in Stephen's interpretation; in accordance with the theories of Freud, he tries to find in the playwright's personality and in his life the sources of everything reflected in Shakespeare's work. Thus he argues that Shakespeare carried over into the outer world and reflected everything that was in his inner world: in particular there seemed to live in his soul the moneylender Shylock ("The son of a maltjobber and moneylender he was himself a corn-jobber and moneylender . . . and exacted his pound of flesh in interest for every money lent"), the executioner also lived there ("Sumptuous and stagnant exaggeration of murder"), and Iago likewise ("ceaselessly willing that the moor in him shall suffer"). Basing himself on the sup-position that Shakespeare's wife, Anne Hathaway, was unfaithful to him with his brother Richard, Stephen holds that it was because of this that Shakespeare created the image of the evil king—Richard III—who seduced Ann, widow of the prince murdered by him. The thought "all in all" is united also with the Freudian motif of the father and the son, to which the author gives his attention throughout the entire book, drawing parallels from various provinces, beginning with the Homeric epic and ending with the Bible and the Gospels. Stephen strives to prove that Hamlet is the spiritual son of Shakespeare and at the same time is also Hamnet, the playwright's son who has died. Hamlet's father, who was devoted to his brother Claudius and to his wife, is likened to Odysseus, whom Penelope's suitors want to ruin, and at the same time to Shakespeare, deceived by his wife—the "Strat-ford Penelope." In this chain of analogies the author subsequently in-cludes Bloom, too. Bloom, who is identified with Odysseus, and whose marital rights have been transgressed by Boylan, his wife Marion's lover, is also likened at the same time to Shakespeare, for Bloom's son Rudy died as a child, as did Shakespeare's son Hamnet.

Stephen continues to widen the sphere in which his theory ap-plies: "Maeterlinck says: *If Socrates leave his house today he will find the sage seated on his doorsteps. If Judas go forth tonight it is to Judas his steps will tend.* Every life is many days, day after day. We walk through ourselves, meeting robbers, ghosts, giants, old men, young men, wives, widows, brothers-in-love. But always meeting our-selves."

Further, Stephen expresses the thought that God, too, having created the world, is also "all in all in all of us, ostler and butcher, and would be bawd and cuckold too but that in the economy of heaven, foretold by Hamlet, there are no more marriages. . . ." Stephen sets forth his views in just as doctrinaire a fashion as at one time—in his preceding novel—he set forth a program of aesthetics from which, according to Lynch, proceeded "scholastic stink." Shakespeare is drawn into a circle of pseudo-scientific studies—contemporary and mediaeval (they are even compared: Thomas Aquinas, says Stephen, wrote about incest from a standpoint differing from that of the new Viennese school). With the help of Freud's theory narrowing and distorting what was for him a whole world (it is necessary only to remember that in former times, weary of Aquinas' formalism, he found joy in works of the Elizabethan age), Stephen-Joyce possibly strove, as a representative of the "new art," to break the traditional perception of Shakespeare, making use for his new theory of what appeared to be "the last word." It is not out of the question to suppose that he was not fully convinced by it. It is not without interest that to Eglinton's question whether he believes his own theory, Stephen gives a negative answer. And if in *A Portrait of the Artist as a Young Man* Joyce could take a "detached view" of his program, to quote Lynch, here the "detached view" is given through Haines; after hearing from Mulligan about Stephen's reflection on Hamlet, Haines remarks that "Shakespeare is the happy hunting ground of all minds that have lost their balance." This sentence reveals almost the main aspect of Joyce's attitude toward Shakespeare in the period when he was working on *Ulysses*.

In Shakespeare's work the writer seeks confirmation of the thought about the depravity of mankind which torments his thoughts. According to Stephen, the works of Shakespeare, populated by images of hypocrites, usurpers, adulterers, and murderers, reflect mankind's very history, which is nothing but a chain of crimes, "criminal annals of the world, stained with all other incests and bestialities. . . ." In the work of Shakespeare, Stephen, as author, sees not only history, but also a prologue to the future. Undoubtedly the picture of the First World War rises in Joyce's imagination when he says through Stephen's lips: "Khaki Hamlets don't hesitate to shoot. The bloodboltered shambles in act five is a forecast of the concentration camp. . . ."

Perception of the baseness of human nature, which has formed under the influence of modernist philosophy in crisis, is interwoven in Joyce, as in his hero, with the dogmatism of catholicism about original sin. In all the works of Shakespeare, Stephen perceives the idea of original sin. "Age has not withered it," he says. "Beauty and peace have not done it away. It is in infinite variety everywhere in the world he has created. . . ." Then follows the commentary of the author: "He laughed to free his mind from his mind's bondage."

Stephen Dedalus is the image of Joyce himself, whose consciousness is "in bondage," depressed by the sense of hostility and depravity
of the surrounding world. At the same time Stephen may be regarded
as the prototype of many central characters in contemporary modernist literature. Characteristic of Joyce's hero is the absence of inner
conflict, his spiritual constraint, depression of the will and desires, and
now and then flareups of arrogance. Stephen does not oppose his environment. "Stop struggling," he addresses himself mentally. Evidently
it is for this reason that in *Ulysses* are absent those relations, peculiar
to the realistic novel, between the author and the characters closest
to him, for whose ideals and errors he feels himself responsible.

There is much that separates Stephen Dedalus of *Ulysses* from the
hero of *A Portrait of the Artist as a Young Man.* He does not have the
earlier strength of feeling, nor does he experience "epiphanies," the
spiritual flights and falls. Richard Aldington noted the differences in
the world outlook of Joyce in his early period of creativity and at
the stage when he created *Ulysses.* Aldington wrote that, owing to the
portrayal of the spiritual struggle of the hero, *A Portrait of the Artist
as a Young Man* rose to the heights of tragedy even when the question
was about dirt and poverty. "One felt that here was a man of extreme
sensitiveness and talent getting rid of 'perilous stuff,' throwing off the
evil dreams and influences of mawkish youth to reach a saner, clearer
view of human life." According to Aldington, after studying the character of Joyce's gift he expected genuine tragedy from the writer.
but when *Ulysses* came out, he understood that he was mistaken in
his expectations.[2]

The image of the other major character in *Ulysses*, Leopold Bloom,
is extremely complex—in him there is a crossing of many lines. First
of all he is perceived as a typical petty bourgeois organically tied to
his environment—as a Dublin man-in-the-street. With his commonplace speeches and acts and with his limited thinking, Bloom has been
formed in its own image by the society of which he is part. But at
the same time he is a suffering personality; participating in this society, he is at the same time isolated from it. One of the principal reasons for this is his belonging to a persecuted nation. As the son of a
converted Jew, he is cut off from his people; he is a stranger in Ireland
too. In the broad sense of the word, Bloom is homeless; in the novel
he is compared not only with wandering Odysseus, but also with the
Wandering Jew.

At first the comparison of the Dublin inhabitant with the heroic Odysseus seems a parody. Such an impression is not without ground. But later on it is revealed that this is not the author's main goal, that in the novel there are other, more significant levels of this complex comparison of Bloom's image with that of the hero of the Homeric epic.

Comparing Bloom with Odysseus, Joyce explained to his friend Frank Budgen (who later published a book about Joyce) that Bloom is well-wishing, attentive to people, and has feelings of justice. He is cautious, quick-witted, shows stability, is capable of opposing crude chauvinism. These features are shown in Bloom's attitude to his surroundings. He is a man who has not absorbed the cruelty and indifference of the society to which he belongs. We may suppose that coming to a comparison, in this aspect, of images so incommensurable in scale—Bloom and Odysseus—the author implied that the nobility, kindness, and love of peace appear in Bloom in such degree as is given to a "contemporary Odysseus," a "little man" who feels the pressure of the surrounding world. The basic aspect of the image, it seems, is in the fact that Bloom-Odysseus gradually gets to know the terrible aspects of the society in which he lives.

The secondary plan of the novel is tied in principally with Bloom's adventures. Carrying out his usual commissions, he walks along the animated streets of Dublin. Everything he meets on the way is the everyday life of the town. But behind the everyday hides the terrible —the laws and customs of bourgeois society.

In the episode "Hades," which corresponds with the eleventh book of the *Odyssey* (the descent of Odysseus into Hades), an ordinary cemetery is perceived as a symbol of the ghastliness and decomposition of the bourgeois world. The sentimental epitaphs on the gravestones and the grandeur of the church service underline with special sharpness the gloomy essence of this scene. Religion and commerce come together in Bloom's thoughts when he recalls how priests are dead set against crematoria, for they are "devilling for the other firm." The appearance of Patrick Dignam in his coffin gives birth to a formula in which is rephrased the English saying that the Englishman's house is his castle and gives an idea about the Irish in their land: "The Irishman's home is his coffin." Bloom's thoughts about the "improvement" of the burial ritual—about certain street cars which would deliver the dead directly to the graves, about the setting up of grave telephones in case of an awakening from a lethargic sleep, about installing gramophones with records of the voices of the dead—seem to say that in the end all the achievements of science serve the demands of death.

In the episode "Aeolus," the chatter of idle journalists, "windbags," is associated with the winds that Aeolus commands. Hollow rhetoric reigns in the office of the editor of the *Freeman's Journal*, where articles full of false sentiment are read and where Professor MacHugh, a figure in Ireland's renaissance, holds forth about history and culture. Bloom, who has come to the *Freeman's Journal* in order to turn in to the press an advertisement for a firm, reflects about how the newspaper is made, about journalists who have a weakness for sensationalism—"weathercocks" who turn their nose according to the wind, reporting diametrically opposite information. An ancient song about a goat which comes up in his mind calls forth a judgment: "Sounds a bit silly till you come to look into it well. Justice it means, but it's everybody eating everyone else. That's what life is after all."

This thought becomes the leitmotif of the next episode—"Laestrygonians"—having something to do with the pages in which Homer tells about Odysseus' meeting with cannibals. Here this theme of cannibalism sounds still stronger and more insistent. "Eat or be eaten. Kill! Kill!" is uttered in Bloom's mind when he looks at greedily chewing people in a restaurant. The sight of a tin of preserved meat brings him to thinking about canned human flesh. A chain of similar associations expresses the idea of the cannibal laws of civilized society.

These 'laws' are exposed with great force in the episode "Cyclops," the action of which takes place in a tavern. Here again appears Joyce's confused attitude toward the Irish national liberation movement. Exaggerating the narrowness and chauvinism of some of its figures, Joyce portrays this movement as a blind, destructive power. In the secondary plan of the novel a Sinn Feiner (called "citizen") is associated with the crude giant Polyphemus. At the same time the writer puts into the "citizen's" mouth speeches full of passionate force. In them is reflected the history of Ireland, tortured by the English for centuries: the ruinous consequences of Cromwell's expeditions through the land, the monstrous mixture of cruelty and hypocrisy with which gospel inscriptions were pasted around the mouth of his cannon—"God is love"; hunger in the land, the migration of thousands of Irish driven by need and persecution to America. The whole scene is permeated with a sharp sense of the cruelty of the world.

One of the frequenters of the tavern compares British colonial politics with the practices of the Belgians who in the Congo "rap[ed] the women and girls and flog[ged] the natives on the belly to squeeze all the red rubber they can out of them."

The stamp of petty bourgeois limitations, of reformist illusions, lies on Bloom's attempts to moderate the violence of the "citizen." On the other hand a passionate protest is torn from him against the injustice to which his people are subjected in the capitalist world. "And I belong to a race too," he says, "that is hated and persecuted. Also now. This very moment. This very instant . . . Robbed . . . Plundered. Insulted. Persecuted. Taking what belongs to us by right. At this very moment . . . sold by auctions off in Morocco like slaves or cattles." To the statement of one of those present that it is necessary to oppose injustice with force, Bloom answers: "But it's no use. . . . Force, hatred, history, all that. That's not life for men and women, insult and hatred. And everybody knows that it's the very opposite of that that is really life." Here we see the point of view of the author, his conviction of the uselessness of struggle.

The end of the episode is carried out in the spirit of farcical parody. The "citizen," filled with antipathy for Bloom, upset—partly by his declaration that Christ was a Jew—throws a tin biscuitbox after Bloom who is going off in a cab, but blinded by the sun, misses him (a parallel with the blinding of Polyphemus). The cab turns into a chariot and Bloom, like Elijah the prophet, is borne to heaven "at an angle of forty-five degrees over Donohoe's in Little Green Street. . . ."

The majority of the episodes we have examined are distinguished by the fact that here, on the secondary level, are incarnated characteristic features of bourgeois society and its brutal laws. The writer's sharp sensing of baseness and violence in all corners of the world gives rise to general symbols. But the effect of these images is weakened, for on them lies the stamp of the author's notion that such are the laws of human life. This world outlook of Joyce's is the source of the contradictions in *Ulysses* and fetters the author's creative power. As a result, the value of each of Joyce's artistic aims is reduced. This can be seen also on examining the first level of meaning in *Ulysses*.

There are many scenes in the novel in which life in all its reality is incarnated. This reality vividly rises before one's eyes in the first episode—"Telemachus"; the very first lines give a notion of it: the morning scene on the parapet, the view of the bay and the "awaking

mountains," the sunlight reflected on the nickel shaving bowl, forgotten on the parapet. "Palpably real" also are the inhabitants of the
tower—the jovial Mulligan who, unburdened by reflection, simply en-
joys life, Stephen Dedalus with his inner discord and sharp sense of
being the son of a land enslaved, and the cold, inquisitive Englishman
Haines. The motif of English rule over Ireland, which was latent in
the collection of short-stories *Dubliners* ("Ivy Day in the Committee-
room," "After the Race"), now sounds more clearly and finds expression in the image of Haines. This image is far from the stereotype of
the colonizer. Haines is a cultured, courteous man who has come to
Ireland for the purpose of research. But in his every gesture is seen
unshakable confidence in his superiority, bred in him and his like by
centuries of British colonial imperialism. The entire situation, in which,
as it were, the disposition of forces is marked and the source of possible
conflict hidden, is perceived as an introduction to the epic whole. It
gives rise to the feeling that the writer, having created this scene,
began to fulfill his artistic intention, which afterwards, during the
course of several years of working on the novel, was in some way
bertayed or rejected. The vivid, convincing opening episode does not
have its equal in the novel.

Dublin is portrayed as a living organism—the focus of petty bourgeois life is a "boiling pot" of small interests and passions. We recognize the town here and at times also its characters in preceding works
of Joyce's (thus at the cemetery the grave of Mrs. Sinico brings to
mind her tragic story). *Ulysses* places before us the characteristic
features of the town and its inhabitants with their secret little sins and
their outward decorum, with their "spiritual interests" focussed on a
bet on some occasion, bets on race horses by correspondence, and on
popular novels (names of books on a bookstand give a notion of that:
The Awful Revelations of Maria Monk, Fair Tyrants, Sweets of Sin).
Over all this rises the State (Joyce brings it to mind parodying the
standard loyal journalistic style of reporting the journey of the Vice-
roy of Ireland through the town) and the Church, which subjects
souls to itself: divine service, the sacrament, confession—great weapons
in its hands.

In sketching the portraits of Dubliners, the author laconically,
through a detail or two, gives a picture of the whole: "Buck Mulligan's
primrose waistcoat shook gaily to his laughter"; Mr. Deasy "turned
his angry white mustache toward them." The characteristic figures on

the streets of Dublin are engraved by "instant snapshots." Thus is "snapped" William Brayden, Esquire on his entrance into the editorial office of the newspaper, which depends on his financial support: The figure "passed stately up the staircase steered by an umbrella, a solemn beardframed face. The broadcloth back ascended each step. . . ." Two images from the funeral procession are picked up by the author's eye: "Leanjawed harpy, hard woman at a bargain, her bonnet awry. Girl's face stained with dirt and tears, holding the woman's arm looking up at her for a sign to cry. Fish's face, bloodless and livid." The image of Boylan, which comes up from time to time in the hurly-burly of Dublin, is composed of very unimportant features, caught by the author by the way—straw hat glittering in the sun, red carnation in his teeth, an advertisement quickly dictated to the typist—but there results a comprehensive idea of the flashy commonplaceness of the insolent provincial Lovelace and successful businessman.

Joyce's realistic skill attracted the attention of Bernard Shaw when he read a part of *Ulysses* printed in the journal *Little Review*. In 1921 the playwright wrote in one of his letters that a repellent but true picture of Ireland is given in the novel. He would have liked to make every Irishman read this book so as to satisfy himself whether any one of them could bear such a spectacle—his own reflection in the author's mirror. As Richard Ellmann describes Shaw's reaction, "At least someone had possessed the courage to write it down. . . ."[3] Later, in a talk with his biographer, Archibald Henderson, Shaw said that he was attracted by the true, documentary portrayal of Dublin, which he knew in his youth, and by Joyce's outstanding literary skill. Shaw remarked, however, that he could "find no interest in his [Joyce's] infantile clinical incontinences."[4]

But the pictures in relief of Dublin and its inhabitants are perceived against the general background of the novel rather as fragments. The author does not set himself the aim of realistic re-creation of reality. He gives the life of Dublin as a "model" of the whole life of man, which, like the history of mankind, appears to the author to be a closed circle. Herein lies the philosophical basis of the novel.

Joyce's world outlook was favorable soil for philosophic theories having a subjective, idealistic base. In the early years of the twentieth century, particularly in the period when, together with Oliver St. John Gogarty (prototype of Buck Mulligan), the writer, like his hero, lived in a tower, the idol of their circle was Nietzsche with his theory of an irrational myth, the cult of the superman who stands beyond good and evil. Later on Joyce got acquainted with Schopenhauer, with the philosophy of intuitionalism of Bergson, who depreciated the role of reason, science, and logical thought and insisted on knowledge by way of "inner contemplation," and with the philosophy of Whitehead, who held the only reality to be that of sensation. Above all, however, Joyce was interested in the metaphysical historico-philosophical theory of Vico (developed in his book *The New Science*) in accordance with which all peoples of the world, after passing through the same cycles of development, return to a primitive state, while the history of mankind is an eternal rotation and moves in a closed circle. This theory, put forward in the eighteenth century, came in the nineteenth and especially the twentieth centuries to attract the interest of reactionary bourgeois philosophers, who were interpreting life and history of society subjectively. In particular, Spengler, who in his book *The Decline of the West* presented the history of society as a process of the beginning, flowering, and decay of separate, closed cycles, proclaimed the decline of contemporary European civilization. To the question whether he believed in the "new science," Joyce answered that he didn't believe in any science, but that reading the books of Vico—as opposed to reading Freud and Jung—stimulated his imagination.

The philosophy of recurrence has central importance for *Ulysses*. The rapprochement of the images of Stephen Dedalus and Bloom, who, it would seem, were conceived as antipodal figures, is in part tied in with this philosophy.

In examining this problem, we should first of all dwell on the rational explanations. Stephen and Bloom are outside this society where the loyalty of Mr. Deasy and the insolent Boylan triumphs; the primitive "little man" and the artist with a sensitive nature are both lonely and depressed, each in his own way is an "exile," each is "homeless."

But in conformity with his world outlook, the author also brings together Stephen and Bloom, who roam the town from morning to night, as figures in the eternal cycle of life. About this, the thoughts of the protagonists testify first of all—they perceive life as a senseless, ever-renewing cycle in which birth and death take turns. Wandering on the shore, Stephen sees two midwives descending to the shore—the sight of them is associated with birth; the carcass of a dog stretched on the shore and the "white as salt" body of a drowned man that has floated to the surface brings to mind death. In the episode "Laestrygones" this thought is conveyed through the inner monologue of Bloom, who, walking the streets of Dublin, reflects about the fact that everything repeats itself from day to day. The flood of pedestrians moves there and back. Patrick Dignam died this morning, while in the maternity home Mrs. Purefoy is about to bring a child into the world.

It is not given to the two major characters of the novel, one gathers, to break out of the closed circle. Each of them is a passive victim of circumstances—to use an expression of Joyce himself in his story "Araby," "a creature driven and derided by vanity."

The history of mankind similarly is perceived by Joyce's heroes as a recurring cycle. This thought, expressed in the inner monologue of Stephen ("Hold to the now, the here, through which all future plunges to the past") is stated by Bloom in a more stereotyped form: "History repeats itself . . . Names change: that's all . . . Nothing new under the sun."

The correspondence between the inner monologues of Stephen and Bloom makes itself understood not only by the fact that through them the author expresses his own thoughts. By means of their inner monologues are established also certain irrational ties between the heroes, in preparation, as it were, for the meeting of Stephen-Telemachus (who has broken with his own father) with his spiritual father in the person of Bloom-Odysseus. During the greater part of *Ulysses* the heroes of the novel do not know each other, do not socialize, although their paths in the Dublin crowd repeatedly cross. Nevertheless, between them is established a mysterious contact. Sometimes in their inner monologues there float up ideas about the same things, for instance about "Turko the terrible" out of a pantomime, etc. Mentally they utter the same phrases. Thus in the episode "Laestrygones," Bloom, imagining a butcher shop with bloody carcasses, says to himself "Rawhead and bloody bones"; Stephen cries out this same phrase when the fearful vision of his mother appears in the episode "Circe." The images of a fox and a dog who scratch the ground, images which pursue Stephen in connection with thoughts about his dead mother, correspond to the image of scratching rats—devourers of corpses—in the imagination of Bloom. The meeting of Bloom and Stephen, which takes place only at the end of the novel (episode "Circe"), is presented as their mystical union. At the moment when Bloom bends over Stephen, who, hurt in a collision with drunken English soldiers, is stretched on the ground, there arises in Bloom's imagination the face of his

mother and the words of a song about Fergus. At the very same moment against the background of a wall, there appears a vision of Bloom's
dead son Rudy. This must mean that Bloom has found his spiritual son.
Odysseus is united with Telemachus.

The union of the protagonists, however, does not at all mean their
genuine spiritual closeness, their liberation from the closed circle of
life. Their meeting resolves nothing, the cycle continues, each of them
is lonely as before, whatever the ties—real or artificial—which the author
established between them. In the episode "Ithaca," where Bloom brings
Stephen home with him, the heroes part and the author lets it be understood they will meet no more.

The thought that Stephen is at the same time Telemachus while
Bloom is Odysseus is in essence tied in with Stephen's thesis in the episode "Scylla and Charybdis"—"all is in all"; as is clear from the latest episodes, it also fits into the formula "each can be each" (the ironical continuation of this thought may be heard in the inner monologue of
Bloom.—No one is any "thing"). The meaning of Stephen's saying is
that Shakespeare, Bloom, and Jesus Christ are different bodily coverings
of the same essence. When in the episode "Circe," in which Bloom is
made fun of as a cuckold, he walks up with Stephen to a mirror, in it
is reflected the gelled, paralyzed face of Shakespeare, crowned with
antlers.

The idea of equating everyone with everyone bears direct relation
to the pessimistic outlook on man characteristic of Joyce's postwar
work. If in the period when the writer planned the novel he pictured
Odysseus as an image of humaneness, then now, when mankind in all
ages seems to him criminal, the shadow of this idea falls on Odysseus
too. In the light of such a concept, the rapprochement of Stephen and
Bloom may also be perceived as the author's wish to show that there
is no difference between high and low. Indeed, he "lowers" the image
of Stephen, noting such of his characteristics as serve this aim—right
down to physical uncleanness. Stephen begins to be covered with the
same slime as Bloom is immersed in.

The attitude of Joyce toward man dictates a naturalistic method
of depicting him. To a certain extent this is justified; the very detailed
description of the way of life, of the domestic morals and manners
of Bloom and Marion, gives a notion of the quagmire of petty bourgeois commonplaceness. But at bottom the author's naturalism is perceived as an expression of his disgust with man.

By disgust for man there is called forth in the novel also what in aesthetics we may call ugly, and which afterwards became an ordinary feature in modernist works. Thus in "Hades" the author with sadistic stubbornness fixes his attention on everything that is monstrous and revolting. Bloom imagines all stages of the decay of corpses ("Turning green and pink, decomposing. . . . Then a kind of a tallowy kind of a cheesy. Then begin to get black, treacle oozing out of them . . ."). In this way the author strives to call out disgust—an emotion which at one time he excluded from his aesthetic program. Here also we have features characteristic of contemporary modernist literature—grotesque use of the gloomy and the sinister by means of contrasting comparisons on the basis of purely superficial associations. Bloom's thought about grave pits, swirling with maggots, is immediately associated with the words of a banal song: "All dimpled cheeks and curls, your head it simply whirls."

As is characteristic with the author, his attitude toward man and everything human shows in the concluding episode—"Penelope"—which presents the confused inner monologue of Marion, and where for forty-five pages there is not a single mark of punctuation. Marion's monologue, made up for the most part of recollections about her lovers, begins and ends with the word "yes." In a letter to Budgen, Joyce explained that the word "yes" expresses Marion's character. And if Goethe's Mephistopheles is the spirit who always denies (Ich bin der Geist, der stets verneint"), then Marion is the flesh which always consents ("Ich bin das Fleisch, das stets bejaht").[5]

Earlier, comparing the *Odyssey* with Goethe's *Faust*, Joyce had approached it with the criterion of high humanity; now he lowers the very understanding of humanity. In a letter to Frank Budgen in February 1921 he wrote: "The last word (human all-too-human) is left to Penelope."[6]

To the difficult search in *Faust* for a positive principle to which the restless spirit of man comes through denial, Joyce opposes the "yes" of Marion, signifying something all-accepting, infinitely unfastidious, low, animal. Here actually is sensed the obtrusive purpose of bringing to naught both the poeticalness of the true image of Penelope in the *Odyssey* and Goethe's idea of "the eternal feminine." The image of Marion, the female-woman, petty-bourgeoise incarnate, indisputably embracing the features characteristic of a certain type, is brought forward as something universal. Not accidentally does the author leave the last word to his Penelope.

Joyce's unbelief and nihilism, born of despair, work their way into the first plan of the novel. Even in his play *Exiles*, which came out not long before *Ulysses*, Joyce revealed his interest in psychological and moral questions, in vital situations which give rise to complex and even tragic conflicts, and posed the problem of the contrast between egotistic and sacrificial love. In *Ulysses* he rejects the category of the tragic, even in the sense in which it was contained in his aesthetic program in *A Portrait of the Artist as a Young Man*, which demanded a static character for tragic emotion. In *Ulysses* there is no longer any talk about a high or a low level of morality in people, about the problem of human relationships, about the character of love. Here in general there is no love, there are only sex relations. Nor is there moral judgment of people, for the moral norm from the viewpoint of which they could be judged is absent. In *Ulysses* the humanity and warmth which were felt in *Dubliners* and in *A Portrait of the Artist as a Young Man* are lost. Only distantly are we reminded of them in the scene of Stephen's chance meeting with his younger sister, who is examining a French textbook on a bookstand after she has tried to sell some domestic goods and chattels at an auction. She wants to learn French, but at the same time she realizes that it isn't possible for her. The few sentences she exchanges with Stephen resurrect in the mind the heartache that in Joyce's preceding novel was aroused by the images of children who were already weary at the beginning of life's journey.

In *Ulysses*, too, is expressed Joyce's own sensitive feeling for beauty and his gift of creating a visual image. In excellent rhythmic prose is conveyed, for example, the appearance of the ship Stephen looks at when he is taking a walk along the seashore. "Moving through the air high spars of a threemaster, her sails brailed up on the crosstrees, homing, upstream, silently moving, a silent ship." But preference is now given to ugliness.

The contradictions of Ulysses affect also the method of portraying the inner world of his characters.

As Richard Ellmann tells us, Joyce alludes to the fact that for the technique of inner monologue he is indebted to the French writer Édouard Dujardin, author of the novel *Les Lauriers sont coupés* (1887). At the same time Ellmann expresses the opinion that inner monologue in the works of Tolstoy may possibly, in some degree, have served as a starting point for Joyce's experiments in the given province and that here a sort of push may have been given by Stanislaus Joyce's literary exercises in his journal, which he showed to his brother; under the

influence of Tolstoy's story "Sebastopol in May, 1855," in which are
given the thoughts of Captain Praskoukine before death, Stanislaus
tried to give a man's thoughts at the moment when he is falling asleep.

In Joyce is absent—principally because of a different attitude toward
life—the especially characteristic type of Tolstoyan inner monologue
in which is conveyed the spiritual state of a man at a moment of inspiration, shock, threatening danger, inner conflict, or tormenting dissatisfaction with himself—"purges of the soul"—at a decisive turning-
point of life.

At the same time Joyce has his discoveries in the sphere of depicting the psychology of his characters. He depicts the psychological
process spontaneously, without the author's commentary. Characteristic of the writer is a flexibility of transition from the traditional forms
of story-telling in the third person to the speech of the acting person,
and from that—to inner monologue. Such mobility gives an impression
of real synchronization of uttered and unuttered speech—of what is
spoken and what the hero at the same time thinks. In this way Joyce
gives a true psychological picture. We can take as example the scene
of the conversation between Stephen Dedalus and Mr. Deasy, where
the words of the latter take turns with the unuttered speech of Stephen,
with his words spoken aloud, the author's speech, and then again
Stephen's thoughts. The thrifty Mr. Deasy, after paying the usual
wages to Stephen, who has been working at the school three months,
advises him to handle his money more carefully and get himself a
money-box.

"Don't carry it like that," Mr. Deasy said. "You'll pull it out somewhere and lose it. You must buy one of these machines. You'll find
them very handy."

"Answer something."

"Mine would be often empty," Stephen said.

"The same room and hour, the same wisdom: and I the same. Three
times now. Three nooses round me here. Well, I can break them in
this instant if I will."

"Because you don't save," Mr. Deasy said, pointing his finger. . . .

Through the inner monologue, Joyce gives the reader an emotional
reaction. In the episode "Telemachus," Stephen's thoughts about his
dead mother, about the fact that he did not fulfill her last request, are
impressive. For the few instants Stephen stands leaning on the parapet
of the tower, there rises before him the image of his mother, called

up in memory by Yeats' song "Who Goes with Fergus" which Mulligan sings. The bay "lay behind him, a bowl of bitter waters. Fergus' song: I sang it alone in the house, holding down the long dark chords. Her door was open: she wanted to hear my music. Silent with awe and pity I went to her bedside. She was crying in her wretched bed. For those words, Stephen: love's bitter mystery. Where now? Her secrets: old feather fans . . . amber beads in her locked drawer. A birdcage hung in the sunny window of her house when she was a girl." Inner monologue also serves Joyce as a means of indirect characterization of the protagonists. The psychological portrait of a petty bourgeois is drawn at the beginning of the novel in the inner monologue of Bloom. Here are his trivial maxims ("black conducts, reflects heat," "eyefocus bad for stomach nerves"), telling that he is filled with the consciousness of his "culture," and his practical calculations—attempts to compute when he is passing a brewery how much one can make on porter, or his regrets over having forgotten to ask an acquaintance for a train ticket to the town where his daughter has a job, and his thoughts about secret intrigues. Sitting on a bench in an empty church, Bloom thinks: "Nice discreet place to be next some girl. . . ." At the cemetery the thought comes to him: "You might pick up a young widow here. . . ."

Basically, however, in *Ulysses* that form of depicting spiritual life prevails which the definition of William James fits best of all—"stream of consciousness." Joyce reproduces an endless series of associations, one hooking into the next—a process which Freud called "free association." Thus, silk in a shop window brings to Bloom's mind that silk manufacture was started in England by the Huguenots after being driven out of France. This in turn calls up in his memory a motif from Meyerbeer's opera "The Huguenots." He starts to sing. "Great chorus. Tara. Must be washed in rain water" (here his mind reverts to silk); then an aria of the opera again floats up, etc. This sort of chain of associations is inherent in human consciousness, but taken as the base of depicting spiritual life and becoming the goal, it is perceived as a fruitless and tiresome thing. Stephen Dedalus' "stream of consciousness" is exceedingly overloaded with associations from history, philosophy, literature, mythology, out of the Bible, the Gospels, formal logic, and the theological tracts of mediaeval theologians, especially Thomas Aquinas. In the midst of this complex interlacing, there float up phrases in French, Latin, Italian, and other languages. Sometimes one gets the impression that this is a demonstration of the author's erudition. Rational, logical thinking is pushed aside. Mental tightrope-walking takes the place of the fruitful work of thought.

A huge place in the spiritual life of the characters in *Ulysses* belongs to memories. In many instances there is no need for them either in order to explain events, or to develop the action, or to throw light on character. The big role of memories is chiefly to be explained by the writer's idea about the isolation of the protagonist's inner world, of its independence of reality, which the author considers immaterial. Time—and here we have echoes of Bergson's philosophy—is not regarded as an objective category, as a measurable extent. In their memories the heroes of *Ulysses* depart from reality for a long time, and for this reason nothing changes. Into the one day during which the action of the novel takes place are "packed" years and millennia: the heroes' past, the past of Ireland and of all mankind is re-created in the consciousness of Stephen Dedalus and Bloom. As a result, minutes and hours stretch out to infinity. This is something that investigators of Joyce's work put down as a merit, in particular Stuart Gilbert and Marcel Brion, holding that he broke through the frame of the categories of time and space and with his glance embraced the cosmos. In this way Joyce creates the illusion of independence from time characteristic of subsequent modernist writers.

Erroneous also is the modernist novelists' and critics' conviction, similarly tied to the work of Joyce, that in contradistinction from representatives of realism, modernist writers, basing themselves on the theories of Freud, delve deeply into the psychological life of man. Deep delving into human psychology is exactly what there is not in the works of modernists who follow Freud. Arguing that the true—biological—essence of man, at the base of which lies sexual instinct, is repressed by social life, which is hostile to it, and is forced into the "subconscious," they isolate personality from social life in their works and thereby impoverish it. Alienating his characters from reality, carried away by Freudian "free associations," Joyce portrays the human consciousness as more confused and illogical than it is in life and does not clarify, but rather obscures, the picture of his protagonist's spiritual life. The process of fixing everything that the "stream of consciousness" carries along, without selection of the main, leads to depersonalization of the character. In this way a paradoxical situation arises: the individual, exalted by modernist literature, loses his individuality. The human psyche becomes merely a receptacle of vague sensations.

Joyce was one of the first writers who went over from the realistic method—in which the depiction of the process of consciousness is a function tied to character and its acting role—to the portrayal of a passive, static "state of consciousness." It is this method that the opponents of the realistic novel now hold to be the only one possible. Consider a comment by Nathalie Sarraute, representative of the school of the "new novel," which considers Joyce its "spiritual father." In an essay about the evolution of the European novel "From Dostoievsky to Kafka" (contained in a collection of her essays *The Age of Suspicion* [1956]), she declares that this evolution seems to lead to the rejection of the concept of character in the contemporary novel; this concept, she says, was brought to naught by the theories of Bergson and Freud. According to Sarraute, Joyce had done with characters, fixing his attention on the psychological state and not on the person, who serves merely as a support for this state. She reproaches Joyce only with inconsistency: in other words, that he, like Proust, did not sufficiently destroy his characters.

In *Ulysses* there is also another negative result of the author's acquaintance with Freud. Following Freud, applying conclusions about the peculiarities of a sick psyche to healthy people, and holding that man's behavior is conditioned by one or another "complex," Joyce shows a tendency to give the appearance of "fixed ideas" to thoughts and feelings which at first are perceived as quite natural (for instance, Bloom's thought about his father's suicide, about Marion's unfaithfulness, about the fact that he lost his son, who lived less than a year).

Stephen's psychologically justified memory about his mother, permeated with spiritual pain, becomes a fixed nightmare. Touching in its humanity, the image of his mother, uniting with the image of the Catholic Church which he rejected, acquires terrible outlines. "In a dream, silently, she had come to him, her wasted body within its loose graveclothes giving off an odor of wax and rosewood, her breath bent over him with mute secret words, a faint odor of wetted ashes. Her glazing eyes, staring out of death, to shake and bend my soul . . . Vampire! Ghoul! Chewer of corpses!"

In one of the episodes the author reveals his device, making Haines express the supposition that Stephen has an idée fixe. "They drove his wits astray by visions of hell," explains Mulligan, meaning the Jesuits with whom Stephen studied. And Haines agrees: "Eternal punishment . . . I see. I tackled him this morning on belief. There was something on his mind, I saw. It's rather interesting. . . ." It is characteristic that in this connection Haines casually mentions an interesting conclusion of the professor from Vienna. Joyce connects various perversions with the images of his heroes. Bloom represents a distinct type in sexual pathology. Stephen is registered as a homosexual; into his inner monologue is woven a memory of experiencing "Wildean love, which dare not name itself." A hint rises in the novel about an "Oedipus complex"; the image of Stephen's mother is connected—in a far-fetched way—with an idea about incest. All in all, there is created an impression that the author is experimenting with the help of a "fashionable" theory. The impression is confirmed by the remark of Ellmann about Joyce being inclined to regard inner monologue rather as a stylization than as a comprehensive picture of consciousness. What is more, Ellmann quotes a talk between Joyce and Stuart Gilbert, to whom the writer said that from his point of view it was immaterial whether the technique of inner monologue was truthful or not—"it has served me as a bridge over which to march my eighteen episodes, and, once I have got my troops across, the opposing forces can, for all I care, blow the bridge sky-high."[7]

But the whole point is that by putting all kinds of "loads" upon inner monologue, Joyce himself blew up what he achieved. His special gift of sensitively portraying the inner world of his characters he brought as a victim to Freud's scheme of complexes. Features tied to the Freudian concept of man are artificially "superimposed" in *Ulysses* on the spiritual life of his heroes, and this leads to its standardization and deadening.

Thus the negative influence of Freud on Joyce is indubitable, no matter on which level he used Freudian theory and no matter what his attitude toward it was (according to the testimony of Herbert Gorman this attitude was rather ironical, as it was toward Jung's theory, with which Joyce was very well acquainted when he lived in Zurich, it being the centre of the psychoanalytic school of which Jung was head). His relation to Freud, whose notion of man corresponded with the frame of mind of many West European intellectuals in the period of spiritual crisis, was itself significant. Freudianism justified withdrawal from the disturbing social reality and made its interpretation unnecessary. The same can be said about Jung's theory, too, which rejected the idea of development and brought in the idea of the "collective unconscious," in the depths of which primitive images are preserved—"archetypes" tied to man's prehistoric past, to ancient beliefs and myths, and having no relation to outward experience. The influence of this theory was expressed in *Ulysses* principally in the episode "Circe."

In this culminating episode (corresponding with the tenth book of the *Odyssey*, where Circe turns Odysseus' companions into a herd of swine), the strength and the weakness of Joyce are expressed most strikingly. The action takes place in the red light district of Dublin.

Here is sensed most sharply the author's idea of the bourgeois world as something terrible, monstrous. The atmosphere of obsessive dream filled with anguish is created by the very first lines, which draw a picture of the street on the approaches to "nighttown," symbolizing the bourgeois world—a world of sin and human degradation. In semi-darkness, stunted, unhealthy-looking men and women, squabbling, grab up remains of food from an ice gondola. On the ground, beside a dust-bin, a drunken man is snoring; and right here, too, an old woman and a dwarf are ramming rags, bones, and bottles into a sack. On the door-step of one of the flimsy houses sits a bandy-legged child. The noise of a crashing dish sounds, a woman's scream, the oath of a man. In the window of a room lit by a candle stuck in a bottle, a slut combs the tatts from the hair of a scrofulous child. In this prologue of sorts to the episode "Circe," we meet perhaps for the first time in Joyce's work such a terrible reminder of those who are in "the lower depths."

For many pages in "nighttown" there lasts, in the words of E. M. Forster, a joyless orgy. The episode is given dramatic form; scene quickly gives way to scene as in a movie. In the kaleidoscope of chang-ing images, a monstrous phantasmagoria unfolds, a picture created on the basis of Freud's and Jung's theories. Instincts which are fettered by prohibitions free themselves, burst out, and there materializes what was hidden in the depths of the "subconscious" of the novel's heroes—ideas tied to primitive animism, ancient cults, myths. Impressions which have stuck in their memory are realized, people appear with whom they were associated recently and in the distant past. Gloomy gro-tesque gives way to farcical scenes, to buffoonery, in which Joyce's gift for comedy shows itself. Among the figures presented here is that of the English King Edward VII, who sings the anti-monarchist street song "Coronation Day."

Stephen's "fixed ideas"—problems of homeland and religion—are incarnated in terrible images. On the scene appears Ireland—"poor old woman," who has taken on the aspect of a witch. Stephen cries: "I know you, gammer! Hamlet, revenge! The old sow that eats her far-row!" But with the wail: "Strangers in my house!" she forces Stephen to take a dagger. There arises a vision of Stephen's mother in a gray shroud, with holes instead of eyes, a sunken nose, toothless mouth, smelling of wetted ashes. A green crab with red eyes—incarnation of the disease from which she died—sticks its claws into Stephen's heart. The vision of his mother, symbolizing the terrible power of the Catholic Church, demands repentance from Stephen. The writer seems to experience perverse pleasure in disfiguring the poetic image created by him in the beginning: the half-decomposed corpse reminds Stephen of the words of the song at which his mother wept—"love's bitter mystery." In the frenzy of Stephen, who cries out the satanic formula of rejection: "Non serviam!"—"I will not serve," one feels that, having broken with religion, he still feels its power. It is possible that faith, still smouldering in the author's soul, lends peculiar power to the bacchanale of blasphemy in "Circe"—this is a parody on a church ceremony, the "black mass."

The English essayist and critic John Middleton Murry has remarked perceptively that *Ulysses* is a manifestation of the torturing liberation of an artist with a tormented soul from the power of the Roman Catholic Church, from prohibitions and fetters which have become flesh of his flesh. It is indubitable, however, that this liberation is not at all complete. The remark of Aldington in his article on *Ulysses* is interesting: he thinks that the Catholic religion had an effect on Joyce's attitude toward man. Aldington writes that even in Tertullian—a Christian writer, ascetic, and wild fanatic—he "can find nothing . . . which shows such repugnance for humanity, which teaches such abhorrence of the human body, and particularly of sexual relations" as one sees in *Ulysses*.[8] We can conclude that the religious idea of man's being drawn toward evil by force of his original sinfulness—an idea he had been familiar with since childhood—united in Joyce with the dark view of man inherent in modernist philosophy and also with the inclination to attribute to human nature all responsibility for the evils of the real world.

Among the scenes tied in with Bloom, there stands out the one where he figures as the representative of the bourgeois society that nurtured him. The depiction of Bloom's "materialized" dreams—his election as lord mayor and at the same time as president and emperor—is a sharp satire on bourgeois democracy. As the "greatest reformer in the world," Bloom announces the beginning of a new "heavenly era," promises his subjects that they will enter a golden city—the new Bloomusalem. Here is shown the seamy side of democracy, its hypocrisy: while the new Bloomusalem, a colossal building with crystal roof, is being built, many houses are torn down whose inhabitants, left homeless, are resettled in barrels and boxes bearing the initials L. B. Bloom's private guard presents various gifts to those around him: alms which it is customary to distribute to the poor during Holy Week, commemoration medals, memorial days, temperance badges, free bones for soup, billets doux in the form of cocked hats, remission of sins for forty days, false coins, theatre passes, and season tickets for the tram. Mockery of the poverty of bourgeois culture is contained in the following list of gifts: cheap reprints of books in the series "Twelve Worst Books" —*Froggy and Fritz* (politic), *Care of the Baby* (infantilic), *50 meals for 7/6* (culinic), *Was Jesus a Sun Myth?* (historic), *Expel that Pain* (medic), *Infant's Compendium of the Universe* (cosmic), *Let's All Chortle* (hilaric), *Canvasser's vade mecum* (journalic), *Loveletters of Mother Assistant* (erotic), *Who's Who in Space* (astric), *Songs that Reached Our Heart* (melodic), *Pennywise's Way to Wealth* (parsimonic).

The description of Bloom's behavior is a satire on the methods of the bourgeois candidate for elective office who seeks popularity: Bloom shakes hands with a blind stripling, embraces an old couple, plays pussy-fourcorners with ragged children, kisses the bedsores of a palsied veteran, tickles a baby, consoles a widow, eats a raw turnip offered him by a farmer, and gives his coat to a beggar. Later he develops plans for social rebirth: three acres and a cow for all children of nature, bonuses for all, general amnesty, weekly carnivals with the right to wear masks, free money, free love, free lay church. Amid exclamations of approval, Bloom gives wise counsel. Thus, to the question of one of those present as to what he is to do about his taxes, Bloom replies: "Pay them, my friend." The keeper of a street museum drags in a cart with plaster figures of the new muses: Commerce, Operatic Music, Love, Publicity, Manufacture, Liberty of Speech, Plural Voting, Gastronomy, Private Hygiene, Seaside Concert Entertainments, Painless Obstetrics, and Astronomy for the People.

But this way of portraying Bloom soon breaks down and new features come to the top. Here are demonstrated Bloom's various "complexes"—his masochism, his secret desire to be betrayed, his feeling of social and secular guilt, etc.

In the episode "Circe," criticism of bourgeois society attains the greatest sharpness, and along with that it is very clearly shown that the author means all mankind. The effect of the satirical exposure of the bourgeoisie is reduced, for, on account of Joyce's tendency toward erroneous generalization, "Bloomism" appears to be something universal and final. "Nighttown" is the incarnation of the capitalist world and at the same time it is the night of mankind, whose sins and crimes reach the apogee which precedes destruction. It is characteristic that the end of the world is proclaimed in this episode by a primitive man. He throws tiny planets like roulette balls and shouts, imitating a croupier: "Les jeux sont faits! . . . Rien n'va plus!" Thus the author lets it be understood that mankind returns to the point of exit, that the circle closes.

The world outlook of the artist, whose consciousness is traumatized by the notion of life as a senseless cyclic recurrence, by the idea of the ruin of civilization, has a spontaneous effect on his work—it becomes a limited sphere for him, separating him from life.

The second half of *Ulysses* tells us that the author locked himself more and more in his creative laboratory. Formalistic experiments are becoming an end in themselves; symbols full of meaning are crowded out by unjustifiable, far-fetched symbols. Thus the essence of the episode "Oxen of Helios," the action of which takes place in a maternity home, is a symbolic representation of stages in the human embryo's development; for this, examples of prose characterizing the development of the English language are presented in the conversation of the acting personalities—parodies on the style of ancient Anglo-Saxon chronicles, on the works of Mallory, Pepys, Mandeville, Defoe, Swift, Fielding, Dickens, and other writers. Here too are given parodies on the style of detective novels and "horror novels," examples of contemporary jargon are brought in, etc. In themselves, these parodies are very successful, they testify to Joyce's satiric gift, but taking up, as they do, many pages, they turn the episode into something boundless.

An analogous phenomenon is seen in the episode "Cyclops"; its text stretches out endlessly with inserted parodies, the aim of which is to give a notion of the "gigantism" of the Sinn Feiner, who holds forth in a tavern about the past greatness of Ireland. Here are sketched descriptions of unusually strong and strapping heroes in the Irish sagas, of numerous fat herds, etc. In this same episode are parodied stereotypes of the bourgeois press: the chronicle of world events, accounts of the meetings of various societies, and pseudo-scientific researches. An impression of depressing futility is made by the episode "Ithaca," which is built at the same time in the form of a catechism and an arithmetic textbook. The questions and answers which follow one another explain the actions of the heroes with the help of technical terminology and mathematical formulas.

Such exclusive attention to literary methods, their artificiality and exaggerated importance, which constitute the essence of formalism, bespeak the fact that with Joyce form moved out into first place. The writer's hopeless view of reality and the break with it lead to the artistic work's becoming for him a "thing in itself," that autonomous province which seemed ideal to Roger Fry. Joyce's protest against bourgeois society in the end turns into formalistic revolt. Form acquires a function opposite to that which it is called to fulfill: instead of more fully and clearly expressing the content, it becomes a barrier, shutting the artistic work off from the outside world. The artificial symbols of *Ulysses* act as such a barrier, for, although they seem to offer themselves for meaningful interpretation, they actually reveal nothing.

Apart from the *Odyssey*, which serves as the base of the secondary plan of the novel, Joyce at the same time brings to it other meanings and analogies. Thus, in accord with Gilbert's explanation, each episode of *Ulysses* corresponds to some organ or part of the human body, to some aspect or sphere of knowledge, and is tied to the idea of a certain color, to a certain symbol, and written in a special style. Thus, the episode "Nestor," opening as a lesson in history, corresponds with the study of history, the episode "Aeolus" is the art of rhetoric (in his arguments, Professor MacHugh makes use of rhetorical figures). In the episode "Lotus-Eaters" a flower appears as a multi-level symbol. Here it is made clear that the family of the grandfather of Bloom (from the German word "flower") was originally—before his migration from Hungary to Ireland—Virag (which in Hungarian means flower). In this episode Bloom gets a letter by general delivery in the name of Flower—thus he called himself to his sweetheart, hiding his real name. In the letter he finds a dried flower. The image of the flower keeps rising all through the episode. Apart from this, a multitude of other symbols are scattered through the novel. Moreover, each of them has many meanings. Thus, two crossed keys, the representation of which serves one of Bloom's clients as a trade mark, appears also as the symbol of the Apostle Peter and the emblem of the Isle of Man; at the same time, in accord with the deciphering of Joyce's interpreters, it is the emblem of man's solitariness.

According to the author's thinking, the universal and all-embracing character of the work should be clear when perceived as a whole, when the various organs and parts of the body, joined together, portray man, while the various arts and studies jointly call to mind man's activity.

The pedantry with which Joyce creates in *Ulysses* the system of schemes which cost him such immense labor forces us to recall the scholastic reasoning of Stephen Dedalus with regard to his aesthetic program in the preceding novel. At the same time the complexity of this system brings to mind Stephen's appeal to Daedalus—to the "old artificer," builder of the Labyrinth.

In constructing his system of correspondences, Joyce establishes a purely formal relation of the parts. Instead of organic ties, corresponding to reality, we find a mechanical hooking together. In the morning, when Stephen walks along the seashore, he sees a ship returning to Ireland; during the day a crumpled ball of paper thrown away by Bloom floats by the ship, while at night Stephen and Bloom meet a sailor who was that day discharged from the ship. Throughout the novel one image or another, one or another expression or word, at a certain moment floats up anew and has something in common with other ideas and words.

Striving as much as possible to widen the sphere of what he considers ties, Joyce moves from earth to heaven and back again to objects and people. The tin biscuit box thrown at Bloom by the Sinn Feiner in the episode "Cyclops" becomes a meteor whose fall causes destruction; when in the episode "Ithaca" Bloom and Stephen are looking at the sky, they become at the same time wandering heavenly bodies.

Falsely interpreting the idea of the all-embracing, Joyce considered that in *Ulysses* he had succeeded in embracing all life. "If *Ulysses* isn't fit to read," Joyce said, "life isn't fit to live."[9] It is as if in his schemes for *Ulysses* he strives to put life, which he regarded as chaos, into good order after setting it in the frame of the novel. It is thus that one of Joyce's first critics—T. S. Eliot—discussed *Ulysses*. In his article *"Ulysses*, Order and Myth" (1924), he proclaimed that the realistic novel, which reflects socially-conditioned reality, has outlived itself, and only by means of turning to myth, as Joyce does, is it possible to bring order into the chaos of contemporary life.

Harry Levin examines the ramified system of correspondences of *Ulysses* as a means of achieving "order," a certain genuine unity, and universality. "By means of these mechanical contrivances," he writes, "the book achieves an organic quality . . . we see how men are related to things. Nothing is irrelevant. Everything moves in its appointed orbit. The most ill-assorted phenomena are equally parts of an all-encompassing whole."[10] In Günter Blöcker, who is one of those critics who do not regard the representation of concrete social reality and the creation of characters as a significant function of literature, we meet with a similar discussion of the all-embracing. In Blöcker's opinion, Joyce's inner monologue examines the individual soul at the moment when it passes into the universal soul. "Through a subjective series of associations, we gropingly make our way into the Universal." Associating himself with the views of Thornton Wilder, Blöcker says that the theme of the contemporary novel is not individual existence but existence in general. In his view, the solitary event, which even in the nineteenth century was the genuine theme of the novel, becomes only the sign, only the reference point, a tiny point in the planetary system of contemporary thought and creative work.

Joyce's striving for a falsely apprehended breadth, for universality, his marked tendency to regard man not as a representative of his class, epoch, and nation but as part of the Universe, has been raised to the level of a principle by contemporary modernist critics; the type of novel which Joyce wanted to create has received the name "total."

As one manifestation of Joyce's inclination toward universality, we should also examine in the novel his efforts to pass beyond the frame of literature—into the province of another art. Music attracts him and other modernist writers after him as a province which in their opinion least lends itself to decipherment and logical explanation, and is most convenient for abstraction. The tendency to intrude into the province of music shows itself first of all in the attempt to be guided in a literary work by the principle of musical movement and composition.

In this respect the episode "Sirens" is characteristic. By association with the singing sirens in the *Odyssey*, there is much singing here: girls working in a bar and certain guests sing to the accompaniment of a piano. But this is not the whole point. According to Joyce, in constructing the episode "Sirens," he employed the technique of the fugue, where the themes are counterpointed against each other, with repetitions coming at various intervals in various timbres. We have the theme of girls who sit side by side behind the bar—"bronze by gold"; it corresponds to the color of their hair—with a bronze shade in one and golden in the other. The girls giggle from time to time; in keeping with this, their theme becomes "bronze gigglegold." The theme of Boylan, who has come into the bar—"jingle jingle jaunted jingling"—is associated with the ring of the coins which he jingles in his pocket. A sound grows in crescendo: "Tap. Tap"—it is the sound of a cane on the sidewalk as a blind tuner approaches the bar. A great many themes are announced, repeat themselves, and flow together in various combinations. As a whole, however, the combination does not produce the impression of a fugue, it testifies only to the futility of operating in the province of literature with the means of musical language: thereby the laws of each of these aspects of art are violated. The episode as a whole testifies also to the failure of the attempt to subject content to form.

Here is shown in the greatest degree a tendency which appeared in other episodes of *Ulysses,* and which in the end assumes abnormal form—the author's inclination to experiment in language.

Joyce possessed unusual sensitivity to the musical quality of words. With their help he creates living, visible images. He is equally successful with poetic metaphors (the waves of the sea, for example, are perceived by him as "white-maned seahorses, champing, bright windbridled . . . steeds . . .") and clever word-building of a satirical nature. Thus the Sinn Feiner in the episode "Cyclops" talks about British civilization in the colonies as "syphilization," and Stephen calls the British empire "brutish empire." Joyce shows unusual versatility, the ability to give a word flexibility, to get the utmost possible changes out of it. But the word for Joyce stops being a means to the greatest expressiveness of thought; very often it does not organically unite with the texture, it becomes autonomous and serves to veil the meaning.

In the novel there are attempts to break up language into its original elements, to turn it back to its primordial mythological nature. On the other hand, in his linguistic experimentation in *Ulysses* Joyce goes basically along the same path as the Russian and West European futurists did before the First World War: here a game proceeds in consonances, in the creation and combination of words on the basis of chance subjective associations, the use of words in a dual sense, breaking the norm of literary language, shattering of syntax, violation of logical ties between words, the introduction of barbarisms. Sometimes Joyce makes broad use of ancient Greek, Latin, Hebrew, French, and Italian words, at times uniting them with English, and also of archaisms, dialectic words and idioms, thereby weighing down his English prose. Worshipers of Joyce hold that he liberated the word from its too narrow boundaries of space and time. But in striving to broaden the possibilities of language, to make it all-embracing, the writer in fact comes to destroy it.

In *Ulysses,* Joyce also lays the basis for the destruction of the epic structure of the novel, for the annihilation of the novel as genre. In the struggle between two tendencies in his work—objective portrayal of reality and its subjective vision—the latter wins out. The position of Joyce—of the artist who retreats into his personal world—his rejection of objective criteria, his egocentrism, and his absence of inner discipline determine also his attitude toward his readers, which differs radically from the position of realist writers, for whom intercourse with readers and striving to be understood by them constitutes an important part of the creative credo. As Joyce's biographers tell us, he said that *Ulysses* must be read many times to try to grasp its meaning. Such an attitude toward readers—they are asked to have a set of keys to the "cipher" of the work—means aiming at a few "elect." This becomes the norm for the contemporary modernist. The type of work contemplated in *Ulysses*—locked up, fenced off from reality, having no aim outside itself—they regard as a model. Deeply convinced that he put everything at the service of art, Joyce in essence was unfaithful to that very art, to its basic function.

The tendencies marked in *Ulysses* get their final expression in *Finnegans Wake* (1939)—a novel which Joyce wrote during the course of seventeen years. This is the book of a writer for whom social criteria of value do not exist, for whom life represents senseless buffoonery. Isolated in his creative laboratory (his isolation was aggravated by almost complete loss of vision), Joyce, according to Ellmann, noted some three years before finishing his book that for him it was a greater reality than reality itself. Before the novel came out as a separate edition, it was published, in the years 1927-1938, in the French journal of aesthetics *transition* under the title "Work in Progress." In November 1928, H. G. Wells, who at one time so warmly responded to *A Portrait of the Artist as a Young Man,* sent Joyce a letter—apparently after acquaintance with a part of the last novel. Wells wrote that with all kindly feelings for Joyce and with respect for the writer's talent, he had to confess that their paths were diverging. Wells' letter speaks of the collision of two outlooks on the world, of the abyss between artists of a diametrically opposed turn of mind, with principally opposite attitudes toward the problems of literature.

In *Finnegans Wake,* Joyce's striving for universality and "cosmic" significance is sharply expressed—in it are incarnated the ideas of "all is in all" and "each can be each" which revealed themselves in *Ulysses* and also the idea that man's life and the history of mankind are an eternal rotation, a closed circle. The characters in the novel—the Dublin tavern-keeper Earwicker, his wife Anna Livia Plurabelle, their daughters and sons—come forth in the most different aspects. Thus Anna Livia, and at the same time Eve, Isis, Isolde, are the river Liffey, which runs through Dublin, the river of time, whose circling current carries fragments of dead civilizations and the embryos of future cultures. Just as he fuses images into one, so Joyce unites in his book a great many languages into a general language, a "language over languages." On this account the book does not yield to the understanding without special "keys" which investigators of Joyce's work have put together for it. *Finnegans Wake* is the logical end of the road on which Joyce started in *Ulysses,* the dead end of his work, as H. G. Wells said.

Modernist critics, who proclaim the weakest innovations of Joyce as a model for the "new literature," do not see the contradictions in his work—the result of the artist's inner struggle. Beyond the barriers of their attention remains everything that Joyce suppresses for the benefit of false theories and which constitutes his power: sharp perception of the evil reigning in the world and its satirical exposure, the gift of creating living reality, of revealing man's spiritual life, of creating poetic images, and—most important—warmth and humanity. The suppression of these sides of his talent by the writer is apparently considered by those who represent the dehumanization of literature as something to be expected in the natural course of events.

REFERENCES

1. G. Borach, "Conversations with James Joyce," *College English,* XV (March, 1954), pp. 325-327.
2. Richard Aldington, *Literary Studies and Reviews* (New York, 1924), p. 197.
3. Richard Ellmann, *James Joyce* (New York, 1959), p. 522.
4. A. Henderson (ed.), *Table-talk of G. B. S.,* (New York, 1925), p. 109.
5. Stuart Gilbert (ed.), *Letters of James Joyce* (New York, 1957), p. 170.

6. *Ibid.*, p. 160.
7. Ellmann, *op. cit.*, *p.* 543.
8. Aldington, *op. cit.*, p. 198.
9. Ellmann, *op. cit.*, p. 551.
10. Harry Levin, *James Joyce: A Critical Introduction* (Norfolk, 1960), p. 120.
11. Günther Blöcker, "James Joyce," *Neue deutsche Hefte. Beiträge zur europeischen Gegenwart,* herausgegeben v. Günther und Hartung. Heft 31, Januar, 1957, S. 539.

THE ARTS AND THE PERSPECTIVES

OF SOCIALISM

INTRODUCTION

What might one expect of an art adequate to the needs of the new period in history? While continuing to furnish an imaginative interpretation of specific and social man (the traditional subject matter of literature), it would exhibit a new relationship to the present moment in history. Among other things, it would provide some insight into the fundamental differences between the competing social systems; it would point to the nature of those characteristics of capitalist society that stand in the way of fulfillment of human needs; it would also show the main line of development toward socialism. The new literature would function as an indispensable component of the process of revolutionary change. Even more important than its criticism of capitalist society might well be its contribution to the task of creating a new socialist society. All these purposes it would accomplish, one need hardly say, not as a substitute for sociology, but while maintaining the specific character of art.

One way in which the new literature could perform its task would be to reflect and at the same time shape the new socialist humanism that develops as part of the struggle to create a new society. That is, the new literature should reflect, interpret, and shape new modes of life that come into being as man assumes responsibility for his own social development. It should be a prime agency in the formation of an historically concrete image of socialist man.

These are some of the things one might expect. Let us turn now to elements of contemporary theory in regard to socialist realism. It is in fact looked upon as a literature that corresponds to the interests of broad masses of men involved in this stage of historical change; it should be capable of reaching out to them and responding to their needs; it should help create a social vision that will enable them to participate fully in the task of creating a new social order. This literature would of necessity have a relationship to the role of the leading rev-

173

olutionary forces involved in the building of a new society. It would have a close relationship to leading organizations. Being close to the concrete experience of building the new society, it would reflect the changed image of man and the new consciousness that emerge when man discovers that he can in fact regain control of the historical process.

One would expect more insight into the causal nexus in the literature of socialist realism than in critical realism, not to speak of modernism. It can be taken for granted that in socialist society understanding of the causal nexus is more accessible to the average citizen than under capitalism, and the writer in consequence will have a better chance to grasp the fundamental movement of society. The writer will in many circumstances be more closely related to those responsible for social change and better acquainted with the objective forces that have to be brought under human control.

It is expected, again, that the new literature would have a changed character in its representation of the "typical." That is, it would give a different account of the highly representative experience of our time, especially as we begin to move toward a society in which antagonistic class contradictions have been eliminated. The new social and moral unity of the people must necessarily bring about a change in the kind of representative experience that the concept of the typical implies. The initiative, creativity and confidence that grow out of successful performance of the tasks of social construction would also be expected to give rise to changes in the typical. These new features of man's experience would necessarily be reflected in the more personal and intimate sphere of life, that of private relationships, love, and friendship. Here also changes in the typical are to be expected.

An advance is expected also with regard to artistic truth, not because the new literature would have a more direct relationship to reality but because of a changed artistic method. A closer relationship between literary creation and the scientific understanding that makes possible the guidance of the historical process would in itself make possible a strengthening of connections between the truth of art and the truth of life. (The principle involved here may throw light on how it is that Steinbeck in *The Grapes of Wrath* was able to develop qualities of artistic truth from many points of view in advance of what is to be observed in a novel like, say, Ellison's *Invisible Man*.)

What are some of the other points being stressed now with regard to socialist realism? It is a literature that seeks to interpret the present in the light of the future. The writer has an understanding of the kind of society man has the capacity to create as he becomes subject of history, and in describing the present he is able to see in it the potential for a new epoch of freedom. This perspective enables him also to understand the impediments in the way of social advance and to portray them in such a way as to help smooth the path of advance. One has in mind here of course not the kind of analysis that would be expected of a party congress but something much more intimately concerned with the lives of concrete men and women, though at the same time the social and individual are of course interrelated. Literature of this kind would itself constitute a powerful creative force in the period of transition.

The new literature would have a partisan character. The point brings us to the common objection that partisanship and objectivity are mutually exclusive. The Marxist view here is that it all depends upon what class interests you are identified with. To be a partisan advocate of a class that must misrepresent objective reality in its own interests will obviously mean that the partisanship and objectivity exclude each other. For the Marxist-oriented revolutionary class at this moment in history, on the other hand, partisanship and objectivity form an inseparable unity. This class has an objective interest in getting the most truthful picture possible of the laws that operate within the process of social change and of the specific reality in every area. It must get this picture in order to advance its own partisan interests. So partisanship and objectivity go together. Each requires the other.

If partisanship has a class character, what does it mean in a society that is now passing beyond the stage of class antagonism? This is a situation now beginning to emerge in some of the socialist countries, where increasingly the population comes to be divided into two broad classes, the working class and the collectives of farmers, and where the social interests of these two classes are in fundamental harmony. We here approach a situation in which partisanship would be on behalf not so much of a class as of an ideology that represents the interests of society as a whole. But this already looks toward the future. In the present world situation the socialist societies are allied with the working class in the capitalist countries in their struggle against imperialism, and it is still true that the working class plays a leading role within the socialist countries. The concept of partisanship on behalf of the interests of the working class remains applicable.

What are the special reasons for insisting upon partisanship in socialist realism? It is partly that only this kind of commitment will enable one to grasp the role of the working class in history. The non-partisan spectator is likely to think of the working class primarily as exploited; only the partisan sees that this class has the capacity to dominate the historic process. Partisanship is needed, Pracht and Neubert argue, if the writer is to get an understanding of the social machinery. Two things in fact are required to achieve this understanding, first, a theory of society and history (Marxism), and second, partisan participation in the engineering of social change. In a socialist country the party constitutes the most important moving force in society. If the writer is to understand social movement, he must be connected with this most powerful source of change.

Partisanship and ideological commitment go together. Pracht and Neubert feel that the point made by Engels with reference to Balzac, that the writer with a retrograde ideology may nevertheless develop a progressive world view, is not likely to be widely applicable today. In a time of philosophical stability, Johannes Becher has said, the ideological commitment of the writer would have less importance than it does today. At such a time the writer might be able to trust the Zeitgeist. But in an epoch of revolutionary transformation the writer without ideological commitment will always be likely to run into the danger of serving a false cause. In an epoch of revolutionary transformation it becomes difficult for everyone, the writer included, to find his way. That is why writers must now ally themselves with those theorists and men of action who occupy key positions in the building of a new society.

Important features of the concept of socialist realism are brought out in Mittenzwei's account of differences between the protagonists of the "Brecht-Lukacs Debate." In the important controversy of the 30s described in this essay, one issue was the relationship between socialist realism and the independent role of the working class. Lukacs, Mittenzwei argues, underestimated the importance of a separate working-class program, in part because united-front politics led him to stress goals shared in common by the working class and bourgeois progressives. So he came to minimize both the class contradictions of bourgeois society and the need for a separate program on the part of the working class. Or to put this in another way, Lukacs placed too much stress on the contradiction between bourgeois democracy and fascism and too little on the contradiction between bourgeois democracy and working-class ideology.

As a consequence, Lukacs came to regard the tradition of 19th-century realism as a source of criteria for realist art in general. This led him to condemn flatly the work of 20th-century modernists like Joyce and Kafka. Brecht, on the other hand, is not willing to take 19th-century bourgeois realism as a model, nor is he ready to join Lukacs in blanket condemnation of 20th-century modernists. On the contrary, he takes it for granted that much of their experimentation can be appropriated in socialist realism. Brecht asserts that in his praise of 19th-century realism and his condemnation of 20th-century modernism, Lukacs was in fact setting up formalist criteria.

Conscious of the need for a separate working-class ideology, Brecht gave much thought to the distinctive features of a class-oriented literature. At the conclusion of the present article, Mittenzwei presents Brecht's ten working theses on socialist realism. It is an art that considers its public; it takes into account the degree of intellectual aptitude and receptivity in the audience. Devoted to human advance, it detects and communicates the historically significant; it concentrates on change and development; it sees things in historical context. Guided by Marxism, it discloses the contradictions in men and the material base. It offers practical insights into the social mechanism; it penetrates to the causal nexus. It is a militant art. It contemplates reality from the point of view of the working class and its allies.

A lesson for today in the Brecht-Lukacs debate, in Mittenzwei's view, is that the working class, even when accepting the program of a united front, should insist on its separate ideology and revolutionary mission, on a separate aesthetics, and a distinctive class-oriented literature.

The article includes other examples of the relationship between ideology and aesthetics. Mittenzwei believes, for example, that because of an uncritical attitude toward bourgeois democracy Lukacs came to think of typification as more or less identical in bourgeois and working-class literature, whereas in fact, the typical in proletarian or socialist literature develops a distinctive character of its own.

In his exploration of the connection between ideology and aesthetics, Mittenzwei throws light also on the question of the closed and open form. He asserts that Lukacs put more stress on the unity than on the contradiction between appearance and essence and was insufficiently

178 MARXIST LITERARY CRITICISM

aware of the element of contradiction *within* the underlying forces that determine the movement of society. In consequence Lukacs came to regard the novel as serving to disclose a unity of appearance and essence; this meant that he thought of the novel as a closed form, serving as a vehicle for a completed and ultimately static view of reality. Brecht, on the other hand, more aware of the discord between appearance and essence (the contradiction as opposed to the unity), and more aware also of inevitable contradictions in the underlying forces of society, became an advocate of open forms, where the purpose of the writer is not so much to develop a completed insight as to encourage the spectator to take a fresh look at social relationships in their flux.

Brecht and Lukacs differ also in regard to catharsis. It is Mittenzwei's contention that Lukacs retained a conception of a uniform ethical essence in man, despite disclaimers. He accordingly came to think of catharsis as providing an insight into man's unchanging nature. For Brecht, on the other hand, the object of art was not so much to help the spectator to "know himself" as to make him aware of a potentiality for change. In order to prevent the kind of identification with the protagonist that accompanies catharsis, Brecht developed his "distancing effects."

The articles on socialist realism by Erwin Pracht and Elisabeth Simons sum up major theoretical questions debated in the German Democratic Republic during the past few years. Both put stress on the important role of literature and art in the period when a new society is being created. Simons, for instance, speaks of how it has been possible to bring more and more activities under social control and of how a start has been made toward the socialist Aufhebung of alienation. She takes note of the greater role of the individual corresponding to a strengthening in the collective.

Need for an independent aesthetic. The function of the emerging literature, Simons says, is to help create a new consciousness, a new socialist personality, in the end a new reality. This takes place in a period when non-antagonistic contradictions are beginning to replace the antagonistic contradictions of class society. The emerging literature will hardly perform its role without the aid of an independent aesthetic, whose function will be to guide and encourage new forms of literary expression, to help writers discover their true subject matter and select literary forms appropriate to it. Writers will necessarily be seeking different means of representation, different plots, different conflicts. It is important, therefore, that socialist critics reject the "revisionist" view (for which Ernst Bloch served as one spokesman) that there is no important distinction between socialist and bourgeois aesthetics.

New themes. The themes most commonly treated in G. D. R. literature till now, according to Pracht, have included the effort to master the immediate past (a theme embodied in a vast anti-fascist literature) and, more recently, the theme of commitment to socialism and discovery of its productive character as a social system. Pracht feels that while the new literature offers a good account of "spontaneous" consciousness (*Ole Bienkopp*), it has been less successful in presenting characters who have succeeded in ridding themselves of mistrust concerning their own strength. He has in mind primarily the well-informed, scientifically guided leaders in the construction of a new society. They are men resolved, in the spirit of Marx's famous eleventh thesis on Feuerbach, not only to understand the world but to change it. They exemplify a new kind of activity and a new state of consciousness. It is hoped that socialist writers will turn to the study of these men.

Simons adds something to what Pracht has said about the themes of the new literature. She notes a change in the kind of protagonist writers have selected; first came the leader of the class struggle fighting against inhuman odds or undergoing terrible hardships, then the protagonist who makes the historic decision for socialism, then later the one who, having already made this decision, comes to represent aspects of the newly emerging image of man.

Pracht voices the hope that headway will be made in the treatment of certain other themes, one of these being the new perspective in regard to the future. If he is to create this perspective, the writer must himself acquire "the vision of the leader and the planner." It should be part of his responsibility to discover the potential within the present, the foreshadowing of a society yet to be built. A literature that supplies such perspectives helps to create what is to come. It awakens potentialities as yet dormant.

The question of form. The inevitable rivalry between East and West Germany has led some members of the literary community to occupy themselves unduly with questions of form, in Pracht's opinion. This he regards as partly regrettable because the importance of the new subject matter tends to be neglected when formal matters are given too much stress. It is unfortunate, he feels, that formal considerations tend to be uppermost when East German writers are compared with West Germans like Heinrich Böll. East German writers should not feel at a disadvantage when you consider that many of them, like Dieter Noll, the author of *Die Abenteuer des Werner Holt*, are attempting "to master a subject matter which has not yet entered Böll's field of vision."

The task today, Pracht asserts, is to develop a literature appropriate in its content and vision to the mighty developments taking place; at such a time questions of literary form may properly be regarded as of secondary importance. Writers attempting to take command of a subject matter that has not yet been interpreted in art (the new human nature and the new social relationships in a classless society) may well appear to lose something in artistic quality. So far as aesthetic control is concerned, in other words, a break in continuity may be expected. Pracht makes the point also that the documentary may turn out to constitute an important literary genre during the transitional period.

Simons also discusses the question of how receptive the new literature should be to formal influences emanating from contemporary writing in the West. The question was at issue, as we have seen, in the Brecht-Lukacs debate. Simons expects that socialist writers will increasingly experiment with stylistic innovations pioneered in bourgeois literature. While formal experiment in the West is to be explained partly by the absence of a new literary vision and of a new reality to be mastered, such experiments may nevertheless be adapted for the purposes of realism. Horst Redeker has pointed out that bourgeois literature, in its constant search for new forms, has experimented with new ways of representing the altered character of space and time in a period when the scientific understanding of these matters has been transformed, and he predicts that some of the technical innovations will be appropriated in socialist literature.[1]

Yet all Marxist critics are aware that technical imitation may have an adverse effect on content. Hemingway's style, for example, was taken up by some socialist writers dealing with the experience of World War II, but when they imitated the Hemingway style they found themselves adopting to some extent Hemingway's world view.

Intelligibility. How important is it that the new art be intelligible? Pracht rejects the notion that the obscurity in much contemporary art is to be attributed primarily to the complexity of the modern world. Bourgeois scholars make this point and even question the possibility of adequately picturing present-day reality. Pracht agrees that it is harder to understand social reality now than it was in the 19th century. Appearance is further removed from essence. Brecht gave an example when he spoke of a modern factory, where the realities of ownership are customarily hidden from view. The worker has no way of knowing who owns the factory or, in the ultimate sense, who exercises power there. Pracht mentions also certain other problems that make for difficulties in communication. One of these is that many readers lack the poetic experience. Nevertheless, much obscurity in bourgeois literature is to be explained not simply by the complexity of its subject matter but by a class-dominated climate of mystification. Pracht concludes by affirming that "intelligibility remains a basic characteristic of any socialist art."

Literature and science. Pracht argues for closer ties between the two. He would like to see more scientific research in the *influence* exerted by the arts. Investigation of this kind is all the more requisite, he says, because "our class enemy, with the help of mass media such as TV and radio, is constantly trying to influence the population of the G.D.R. in our common language." Again, literature is to some extent held back by the as yet "insufficiently developed prognosis capacity" of the social sciences. Theoretical models of the future course of society are not available. The sciences have not given enough consideration to changes in psychology and emotion that must inevitably come about when men are largely freed from bondage to the manufacturing process. In a word, the writer and the social scientist have parallel roles in exploring the causal nexus in society, and each should contribute to the other's work. Pracht hopes also for an advance in sociology that will put an end to a situation where the writer explores areas of experience that the social scientists have hardly begun to investigate. At present, the writer gets too little help from the sciences, and at the same time discoveries made by writers are commonly neglected by scientists at work in the same field.

The pragmatic function. The term is used here for the effect of a literary work on reader and public. The model function, on the other hand, has to do with the relationship between art and what is portrayed. Elisabeth Simons stresses the importance of the pragmatic function and even more the need to unify pragmatic and model aspects of art. Both ends can be accomplished only if the writer participates in the struggle to transform society. The writing itself is a contribution to the struggle, but the socialist writer should also generally have some experience in organizational work. This is required of him as a human being, for whom the most direct involvement in the tasks of the age constitutes a significant exercise of free activity. It is a way of gaining the ideological understanding needed if the writer is to gain full control of his subject matter. Also participation of this sort will help the writer achieve mastery in the two functions of literature.

The model function. It has been necessary, Elisabeth Simons says, to combat an oversimplified notion concerning the model function of art. Some readers felt that they had a right to object if "typical" characters in fiction or drama might be thought of as reflecting adversely on the group, trade or vocation to which they belonged. In order to show the impropriety of expecting that kind of correspondence between literature and life, it became necessary to examine the varied and complex ways in which the literary model relates to the real world.

On the "critical element" in socialist literature. How should criticism of the existing society be handled in socialist realism? The guideline for an answer is to be found in the principle of partisanship. The partisan writer, it is argued, will not stifle whatever critical observations he has to make, but at the same time he will make them in such a way as to contribute to, rather than obstruct, the advance toward socialism.

Defense against the charge of dogmatism. It is hardly to be expected, Pracht says, that critics removed from the scene would understand the specific problems of the new society; certainly a sympathetic attitude is not to be expected from the West German press. He finds it surprising, however, that some Marxists, "under the pretext of purifying Marxism from dogmatism," identify themselves with West German attacks on developments in the East. Ernst Fischer's characterization of "dogmatism" in the G.D.R. goes along with the assertion that the condition of alienation applies in the new socialist countries in the same sense as in capitalism. Writers like Fischer make a sharp division between an alienated socialist present and a utopian future, then they call attention chiefly to ways in which the existing socialist societies fall short of the utopian blueprint. Pracht believes that such thinking betrays doubts concerning the possibility of realizing socialist goals. The best way to counteract this line of criticism is "to see the whole," as Hegel said, the whole including not only past and present, but future also. Assuredly we must try to tell the truth about the present condition of socialist society, but telling the truth is a matter of extraordinary difficulty. It requires, as Brecht said, courage, knowledge, and talent. Even more, it requires an understanding of the present in the context of both past and future.

The principles of socialist realism have been worked out in most detail with regard to literature, but they are felt to be applicable, with modifications, to all the arts. The literature and art that begin to take shape in accordance with these principles are felt furthermore to be something without historical precedent. To form an opinion about socialist realism, it would not make sense to assess the achievement at this point. The development of a new movement in art may take a much longer period of time than has elapsed since the emergence of this new "method." What is at issue is not so much what has been accomplished as a grasp of the new conception of the function and character of art.

Socialist realism is to be thought of as continuous with the development of realist art, but at the same time it goes beyond this tradition, as has been indicated. It corresponds to, reflects and interprets a new stage of man's command of the historical process, a stage initiated when the working class assumed its role as an agent of revolutionary change. Socialist realism may be thought of, then, as the system of dynamically developing principles, practices, and goals that govern artistic creation in a period marked by a new understanding of the laws of social development and the conscious formation of social reality in accordance with this understanding.

One of its functions is to serve as an ideological weapon in the working-class struggle. No doubt this explains in part the venom with which socialist realism is attacked by spokesmen for the imperialist powers. The effort is to discredit the new principles by any means possible, and so to make them unavailable to the masses and of course to writers also. The struggle over socialist realism constitutes therefore one of the important areas of ideological conflict in our time. Some have seen a connection between the attack on key principles of Marxist literary theory at the Kafka Conference in 1963 and later events in Czechoslovakia. If such a connection does exist, it provides a noteworthy example of the importance that literary and cultural questions may have in the arena of ideological struggle.

An advance in socialist realism requires collective leadership in the arts based on Marxist-Leninist principles. This leads at once to objections. It arouses the fear of "artists in uniform"; collective leadership is envisioned as a matter of decree, and of course it is thought to be a threat to the artist's freedom. But the principle of collective leadership does not mean rule by decree. It means organizing resources of theory and generalizations arising from creative practice in an effort to relate whatever can be learned to the needs of men in a concrete situation. The notion of a threat to the artist's freedom is likely to be associated with the bourgeois concept of freedom, in which freedom and necessity are seen as mutually exclusive. With the Marxist notion of freedom as the product of a command of necessity, it is not nearly so clear that collective leadership must threaten the artist's freedom. If wisely employed, one might argue, collective leadership is precisely what is required in order to augment the true freedom of the artist. Another source of the objection to collective leadership is likely to be an attachment to the principle of spontaneity in social development. In the past, new movements in art, like new directions in society, have generally come about spontaneously. But in most areas of life the principle of spontaneous development is being superseded by a different principle, one that involves analysis, assessment, prognosis, and then the careful plotting out of a course.

It is important to move in the direction contemplated here because of the great formative power of the arts. Everyone who understands literature at all recognizes its power to influence social consciousness and life style. In socialist realism these immense creative potentialities of the arts are to be used in such a way as to contribute to the effort to stave off the debacle that threatens and give organizational strength and direction to the movement whose goal is the long overdue restructuring of social formations.

REFERENCES

1. Horst Redeker, *Abbildung und Aktion: Versuch über die Dialektik des Realismus* (Halle/Saale, 1966).

Erwin Pracht and Werner Neubert

PARTISANSHIP

On the Specific Cognitive Character of Realist Art

When the influence of art and literature is being evaluated, their truth content and their cognitive character have always to be taken into consideration. In world history all realist and humanist art has been a means of spiritual communication between men. Realist art, Brecht says, in its "practical representation" of the world, constitutes an essential medium of orientation in life. Bourgeois writers of the Enlightenment were also quite frank in stressing the cognitive and educative function of literature. They wanted to enlighten men through literary means, to make them aware of what goes on in the world. It was not an individual bent of some of them but an objective historic necessity. In order to prevail in the politico-economic struggle, the bourgeoisie of the Enlightenment had to be aware of the actual *condition of life*, and literature in its own way helped men to find the right —bourgeois—orientation. In the period of bourgeois decadence, the axiom of the inseparability of literature and truth, sacred to the bourgeois writer of that early period, falls into discredit. More and more, for reasons of class alignment, the cognitive character of art is slighted, distorted or frankly denied. Nietzsche, the principal exponent of the bourgeois philosophy of decadence, wrote in a late draft for a new preface to the work of his youth, *The Birth of Tragedy*, with his usual cynical frankness: "Very early I took seriously the relationship of art to truth, and even now I am full of a holy terror when confronted with their schism. I devoted my first book to it; in *The Birth of Tragedy* I believe in art against the background of another faith, namely, that it is not possible to live with truth, that the 'will to truth' is already a system of decadence." When the majority of bourgeois aestheticians and critics and some of the writers avoid in one way or another the question of the inseparable connection of literature and truth, when they distort it or deny it exists, or when they speak of how the artist is confronted with the supposed impenetrability of truth, then they differ from Nietzsche only in being less outspoken and direct.

Many honest bourgeois writers of today with a clear humanist position have resigned in view of the function assigned to the work of art by the imperialist bourgeoisie. The Swiss writer Hermann Broch, who died in 1951, wrote in his novel, *Virgil's Death* (1945): "The writer cannot do anything, cannot help to undo any evil; he is listened to only when he glorifies the world, not when he represents it as it is. Lies, not knowledge, mean fame." Thomas Mann goes farther in his *Doctor Faustus*, which appeared two years later, when Adrian Leverkühn demands that "an order reign among men which will again prepare a fertile ground and an honest adaptation to the work of beauty. . . ." For Thomas Mann reconquest of the humanist *role* of literature and social *renewal* are one and the same thing. We don't have to explain in greater detail that this process of reintegration of art and life, of the artist and the people, can only take place under socialism.

We get a strange impression and the discussion sounds academic when people argue whether literature is "representation," "reflection," "intuition" or "cognition" and whether consequently truth content can be "conceded" to it or not. When the philosophers attribute "cognition" and "truth" only to science, then the time has come to examine more closely the narrowness and one-sidedness of this view. As Brecht writes ironically referring to the debate (Schriften zum Theater, Vol. VII, p. 72), "it doesn't matter in the least whether the main purpose of the theater is to offer knowledge of the world, but the fact is that the theater has to represent the world and that these representations must not deceive. If Lenin is right in his assumption ('the condition for the knowledge of all events in the world in their own movement, in their spontaneous development, in their living essence is the knowledge of them as a unity of opposites'), such representations cannot satisfy without a knowledge of dialectics—and without bringing dialectics to knowledge." Of course art is not knowledge in the sense that science is. If in the past the cognitive function of art was simplified because some aestheticians took science as a model, that is another question. What matters is to determine clearly the peculiarity, the specific character of art as of a spiritual appropriation of the world ("thinking in images"). Thus the difference from science (but not the opposition to it) will appear with greater clarity. The autonomy of art as a specific medium of communication between men will no longer be questioned, neither will art be compared to science in a rationalistic erroneous way. Becher and Brecht were in agreement in demanding that art should be considered and respected as a *creative* activity. This point is of great importance, for what makes art different is precisely *creative cognition*. Art is a spiritual appropriation of the world in a double sense, as Marx had in mind, that is, to appropriate something spiritually as one produces, makes or forms something. This meaning is contained in the etymology of the word poetry ("poiein," to create). At the same time Becher and Brecht both oppose a simplified mechanistic notion of reflection in which the artist is assigned the merely passive function of a mirror reflecting the outer world. According to Brecht, the artist must hold the mirror to the world. For him this is the equivalent of a critical exposition. In so doing the artist cannot remain inactive. His exposition finds its climax in helping to form and to change, in the sense of Marx's eleventh thesis on Feuerbach.

It is, therefore, difficult to understand why today some Marxists, while stressing the creative character of art, refuse to recognize its reflecting character and even sometime do not take account of its cognitive function. *The latter is an inevitable component of the social function of art* (whose nature is very complex). The entertainment aspect (in Brecht's sense) belongs equally to the characteristics of literature as a spiritual appropriation of the world. Knowledge and entertainment do not exclude each other but on the contrary complete each other, or rather they condition and penetrate one another. In the measure that literature entertains, that it gives pleasure, stirs participation, awakens emotions and becomes for reader and spectator a spiritual experience, it is able to fulfill its function of transmitting knowledge. In this context, we should study Johannes R. Becher's assertion, in his "Poetisches Prinzip": "Undoubtedly literature contributes to the formation of consciousness, but it is equally important that it should help form the unconscious and the subconscious. Differing from science, art is able to take possession of the whole man and to penetrate him even when he is not conscious of it. Art is particularly well qualified to call forth an unconscious, dreamlike function in man, which, as is well-known, plays an extraordinary role in the negative as well as in the positive sense. . . . On the one hand we have what man thinks; on the other what stirs in his subconscious self. . . . Now, the work of art is capable of also taking hold of the unconscious and in this way, while possessing the whole man, can influence the formation of consciousness even within what is apparently involuntary, even within the dream. . . ." (*Das poetische Prinzip*, thesis 165). The complex influence of art, which, contrary to science, is able to work on the whole socio-psychic area—that is the moods, passions, feelings, the "mentality" of social groups and classes—has to be the object of further scientific study while socialist realism as a form of artistic creation is becoming more precise and more profound. Art not only transmits knowledge but it can also change knowledge into conviction and thus influence the behavior of man and exert an effect on social conduct. Artistic representation in the sense of socialist realism and social action are mutually complementary and dialectically conditioned agents in the process of the transformation by man of his world.

Artistic Elucidation of
the "Social Causal Nexus"

It goes without saying that the social role of socialist art is not exhausted with the specific cognition of the artist. The educative function of art, to mention only this, acts on the total view of the world of man which is tightly bound with the spiritual make-up, the psychic essence, the moral relationships and feelings of the personality. The spiritual and moral formation of man is a party duty of the socialist writer, a part of the cultural task of our phase of cultural revolution. In this complex of tasks, the cognitive function (and with it the problem of artistic truth) remains the main criterion of realist literature and art.

As Plekhanov wrote more than 60 years ago, "When we say that art is the reflection of life, we express a thought which, although true, is still very vague. In order to understand *in what way* art reflects life, we have to understand the mechanism of life." Only knowledge of the "springs" of social life, of the class struggle, enables the artist, who is gifted and in command of artistic skills, to give a faithful reflection. Engels criticized *City Girl* by Margaret Harkness as not fulfilling its historical task, "as not realist enough," since it shows the working class functioning as a passive mass. As Johannes R. Becher once expressed it, what matters is to recognize and to put across "the concrete definiteness of the subject matter." He goes on: "When we advocate in the arts a realist shaping of reality, as we demand in all areas of human life a true relationship to reality, it is because only in a realist relationship we show a mature approach to nature and our social problems. As we know, classical aesthetics demanded the concrete

definiteness of the objective in the profound belief that what is true
is the concrete and that to make something objective is to humanize
it, while to flee into the abstract is to turn away from the principles
of humanism." (*Von Anderswerden*) "Concrete definiteness of the
subject matter" means finally to include within the creative process
the social forces which *determine* the development of an epoch. This
does not mean to represent as *exhaustively* as possible the aspects and
relationships of life. It is rather to expose creatively what Brecht calls
"the social causal nexus." As Brecht wrote referring to the theater,
"socialist realism means a true representation of reality from the socialist point of view, through the means of art. This representation is
of the kind that enables us to penetrate into the social machinery and
creates a socialist impetus. The greater part of the pleasure that any
art has to give is in the case of socialist realism the pleasure of con-
trolling the potentialities of man's fate through society." (*Sozial-
istischer Realismus auf dem Theater*) Brecht goes on to stress that the
task of socialist realism is to uncover the dialectical laws of motion
of the social machinery "the knowledge of which makes it easier to
control man's fate." Only a work of art which succeeds in its specific
medium in allowing "penetration in the social machinery" can also
transmit a "socialist impetus." However, the artist can only help us
penetrate into the social machinery when he himself understands the
laws of motion of society. In the complicated class conflicts of our time,
these are not obvious on the surface. The artist can grasp them only
under the scientific guidance of Marxism-Leninism. The knowledge
of the "mechanism of life" cannot be obtained under socialism by observation alone nor by the study of scientific literature. The creative
laying bare of the "social causal complex" (Brecht) means for the
writer awareness instead of spontaneity. But awareness means not only
—for writers as well as for readers—*knowledge* of the laws of social development, but also participation in creation and change. And
again this awareness can be obtained only in close union with the party
of the working class. "The party helps the artist most," Walter Ulbricht
said at the second Bitterfeld Conference, "by analyzing in its resolutions the social events of the past and of the present and in setting up
tasks for all in close connection with the people. The clear vision into
the past, the *prospect* that we can show our Republic and each individual, and the anticipation of future social and individual development make it possible for our writers and artists to attain historical

concreteness, an all-embracing vision covering past, present and future, that 'trinity of time' in which Johannes R. Becher, following Gorky, saw the essence of a socialist-realist literature."

Whereas with many realists of the past—let us mention only Balzac —there were contradictions between their political opinions and their total view of the world, such a discrepancy is inappropriate in socialist realism. Socialist realism has as its inevitable pre-condition and base the scientific world view of the working class, the only logical, homogeneous world view of our time. When some "troubadours of skepticism" are made uncomfortable by this ideological connection with the party of the working class, let us ask them: from what and for what do they actually want to be "free"? While expressing "angry" doubts about everything in anarchistic fashion, they think they are "free" from "tiresome" commitments. The freedom they have thus gained is a fiction, as experience proves. As Johannes R. Becher wrote, "*each* poetic conception contains a view of life. . . ." Whoever believes he can free himself from a commitment in outlook to the policy of the party of the working class ends up by being committed to the opposite world view. So Biermann's "third" road has no exit, it leads nowhere. In reality it is the "second" road, namely, the bourgeois position opposing the socialist one.

Partisanship—a Central Aesthetic Category of Socialist Realism

The party is the best organized segment of the people with the farthest reaching world view. Whoever is sincerely committed to the struggle of the people will also adopt the party's point of view. Without being in every case members, the great majority of our writers participate in the realization of its policy (in the large and also in the restricted sense of the word.)

Lenin already wrote on the necessity of involving socialist literature in the tasks and aims of the party. In this connection let us refer to the most detailed and thorough analysis published in German of Lenin's *Party Organization and Party Literature*, namely, Hans Koch's book, *Marxism and Aesthetics*. Hans Koch has elucidated not only the social conditions giving rise to party literature as well as the content, the criteria of the concept of "partisanship," but has also researched its historic development and evolution in the present time. Of course,

Koch's analysis does not exhaust the discussion bearing on the actual content of present-day party literature. While praising Hans Koch's work, Paul Reimann observed that for a definition of the most important characteristics of party literature later works of Lenin must also be taken into account (for instance in what concerns the relationship of socialist literature with our heritage). The Soviet literary critic Stanislav Roshnowsky also pointed out a certain one-sidedness in some of Koch's formulations. He objected to the latter's definition of socialist partisanship: "an open, honest, direct and consistent commitment" (Koch, *Marxismus und Asthetik*, p. 594), as this definition, in his opinion, "applies to only part of the content and essence of this principle, the part that strikes our attention first." Roshnowsky observed that Lenin was not only or primarily concerned with the subjective "commitment" of the individual writer in his literary works but with "party literature," with the tight linking of the writer with the party—*as the new social foundation of his creativity*. He stressed that above all Koch's definition doesn't do justice to the *objective* standards of partisanship. It is not only the individual writer's commitment which characterizes the historically new phase of our literary development but primarily the appearance of a literary society which was not possible before and has now become necessary, of a literature as a phenomenon of society and state, making its imprint on the individual creativity of the writer and thus bringing about a new norm in the sphere of art, whether the writer himself wants it or not. Since the party is the guide of this society, in the criteria of socialist literature it must be presumed to be objective in its judgment. Thus the concept of "partisanship" seen historically acquires a deeper meaning in socialist literature. The tight link of the writer to the party is the necessary socio-political pre-condition for the new way of a literary interpretation of society as a whole. (Cf. Roshnowsky, "Die Kategorie der Parteilichkeit und der sozialistische Realismus in Deutschland." In *Zur Geschichte der sozialistischen Literatur, 1918-1933*. Berlin, 1963, p. 183 ff.) Thus the essential objective criterion for socialist partisanship in works of art must be the degree to which a particular literary expression and its influence harmonize with the struggle and the aims of the party.

Consequently to be partisan means that in life as well as in artistic interpretation the point of view of the party is adopted. This point of view cannot be reconciled with the position of the inactive spectator who feels superior to the situation, gives "advice" and writes off as mistakes everything that contradicts his own notion of the construction of socialism. To be partisan means that the artist, today more than ever, has also the scientific and moral qualities of a planner and leader of social development. These qualities enable him to play a leading role in solving the conflicts of our development. Finally to be partisan means to calculate the results of each artistic utterance, the social influence inherent in the choice of the theme, of the material, of the ideas, characters, conflicts and their interpretation, in order to create a *socialist* impetus.

It goes without saying that in the concept of the "party" the unity of democracy and centralism is also included. In order to determine the limits between what is in agreement with the party and what is contrary to it, as Lenin says in *Party Organization and Party Literature*, we have the party program, the tactical resolutions and the statutes of the party and finally the whole experience of the socialist working-class movement.

The necessity of the point of view of the party for the socialist writer derives from the object of his artistic creativity. Naturally the object of literature is not the same as that of politics and it goes without saying that art is not "illustration" of political or social theses, and yet any artistic grappling with reality must take into account the unity of human and political relationships. "A great writer who knows and represents the whole scale of man's feelings and actions, will not leave out of his works the most important feelings and actions which characterize men today. . . . He can't afford to leave them out. Not because he obeys some external political coercion but because each feeling, each action by the character he represents, whether he *knows* it or not, is colored by what is most important today." (Anna Seghers, Fifth Congress of German Writers, Protocol, p. 62) Socialist construction as a whole is many-faceted. It embraces man's essential relationships in their totality: with his work, community, society, state, nation, nature, etc.; it influences private and intimate relationships and changes man's psyche. It touches upon all conditions with which literature deals. Thus, when the political factor is part of life and determining the development, the literary material demands from the writer the ability to recognize this connection, the dominant role of the political in human life. This recognition makes it possible to evaluate adequately man's behavior. In order to make of the facts of life a base in the representation of important literary conflicts, heroic, tragic or comic, especially in order to stress the justified optimism of our ideas and feelings, the writer should steadily enrich his knowledge of the role of socio-political factors in all areas of life. The best way to achieve this is for the writer to rally openly and consciously to the aims of the party, to be *committed* to the struggle of this party.

Added to this is the fact that the party is the moving force in the changing of all human and social relationships. Literature, while it interprets artistically our present time, cannot ignore the most important subjective factor in society. The party struggle belongs also to history and is therefore entitled to a place of corresponding importance in the sphere of realism.

The demand for a close relationship of the writer to the party derives then from the specific artistic method of socialist realism in literature. In this connection we would like to mention two more factors:

1. Artistic truth (a decisive criterion of socialist realism) is not to be equated with the rendering of a simple material content. It always involves the personal views, feelings and likes and dislikes of a given writer before his subject matter. Although the author himself is an ensemble of social relationships, "belonging to a larger entity" (Marx), thus incorporating relationships that are political or at least essentially influenced by class politics, at the same time, while taking hold artistically of his subject matter, he reflects the process of his own subjective attitude to society in general and to a class in particular. Subjectivity determines largely the specific emotional effect of art. But it must not be confused with subjectivism. The stamp of aesthetic subjectivity and commitment together constitute in socialist art an inseparable unity. It is only when a "functional disturbance" in the interplay of these elements occurs that we have a sliding down into subjectivism. Without a clear partisan vision, there is the danger of seeing everything in rosy colors or of magnifying excessively negative phenomena which seem to impede the advance of the collective; in either instance the results could be artistic utterances which fall short of the truth. The artistic reflection must correspond to the objective development of our life, encompass the gravity and the beauty of our struggle, include the interplay between the old and the new, stress the social forces and create a socialist feeling for life.

2. As an artistic category, literature—in spite of the necessary ab-

straction—must always be bound to the sensuously concrete (see Hegel). The writer must let himself be "caught" by the immediate relationships of life and "yield" to them. However, as appearance and essence never coincide, constant difficulties for a truthful reflection arise at this point and they can only be overcome when to the understanding of the immediacy of intricate relationships in reality, to empirical experience, is added the *knowledge* of conformity to law, when the writer is in a position to go to the bottom of things and finally searches for the kind of experience where the *new quality* of our socialist life is revealed. In the present time when all forms of life are changing, it is more necessary than ever to rise above things ideologically in order to look into them more deeply.

When he adopts the point of view of the leading party, engaged cooperatively in changing and taking responsibility for all events in our republic, the writer is better able to penetrate into the essence of appearances, processes, cause and effect, the accidental and the necessary, in the subject matter of his choice. His vision goes beyond today. The writer is enabled to perceive empirically the present moment not only as a unity of past and present but also as containing a spark of the future. Without this threefold aspect which is incorporated in the best work of our young socialist literature, there can be no socialist realism.

One of the special tasks of literature is also mentioned by Walter Ulbricht, who demanded at the Second Bitterfeld Conference that "the artists' creativity should be concerned in a variety of ways with the work of management up and down the social scale."

Now a literary work does not acquire value from the mere fact that the author's point of view is correct. The partisanship of the writer—as an artist—can only realize itself *within* literature. Partisanship in literature is an aesthetic category. It becomes artistically realized through an interpretation of the material which incites the reader to aesthetic participation. It can only be transmitted to the reader by making truth "manageable" through the reciprocal action of the desires, intentions and passions of the represented characters, through their situation, conflict, decisions, joys and sufferings. Whatever is not re-lived by the artist is unable to activate the reader aesthetically. Next to the selection of themes suitable to the partisan concerns of the writer, we have here the most difficult artistic and ideological problem in the process of literary reflection. The job is to master the inner organization of the material or, as N. Pogodin once said, "to find the proper characters and out of their assigned roles to weave the fabric of the work of art. Then it will start to live and to flower. . . ." (N. Pogodin, in *Kunst und Literatur*, No. 12/1960, p. 1275) Only then can the author steer the imagination, create tension and lead the reader with irrefutable logic to aesthetic cognition. Only then is he capable of giving an artistically valid answer to the questions that are posed by life.

The "Pregnant Point" as an Integrating Factor of Partisanship

Consciousness of his aesthetic and philosophic position is an important part of the artist's equipment. Under the conditions prevailing in our country, Johannes R. Becher's assertion acquires the signification of a poetic creative principle of socialist realism: "We can only look into something when we are *within* the thing itself." The aesthetically fruitful "pregnant point" (Johannes R. Becher) can only be found in the dialectical unity of the ideological and the aesthetic, in the harmony and ideological accord of the writer, that is of the productive "aesthetic subjectivity," with the leading force of society.

In accordance with his socialist convictions and with the views on aesthetics which we stated here, Becher understood by "pregnant point" a capacity, politically and ideologically determined, to represent essential events artistically as part of the *fight for the victory of the new*. As Becher says, "in order to recognize the potentialities for literary influence in our time, . . . a point of view is required. This point of view is the "pregnant point," of which Pascal and Goethe spoke and which they saw not only in the contemplation of works of art but also in the behavior of man creating works of art or in his attitude toward life. The artist must find this focal point, the only position from which an appropriate answer can be given to the ancient question: 'Lord, what shall we do?' What is the need? From one position only can we judge and create artistically where we come from and where we want to go, where we must go. From such a focal point we can be heard, even when we whisper. . . . Only from such a point can we have a total view of the evolution of our century and show it in works of art." (*Das poetische Prinzip*, thesis 211). This new definition of the focal point which is connected with the views of classical

German aesthetics, belongs to Becher's most valuable contributions to
the theory of socialist realism. Becher stresses particularly the dialectics
from a partisan position of the selection of the "focal point" and of the
socialist point of view. "When one misses the right point of departure,
one cannot find the right point of view; the point of view is contained in the point of departure. It is seldom possible to correct later
the erroneous point of departure in order to come back to the right
point of view. The point of departure is the focal point and its importance is primarily to explore the new. . . ." (thesis 285). In Becher's
opinion, to neglect this dialectical process leads to subjective arbitrari-
ness in the establishment of norms and values, and thus to a surrender
of the possibility of any kind of objective standard.

This required conscious socialist position before the complicated
appearances of reality is diametrically opposed to the unstable, hap-
hazardly spontaneous and amorphous swimming in the supposedly
chaotic stream of life. The socialist artist who adopts the creative
method of socialist realism conceives and realizes in his work the decisive pivotal point for the control of social and individual events and
confirms in a deep and convincing way the positive character of human forces in their effort to control society and nature.

As an expression of partisanship the "focal point" clarifies the socialist position before the segment of reality that is being grasped artistically: through and in it, the socialist ethos of artist and writer
becomes transparent. It is true that the "focal point" in the work of
art cannot be exactly "pinpointed." It is expressed as a partisan, historical evaluation of conflicts in the forward movement of socialist society, as socialist, informed penetration of the subject matter, as active
search for the decisive link—in Lenin's words—of an event that can be
made artistically fruitful. In this sense the "focal point" in socialist
partisanship is so to speak continuously transcended. Its particular
prominence, however, is also justified by the fact that it plays a decisive role in the conception of the work of art with its ideological
and spiritual anticipation. "This 'focal point' is really the position that
permits us to survey, to look back and also to have a detailed knowledge, that lets us see past, present and future, that opens our eyes and
likewise opens to us the possibility of getting at the whole truth."
(*Verteidigung der Poesie*). In other words, in the 'focal point,' which
means the socialist partisan position in the diversity of its demands, we
see converging the postulate of deeper knowledge of Marxism-Lenin-

ism, close connection with the party of the working class, the ability to see from the point of view of the leader and planner, the will to serve the cause of socialism through the means of art and finally the human and professional ethos of the artist who is aware of his responsibility.

As a starting point for socialist works we have what Walter Ulbricht said in his report to the 11th plenum of the Central Committee of the German Unity Party: "Nobody can say he has achieved such a position once for all. *It must continually be fought for and tested on each new question.*"

Knowledge of the party's decisions and of the long-range tasks in the construction of socialism, of the socialist cultural policy, helps the artist or the writer in the search for the "focal point," that is, for the adoption of a progressive, active, responsible position in regard to the social and individual events which he represents. Hence any attempt to restrict the active, leading and helping influence of the party of the working class on artistic creativity amounts in final analysis to obstructing socialist art and its humanist concern. Propagation of pessimism, of skepticism, of hidden feelings of alienation, of psychopathic and sexual abandon clashes implacably with the ideological, aesthetic and ethical premises of the art of socialist realism.

As Becher says, "in an epoch that has a firm philosophical foundation, it may happen that the artist does not have to be ideologically committed, that he can trust the 'Zeitgeist' which offers him the possibility to 'move freely in the material.' . . . His freedom consists in his complete agreement with what is historically necessary. His artistic potentiality corresponds to the historic necessity. . . ." But Becher does not allow any doubt that things are different in periods of change, in the revolutionary phases of man's development. "Then the artist must harden his conception in order not to go wrong and not to serve a false cause with his artistic activity. He must discriminate, he must define his position, he must take sides. He has to devote an important, even an essential part of his artistic activity to finding his way within the contradictory and conflicting relationships of his time and get to know on which side the true and the beautiful are. *The artist must then ally himself with the thinker or rather he must be a thinker himself, a thinking artist.* Only then can he move freely in the subject matter. . . ." (Thesis 203). This new hardening of the concept required by the epoch must aim, among other things, at rendering productive in an artistically original and appropriate fashion the scientifically provided knowledge of Marxist-Leninism concerning society and individual.

THE BRECHT-LUKACS DEBATE

"With my friend Eisler, whom some people regard as a pale aesthete, Lukacs has, so to say, wiped the floor, as he didn't show the proper, pious feeling toward the inheritance when the will was executed." This was written by Brecht in 1938 about an article which Georg Lukacs, the Hungarian critic, wrote as part of the discussion of expressionism started by the German emigré review, "Das Wort." Brecht's sarcastic tone by itself indicates that here we have to do with more than an occasional difference of opinion. Brecht then was prompted, primarily by Georg Lukacs' opinions, to clarify his own views as to the problem of realism. In this way, two entirely different, even diametrically opposed concepts of socialist realism took shape. The whole further development of the theory of realism, especially in Germany, was deeply influenced by these two concepts. Within its field of tension, the contradictory process of continuity and discontinuity in the theory and method of socialist realism took shape.

This contrast in aesthetic position, which had been apparent to the careful reader, remained hidden for a long time, since Brecht did not publicize his polemic with Lukacs. If we look up the index of names to the seven volumes of Brecht's *Schriften zum Theater*, we don't see that Lukacs is referred to more often than Emil Ludwig or Louis XIV. Conversely, there is very little mention of Brecht in Lukacs' writings, with the exception of his last important work, *Aesthetics*. Only in his *Skizze einer Geschichte der neueren deutschen Literatur* does Lukacs note that Brecht's concept of a new art failed to do justice to the social content and did not lead toward the desired revival of literature, that Brecht's poetry was "a formal experiment, though to be sure an interesting and clever one." In the preface to the Luchterhand edition, Lukacs confesses that he became acquainted with Brecht's great plays only after World War II and that from then on his views toward Brecht were fundamentally changed, but that circumstances did not allow him to write down his new position. In the English edition of the *Sketch*, he discusses Brecht, misunderstanding him in the same way as in *Aesthetics*. When Lukacs speaks of the great contemporary realists, in his essays written in the 30's and 40's, the name of Brecht is

never mentioned. So one gets the impression that there was almost
no point of contact between Brecht and Lukacs. However, precisely
because of their opposite beliefs, there took place between them a
deep-reaching literary and political argument which, it is true, did not
take the form of direct confrontation and was not conducted publicly
in its most polemical aspects. It is only now, almost thirty years after
the important discussion on literature and art in the journal, "Das
Wort," that the two-volume *Schriften zur Literatur und Kunst* discloses the essence of the Brecht polemic against Lukacs. But this doesn't
exhaust all the aspects of Brecht's anti-Lukacs position; his diaries contain more material on this subject.

Brecht's discussion of Lukacs' theories is not restricted to the 30's
but it assumed its sharpest expression then. After World War II, when
Lukacs' concept of realism played a predominant role, Brecht went on
building up his concept of a socialist realist art, both in practice and
in theory, without polemically alluding to Lukacs any longer. But the
opposition remained, becoming stronger as the differences between
the two concepts of realism were getting deeper. The fight now went
beyond Brecht and Lukacs, whose concepts marked the outline of the
battlefield to which essential problems of socialist literary development were brought. In this way Brecht's discussion with Lukacs assumed the proportions of a full-fledged literary debate. Next to the
Sickingen debate which Marx and Engels directed in the middle of the
19th century against Lassalle, it belongs with the most important documents of Marxist aesthetics. It is the real climax in the evolution of the
Marxist theory of realism. The debate took place within the general
context of socialist literary development. While we have to limit ourselves here to the Brecht-Lukacs exchange, we should point out that
Marxist aesthetics derived stimulation and impetus from a great variety
of socialist writers. Brecht is not the only important author to have
argued with Lukacs on the development of realism. The correspondence between Anna Seghers and Georg Lukacs represents also an extraordinarily important aspect of the fight on realism. There are many
other important connections and side issues in this debate which we
cannot take up here.

The Brecht-Lukacs debate was started by the discussion on expressionism in the review "Das Wort," but that was only a start. The
conflict of opinions on expressionism which started in No. 9 of the
year 1937 and in which 15 writers, critics and artists took part, among

others Ernst Bloch, Alfred Kurella, Franz Leschnitzer, Rudolf Leon-
hard, Klaus Mann, Gustav von Wangenheim, Herwarth Walden and
Heinrich Vogeler, is still of importance today. This literary discussion
is significant less in terms of an evaluation of expressionism than of
the new relationship to the literary past which the Marxists had then
inherited. This discussion was the visible expression of a new phase of
the approach to literature, which nullified the disregard of literary
traditions—an infantile disorder of the 20's. The policy of the Popular
Front formed the socio-political base upon which this development
took place.

All the discussions revolved essentially around one problem: realism.
And so the title Lukacs chose for his contribution, "What is at stake
is realism," was really a program. The First All-Union Congress of
Soviet Writers in 1934, when Gorky launched the slogan of socialist
realism, was at the origin of these discussions on realism. The exchange
of opinions in "Das Wort" must also be considered in the context of
debates on this subject in the Soviet Union between 1936 and 1938.
At that time two well-defined camps were facing each other: Lukacs
and Lifschitz on one side, Yermelov, Knipovitch and Altmann on the
other. We cannot relate here the particulars of this controversy, especially since other writers came up against Lukacs with viewpoints
differing from Brecht's. We shall only stress the wide range and the
far-reaching influence of these discussions.

Brecht attributed great importance to this controversy on realism
which had originated in the Soviet Union and was carried on in the
review "Das Wort." It had started "an international movement," he
writes. It had made clear that neither man nor the world could be
seen clearly if the writer described only the reflection of the world in
man's psyche. Also it was not enough to show how capitalism brought
about a spiritual desert. What must also be shown was "how to conduct an active fight against dehumanization."[1] Brecht's battle-cry was
to use the cultural heritage in the political fight against fascism. Besides, he had other important tactical objections against the direction
the discussion was taking. In a letter to Willi Bredel, editor in chief
of "Das Wort," he complained bitterly against the fact that Lukacs
was attacking him and accusing him of bourgeois decadence. He deplored that under the influence of a small clique led, as he saw it, by
Georg Lukacs and Julius Hay, the important struggle against formalism
was itself degenerating into a kind of formalism. Marxists should be

moved by other concerns, Brecht remarked, than questions of form. As co-editor of the periodical he proposed, largely for political reasons, to put an end to the debate. As the latter had become a battle where the slogans Expressionism and Realism were hurled, he was afraid that the basis of this discussion might become an obstacle to the desired anti-fascist platform of a Popular Front policy. In his article entitled "Praktisches zur Expressionismusdebatte," he wrote: "Old wounds are re-opened, new ones are inflicted, old hostilities and alliances are divulged with mutual accusations. Nobody seems to be convinced, except of his own opinion. So far, everything is in the greatest confusion, the camps reject what they regard as a dirty compromise but go on strengthening their position. Two spectators are left, rather defeated, on the battlefield, the *author* and the *reader*. The latter has read and seen the things that were the object of the fight, the former still has things to write. With pulled-in shoulders, he contemplates the whole array of arms and listens as knives are being sharpened." And Brecht concludes: "Are we to give up theory? No, we will build it up. . . . We will do away with a formalism of criticism. What is at stake is realism."

Brecht's intention in repeating Lukacs' title at the end of his article was to stress that he too was concerned with realism. His objection to Lukacs' concept of realism didn't stem from a defense of formalism but from his opposition to a formalist view of literature. He was quick to observe that Lukacs did not base his concept of realism on the concrete class struggle, but that he used it in the service of a utopian ideal of democracy, thus ending up with formalistic criteria, derived from the past.

The whole extent of the Brecht-Lukacs debate can be clarified only if one examines the diverging political views, especially in respect to the proletarian revolution and democracy. This is where the real causes of the various views lie. But what is needed here is an exact knowledge of the different evolutions of the two thinkers. Whereas Brecht has been recently the subject of many thorough Marxist studies, we do not have yet a critically sensitive over-all evaluation of Lukacs' work. Lukacs himself has through his behavior during the Hungarian counterrevolution contributed to a situation where his writings are more subject to polemic criticism in regard to certain fundamental attitudes than to a detailed study of their significance as a whole. However, Günter Fröschner has recently published a very interesting essay, entitled *Die Herausbildung und Entwicklung der geschichtsphilosophischen Anschauungen von Georg Lukacs* which constitutes an entirely new level of German criticism on Lukacs.[2] Fröschner attacks the view that with Lukacs we have to do with an elaborate system of revisionist concepts. To see in Lukacs only the revisionist or only the dogmatist is to simplify things excessively and to miss the contradictions and the complexity of his views. The Brecht-Lukacs debate cannot be understood in such terms. As Fröschner remarks, "Lukacs as an historian of literature, as aesthetician and philosopher as well as functionary of the Communist Party has earned a great many historical merits which cannot be belittled by the fact that today he cashes in on them in order to peddle better his revisionist political views and to realize them wherever possible. A Marxist interpretation will have to show the dialectic prevalent in this relationship of 'greatness' and 'limitations.' " Although Fröschner's essay deals more with the philosopher than with the critic, it is of extraordinary importance for the effort to determine Lukacs' position in the controversy on realism.

Realism as a Problem of Method

It was in the 30's that the main development of the theory of realism took place. Realism, not as a trend in style but as a methodological problem, was on the order of the day. Now that socialist literature and art could point to early works of international repute, writers, artists, aestheticians and politicians from various countries started discussing the nature of a literature and an art which would serve the interests of the revolutionary working class and of the new society already in existence in the Soviet Union. Thus the 30's became a decisive stage in the development of Marxist aesthetics. This stage, however, was full of complexities and contradictions. But it would be a mistake to consider it only, on the strength of Zhdanov's apodictic and dogmatic pronouncements on realism, as a period of rigidity, of the stiffening of all the great and fruitfully experimental artistic enterprises which appeared so exciting in the 20's and 30's. In this stage of the development of realism, it is true, strong dogmatic tendencies appear, but this is also the time when the essential elements of the realist method are worked out, elements which represent a new quality in comparison with what has come before. This stage owes its existence to the discussion of the most varied concepts, to the contribution of many artists and critics. Those who represented the most solid and far-reaching views were Bertolt Brecht and Georg Lukacs.

Their conceptions of realism are not aesthetic models worked out from the study. Any scientific research which would start from such premises would be certain to go wrong. These two men had their theoretical-aesthetic thinking rooted too deeply in the political reality of their time, in the struggles of the revolutionary working class, to be concerned with "pure" aesthetic questions. In his polemic against Lukacs, as we have seen above, Brecht himself has often used the argument that Lukacs in his aesthetic considerations does not start from the concrete reality and its struggles. Such an objection is only partly right. The fact is that Brecht and Lukacs were starting from totally diverging political conceptions toward their mastering of reality and these are the real source of their different notions of realism.

The years between 1928 and the fascist conquest of power led both Brecht and Lukacs to political decisions which were to determine their entire life. In these years, Brecht went over to the revolutionary working class. His didactic play "The Measure Taken" brings to a focus all the problems which this step involved for certain members of the leftist intelligentsia. From an extreme model situation, Brecht explains his views in regard to the problem of force. His new ideological position led him to a radical break with the bourgeoisie, a class to whom, as he thought, he had nothing more to say. This radical, partly undialectic, way of thinking was evident too in the first years after the fascist coming to power, as evidenced in the "Platform for Leftist Intellectuals." In the nine points of this platform, Brecht holds that only the proletariat can fight against fascism, only those, he stresses, who have broken with the ownership of the means of production and all the relationships associated with it. But already in his speech to the first anti-fascist Writers' Congress held in Paris in 1935, there appeared in contrast to the nine points of the "Platform"—which served as the basis for his speech in Paris—a new turn toward the Popular Front which the Communist Parties were advocating. From then on, Brecht supported consistently the policy of a Popular Front from which he also derived decisive stimulus for his literary activity and his concept of realism.

Georg Lukacs assumed at that time an entirely different position toward the anti-fascist struggle and the proletarian revolution. The problem of force had occupied him in 1919 already when he wrote "Der Terror als Rechtsquelle," marking thus his joining the Communist movement; he was to remain until 1929 a member of the Central Committee of the Hungarian Communist Party. At about the time when Brecht demonstrated in "The Measure Taken" his model case for a decisive revolutionary situation, Lukacs, commissioned by the Hungarian Party leadership, was working out his "Blum theses" in which he linked for the first time the question of the democratic revolution with the fight against fascism. This was a new question which was going to be of great importance in subsequent developments. While Lukacs had already come to a clear and deep understanding of the essence of fascism, his idea of the democratic revolution remained in the image of the classical bourgeois revolution, because of his blurred concept of class oppositions. Fröschner describes Lukacs' notion of the democratic revolution as "a utopian contrast" to the fascist barbarism, guided by the star of "reason" and suffering from a certain abstract imprecision. We cannot go here into the complicated situation which gave birth to the "Blum theses" and the role they played in the Hungarian and international worker movement. What is of interest to us here is the fact that their tendency ran counter to the concepts which Brecht formulated later in his "Platform for Leftist Intellectuals." This divergence in Brecht's and Lukacs' political ideas appeared especially in their choice of ways leading to the overthrow of fascism and to the proletarian revolution. While Brecht evidenced left-sectarian tendencies in "The Measure Taken" and "Platform for Leftist Intellectuals," Lukacs' concept of the democratic revolution was an Aufhebung of the opposition between imperialism and socialism. Toward the middle 30's, as Brecht overcame his narrow concept of the antifascist struggle, Lukacs persisted in his revisionist mode of thinking concerning the character of the relationship between the bourgeois-democratic and proletarian revolution. His concept of democracy as a form of sovereignty covered over the antagonistic class conflicts.

We have had to sketch briefly these different political platforms which allow us to understand the fight on realism between Brecht and Lukacs.

In the field of aesthetics, the idea of progress, which Lukacs detaches from its class context, becomes for him an essential criterion. "The central problem," he writes, "through which the changed attitude

toward history is expressed, is that of progress."³ In accordance with
his notion of "revolutionary democracy," Lukacs sees in the commitment of the bourgeois writer to progress and democracy the actual
center of his concept of realism. Lukacs is less interested in the writer
who has broken radically with his class than in the one who remains
in the spiritual arena of "revolutionary democracy." This explains
Lukacs' lack of understanding for the new methodological paths and
creative devices which Brecht for example brings to the service of
socialist literature. As Lukacs politically envisions a long period of
transition, he sees realism only as the continuation of the great progressive currents of the 19th century. Instead of the discovery and
conquest of a new art arising out of new social relationships, which is
Brecht's concern, Lukacs wants to purify literature from the contamina-
tion of decadence. To this end, his main tool is criticism of ideology.
So his criticism of the late bourgeois conceptions of art doesn't start
with the new possibilities offered by the socialist position to artists but
with the utopian vision of "revolutionary democracy." While Brecht
conducts his polemic against late bourgeois art standing on new shores
and thus achieves a much more commanding position, Lukacs is forced
to a limited fight against decadence by his abstract conception of democracy. This fight was limited due to the fact that he was forever
invoking the great progressive achievements of the 19th century as
a criterion, in the same way as in the political area he had to take the
classical bourgeois revolution as a model for his "revolutionary democracy." We will have to explain below how Brecht, while evolving
his realistic method out of the new social relationships, was capable
of modifying and using certain artistic devices introduced by bourgeois writers. On the contrary Lukacs could see nothing but the ideology of decadence, since his political beliefs prevented him from grasping the new social conditions in which the new ways of writing were
rooted. If his concepts did not permit him to understand fully the new
literary phenomena, his aesthetic analysis is extraordinarily good as
long as it applies to works that remain in the traditional line of the
19th century. Aside from the conceptual conclusions which always
follow his research, hardly anybody has written on the authors of
critical realism with greater depth and insight than Lukacs, and his
merits in this area are incontestable. Brecht, on the other hand, ham-
pered by his polemic stance, often approaches these same authors with
prejudiced snap judgments. Later on, Brecht rendered homage to their

worth but did not penetrate into their not inconsiderable powers of expression and influence.

Attitude Toward Tradition

In his essay "Schicksalswende" Lukacs writes: "The struggle to secure our heritage is the most important ideological task of anti-fascism." The connection between anti-fascism and the cultural heritage which was established in the 30's by Marxist aesthetics is one of the essential preconditions for realism. It is undoubtedly one of Lukacs' merits to have assigned in his work a central position to this relationship and to have fought against any disregard of the cultural heritage. However, he immediately transforms the connection between anti-fascism and the cultural heritage into an imaginary conflict between humanism and barbarism. The class struggles disappear altogether in this opposition. This is the real reason which drove Brecht to attack Lukacs' advice: "Let us go back to our fathers." In 1938 he judges Lukacs' essay as follows: "It is because of the tendency to capitulate, to pull back, because of the utopian and idealistic tendency which still lurks in Lukacs' essays and which he will certainly overcome, that his writings which contain such valuable material are unsatisfactory and create the impression that he is concerned with enjoyment alone and not with the fight, not with the way out, not with the way forward."

In no period of his life was Brecht indifferent to the literary heritage. But he always held authors who relied only on their imagination to be insufficiently equipped. In 1930 already he writes: "Classes and trends which are in movement must try to put their history in order." It was not the neglect of tradition which drove him to polemics but the way in which Lukacs treated certain works of world literature. With Lukacs in mind, he reproaches the "literary pigeon-hole artists" for first cutting up the literary works to make them fit their pigeon-holes. Brecht is reminded of a movie where Charlie Chaplin packs a trunk, closes it and cuts with scissors everything that sticks out. Thus Lukacs with works of art. Realism and decadence are considered as completely separate phenomena and their evolution has very little to do with the class struggle.

Brecht's and Lukacs' antagonistic concepts clashed especially in the attitude toward literary works which Lukacs held to be decadent. For

Brecht, authors like Joyce, Kafka, Dos Passos, Döblin were important. What Brecht valued in them was precisely what Lukacs was forever warning against. Brecht conceded that these writers may not show the whole reality, may not expose the real causes with which socialist realism is concerned, but their grasp of reality is sufficient and one can learn from them; from Joyce for example the use of inner monologue and of change of style, from Dos Passos the montage and dissociation of elements, from Döblin the handling of stream of consciousness, from Kafka certain feelings of alienation. These innovations were related to new developments in reality. But Brecht was in no way thinking of taking over formally these techniques. For him form was not something superficial that can be borrowed here and there. "The form of a work of art," he asserts, "is nothing else but the perfect organization of its content, and its value depends completely on that of the content." That's why he was concerned to divert from their bourgeois context certain techniques of late bourgeois literature and to use them for new social goals. Brecht is aware that this involves considerable difficulty, since technical means are rooted in the concrete content. However, it is not impossible to detach certain techniques from their substantive base in order to use them for new purposes. But of his own experience as a writer, Brecht knew that at the moment of creation often certain formal elements appear together with the content and sometimes even before. This is how he describes the process: "He (the author — W.M.) feels like writing something "light," a poem in fourteen lines, or something "somber" with heavy rhythms, or something drawn-out, or vivid, etc. He mixes words that have a certain taste, brings them together cunningly, plays with them. While building up, he still plays, tries this or that, leads the plot here and there. He looks for change and contrast. He washes the words, for they get easily dusty. He cleans up the situations; they wilt easily. He does not all the time know when he "creates" that he is continuously forming an image of reality or an "expression" of how outer reality affects him. At times he gets stuck and his work suffers, but the dangers of this process still don't make the process itself a false one. Without introducing innovations of a formal kind the writer cannot bring the new substance and the new viewpoints to the new audiences. We build our houses differently from the Elizabethans and the same is true of our plays."

Within this dialectic of content and form, matter and medium, a process of change of function takes place, which is anything but formal, for, as the result of this process, we have a new functional definition of the technical means. Often new means are worked out which may or may not still have something in common with the old ones. (One should be careful not to speak superficially of the appearance of new artistic means and forms which require such a long time until they emerge. Also they do not appear without a polemical or developmental relationship to what is already at hand.) Artistic means that were used to describe the inscrutability of man's condition can be used by the socialist author to show that fate can be influenced. The technique of the montage, the inner monologue and others can serve very different purposes. They may demonstrate the senselessness of man's existence but they can also show how life can be meaningfully altered. As Brecht writes, referring to the works of late bourgeois authors, "socialist writers can get acquainted with valuable, fully-developed technical elements in these documents of disorientation, for they are able to see the way out." And here we have a contrast with Lukacs, who sees in the montage, the inner monologue, the distancing and journalistic elements, a decline of literature, an expression of decadence.

Brecht turns primarily against Lukacs when the latter proclaims that the technique of the 19th century novel is worth studying, but not that of the 20th century novel. But, argues Brecht, if it is possible to detach from their substance certain formal elements in the works of the great realists of the 19th century, it should also be possible with the bourgeois literature of the 20th century. In both cases the formal element is fused to the concrete substance which the socialist writer cannot take over.

Also Brecht felt closer to the bourgeois writers of his time than to those of the previous century who had had to fulfill different social tasks. "To tell the absolute truth," Brecht writes, "I have a harder time to learn from Tolstoy and Balzac. They had other duties to fulfill. Another thing, much of what they wrote has already become my flesh and blood, if I may express it so. Of course I admire these people, the way they acquitted themselves of their tasks. There is much to be learned from them." One can't say that Brecht had no understanding of Balzac's greatness. He valued him, although he was somewhat cautious in appraising the Frenchman's realism. "A great writer and a passable realist," Brecht wrote of Balzac. He has much less understanding of Lukacs' interpretation, where Balzac is praised as *the* realist writer. But this doesn't satisfy Brecht's new social purposes, hence his sensivity to Balzac's weaknesses, above all the monstrosities, the romantic view of the murderous capitalistic competition of post-Napoleonic France, the inflated individualization which presents the complex capitalist competition as conflicts of individuals, one man against "the whole of society." Thus engaged in polemics, Brecht couldn't help pointing out that Balzac had said of himself emphatically that he derived his inspiration from the Indian stories of James Fenimore Cooper. Brecht's criticism exposes real weaknesses in Balzac but in the end he is unfair to him. The solutions which Balzac found for his time, of which Lukacs makes absolutes and models for realism, encounter little understanding in Brecht. But the profound difference between these two interpretations of Balzac is not at all a question of literary taste; it has to be explained by extra-literary causes. For Lukacs, Balzac is the great model case for his kind of ideological criticism. Using Balzac as an example, he demonstrates how a writer can subject his own class to criticism without breaking with it. However, this is an ideological position which Lukacs considers as typical for the "revolutionary democracy" he advocates. What he wants is the critical stance, not the break with the ruling class. It is around this crucial point that he builds his philosophic and critical edifice. Brecht on the other hand, who in the 30's kept telling leftist intellectuals that it was impossible to want both humanism and the capitalistic relationships of production, sees the problems from an entirely new perspective. He is dismayed to be offered as realistic a method based on an individualistic image of the struggles in capitalist competition while what he is trying to show is how the individual more and more emerges as a part of great masses without losing his individuality. Only it is a different kind of individuality from the one Balzac described. For this reason alone Brecht would have to search for new methods. In Balzac he finds no help toward the solution of his problems; writers like Joyce, Kafka and Döblin are closer to him since they do, although from a different ideological angle, deal with the capitalist reality which confronts Brecht. No matter how penetrating Lukacs' analyses of the 19th century realists are, how full of new perceptions which had escaped the bourgeois literary historians, they turn out to be insufficient to interpret through literature the reality of the 20th century. What Brecht was waiting for was cues for the representation of today's world.

The Balzac controversy has to be seen in the context of the two great literary traditions to which Brecht and Lukacs were indebted. Whereas Lukacs emphasizes the 19th century realists and traces a line from Balzac to Tolstoy and Thomas Mann, Brecht's concept of tradition is considerably wider, stressing primarily the early bourgeois writers, along with Shakespeare, Swift, Rabelais, Voltaire, Diderot. Brecht was also strongly attracted by the old Chinese didactic poetry; by Latin poetry, as well as by extra-literary traditions and elements in popular art, that is, by traditions which had no place in Lukacs' concept of realism. It is true that Lukacs does not overlook the merits of the writers of the Enlightenment but he still stresses Balzac's superiority to them. He even blames Balzac for not considering Diderot as a writer. But his abstract praise of the 18th-century authors and of dialectical masterpieces like *Rameau's Nephew* doesn't affect his conclusions. His analysis of the early revolutionary bourgeois writers influences in no way his concept of realism. For him the literary technique which he finds in these authors cannot be reconciled with the realist method which he evolved from the great works of Balzac and Tolstoy.

When Brecht happens to speak of writers who are outside of his line, when he mentions Lukacs' "protégés," so to say, he doesn't proceed with as much delicacy as the Hungarian critic. Especially in his youth Brecht often had adopted a provocative attitude toward these writers: "It shouldn't be expected of me," he writes in the 20s, "to understand *The Magic Mountain!* . . . (The only reason I mention Mann is that he is a typical, successful bourgeois producer of artificial, trivial and useless books.) I concede openly that I would be willing to offer money to prevent the publication of certain books."

Brecht's extreme rejection of Thomas Mann has to be seen in the context of the political and literary situation in the 20s. At that time Thomas Mann faced the young revolutionary writers with an attitude which he summed up in his letter to Count Keyserling in a demand for the "spiritualization of German conservatism." Brecht, who expected nothing any longer from the old world, had only scorn for such a proposal. This is the kind of thinking he found in Mann's novels. Later on Brecht's attitude toward the works written in the tradition of 19th-century critical realism is much more conciliatory. In the 40s and 50s his judgment displays more nuance, as shown, for example, in a conversation with Friedrich Wolf. Speaking of the Aristotelian theater he stressed that "it is also possible to write objective, 'psychologizing' plays by taking chiefly psychological material as the main subject of artistic representation while aiming at objectivity."[4]

The great motto proclaimed then by the Communist Party, to use the cultural heritage for the fight against fascism, was applied better and more effectively by Brecht than by Lukacs. While Lukacs is oriented toward the realists of the 19th century from whose works he derives his conception of realism, Brecht developed his own conception of realism which was both wide and complex. It doesn't derive from certain models providing the norm of realist writing but inquires about the social goals with which art is connected. He is not concerned with artistic means and standards—of which he had a great many, old and new—but with how they will be used. For Brecht the realist method results from the materialist-dialectical handling of literary means for new social goals. "Realism is nothing formal," Brecht wrote in 1938. "One cannot take the form of one single realist (or of several) and call it *the* realist form. This is not realism. Otherwise one comes to the conclusion that *either* Swift and Aristophanes *or* Balzac and Tolstoy were realists." But a realism that refers itself only to the model of a few novels of the last century (for Lukacs mentions new novels only in the measure that they follow his favorite tradition) must remain formalist even when fighting formalism. Brecht, therefore, is quite right to point out the formalist character of Lukacs' conception of realism. Lukacs is in the paradoxical situation of being convinced of formalism himself while fighting against a "formalistic literature." But formalism is inherent in Lukacs' system. Hence Brecht's ironical observation that Lukacs advises writers: "Be like Tolstoy—without his weaknesses! Be like Balzac—but of today." When Brecht writes against Lukacs, "Realism is a concern not of literature only, but a great political, philosophic and practical concern," he leaves out of consideration the fact that Lukacs too with his conception of realism was defending philosophic and political concerns. Only they are different from Brecht's. At that time, at the end of the 30's, Lukacs' political platform could not yet be inferred from his conception of realism. Brecht could then believe that a time would come when Lukacs would get over his utopian views, unrelated as they were to the class struggle.

The attitude toward decadence turned out to be one of the most debated points of the problem of tradition. Here also the contrast between Brecht and Lukacs is startling. Brecht didn't deny the existence of the problem of decadence, neither did he relegate it to the domain of cheap, trivial literature, as some Marxist aestheticians of the 60's are doing. For him, decadence cannot be reconciled with a fighting literature whose task is, in his opinion, to give rise to an impetus toward socialism. In this sense he is a consistent opponent of any decadence. However, he rejects Lukacs' definition of decadence because he finds it formal and non-historical. As Lukacs hails on one hand certain realistic works as the "great models," on the other hand he declares certain works of late bourgeois literature to be prototypes of decadence. Thus appeared the Lukacs constellation of decadents consisting of names like Joyce, Proust, Kafka and Dos Passos. What he reproaches these writers for is not their deep involvement in capitalist alienation, but rather their way of writing, the techniques they use such as distancing, montage, etc. While these authors were unable to uncover essential relationships, their tragic humanism, their stress on man which comes through in their main works should not be denied. Their style is largely experimental. They try to understand man from a different angle. To be sure, their picture of man is narrowed and overshadowed by the limits which late bourgeois writers, unable to break the bonds of total alienation, could not go beyond. If one starts with a conceptual, social definition of decadence, and not with a formal one, then we see a totally different group of writers emerge in our field of vision. True decadence is to be found in the works of Stefan George, Filippo Marinetti, and Gottfried Benn. But this truly decadent poetry is not—as in the case of George—or only incidentally, an object of Lukacs' theory of decadence. Even in the middle 50's, when he wrote the book entitled *Wider den missverstandenen Realismus*, Lukacs sums up conclusions to the contrast between Thomas Mann and Franz Kafka in the following words: "Precisely because today's real dilemma is not the choice between capitalism and socialism but rather that between war and peace, because the immediate ideological task of the bourgeois intelligentsia is to overcome the anguish that has become permanent and universal, the fatalistic terror which is not a realization of socialism but which opposes human salvation, it is easier than it was yesterday for the bourgeois writer to give a positive answer to his own dilemma: Franz Kafka or Thomas Mann? artistically interesting decadence or true to life critical realism?"[5] And Roger Garaudy remarks: "This is the most sectarian book on Marxist aesthetics." One could agree with him if he emphasized more the political starting point than the conceptual peg on which Lukacs rests his evaluation of Kafka. In the 50s, when Brecht was preparing to write an article on Kafka, he observed in the few lines he jotted down: "My intention here is very far from proposing a model." With all the esteem Brecht had for Kafka, he didn't see in him a model for the literature he had in mind. Still his judgment differs essentially from that of Lukacs. Brecht started from the view that the important works of late bourgeois literature, those of Kafka, Joyce and Proust, cannot be considered merely as products of decline. A dialectical way of thinking will always take into account the fact that literary evolution doesn't proceed in clean-cut categories. It often happens that late bourgeois writers themselves uncover revealing currents of reality. They evolve interesting techniques which sometimes do not come to fruition because of their ideological point of view. We have noted above that these techniques can also be used by the socialist writer when he knows how to modify them to serve his own purposes. While aware of the historical situation of the late bourgeois writers, Brecht also stresses the undialectical mechanical method of their writing. He especially criticizes the abstract art which distorts things to the point that they appear strange to the spectator but in their strangeness symbolize only their total lack of function, whereas Brecht is concerned with grasping through his method of distancing the actual essence, the thing behind the things. According to him, the representatives of dadaism and surrealism attempt to use distancing but in their works the objects do not come back to us through the distance.[6] This creates only a sensation of generality but nothing connected with real knowledge of the objects. Art thus dissolves in an ambiguity which can be of use to the oppressor as well as the oppressed. In his article "On Abstract Painting," he writes, "You paint for example something vague and red; some in the public will cry because it makes them think of a rose, others because they see in it the blood of a child hit by a bomb. So your task is done, you have through lines and colors created a feeling. . . . We communists do not see things like the exploiters and their ministering angels. But when we see things differently, it is because the things themselves are different, not our eyes. When we want to teach that things must be seen differently, we have to do it with the things themselves. And we are not satisfied with simply seeing "differently" but we want things to be seen in a certain way, a way which is true, that is, in conformity with the thing. We want to master things, in art as in politics."

The essence of Brecht's method consists not simply in making things appear strange, or even distorting them, but in the step that follows: to bring about clarity of knowledge through the estrangement of things. This is why Brecht objects equally to a dull rendition of reality and to artistic distortion which does not allow us to know things but makes them unrecognizable. During the controversy on expressionism in the 30s, centering on Franz Marc's blue horses, when it was objected that horses are not blue, Brecht remarked ironically that in his opinion this slight distortion of reality was not a crime. But he objected to the fact that Franz Marc's blue horses, who had kicked up more dust than those of Achilles, were made to proclaim a new artistic vision. He didn't consider it as desirable that working men became partisans of the blue horses as a result of their art education. He was aiming at other forces which could awaken art. He is therefore a sharp critic of the tendency in abstract art to make things unrecognizable. Brecht's reaction to abstract painting, which is synonymous with the trends in late bourgeois art, shows clearly how he differs from Lukacs' conception of realism. In that same article, Brecht writes, addressing the abstract painters: "I see that you have done away with the subject in your canvases. No recognizable objects emerge any longer. You give us again the curve of a chair, not the chair itself; the reddishness in the sky, not the burning house. You give us the mixture of lines and colors, not the mixture of things. I must say I am surprised to hear you say that you are communists, people who want to change a world that has become uninhabitable. Your painting would not perplex me so much if, instead of communists, you were the ministering angels of the rulers. Then your painting would not seem incongruous, it would even be logical."

How Art Represents

The aesthetic opposition between Brecht and Lukacs extends also to their relationship to reality. The Marxist point of view emerges most clearly in the attitude toward the mirror theory. However, both Brecht and Lukacs accept Lenin's theory of representation, thus creating the impression that they don't disagree on this question. But, as one follows their exposition on how to obtain a literary representation of our reality, the differences become at once apparent. In Vol. VII of his *Schriften zum Theater,* Brecht gives some illuminating examples of the way he envisions the dialectical process of representation. Like the sketch of a portrait, the image must still be surrounded by traces of other movements and currents. In order to clarify further his conception, Brecht describes the situation of a man who is delivering a speech in a valley, changing his mind now and then while talking, so that the echo carries back contradictory phrases. The examples stress the contradictory character of the process which takes place within the phenomenon of representation and which must be visible in its finished literary form. The living, irreplaceable man, Brecht remarks, should not be identical with his portrait and this contradiction should be expressed in the image. "Representations should in fact efface themselves before the thing represented, the collective life of men," Brecht observes in his "Kleines Organon."

Again, Lukacs conceives this process quite differently since he bases it on another relationship to reality. To the question of what this reality is which the literary work must mirror faithfully, Lukacs answers: "Here the negative side of the answer is what matters: this reality does not consist merely of the surface of the external world that has been immediately perceived, not merely of the momentary accidental phenomena. While Marxist aesthetics gives realism a central position in the theory of art, at the same time it opposes vigorously any naturalism, any trend that is content with a photographic reproduction of the immediately perceptible surface of the external world."[7] This at once connects Lukacs' conception of reality with the relationship between essence and appearance. Fröschner and other critics point out that Lukacs derived his conception of reality from Hegel. However, in his literary essays, Lukacs, going beyond Hegel, emphasizes that essence and appearance are both part of objective reality. But the following reasoning shows to what extent he still adheres to idealistic notions when he discusses the dialectic of essence and appearance. In his opinion the goal of any great art is . . . "to give a picture of reality in which the opposition of appearance and essence, individual case and law, immediacy and idea is resolved in such a way that both are fused into spontaneous unity in the immediate impression made by the work of art, that they *form an inseparable unity for the spectator or reader.*" (My italics – W.M.)[8] Lukacs stresses the inseparable unity of essence and appearance. He sees in it the essential superiority of Marxist aesthetics over bourgeois philosophy of art for which, as a result of its absence of dialectics, essence and appearance are rigid antinomies. In this opposition, Lukacs argues, the bourgeois theoreticians do not recognize the dialectic unity of the contradictions. In this polemic we can only agree with Lukacs; but, as he often does, he stresses unity at the expense of the contradictions. In the total mechanism of his theory of image, the contradiction is almost dislodged by the unity. It is not, as with Brecht, the basic moving element, the spiritual center of gravity, but at best a rhetorical ingredient. Marxist dialectic, however, starts from the contradictory character of essence and appearance. Lukacs, it is true, is far from contesting it, but in seeking an understanding of literary representation, he fails to make fruitful use of the discord between these connected aspects of objective reality as the necessary cause of the whole dialectical process. In his comments and marginal notes (*Philosophical Notebooks*) Lenin observes concerning this problem: "In the strict sense, dialectics is the investigation of the contradictions *in the essence of the things themselves*: it is not only the appearances which are ephemeral, mobile, flowing, limited only by certain milestones, but also the essences of things." Therefore, it is impossible for essence and appearance to form "an inseparable unity," as Lukacs formulates it. The contradiction itself within this unity is a determining force.

While Brecht, following the guidelines of Marxist dialectics, always starts from the position that both sides of reality do not coincide immediately but are distinct from each other, Lukacs makes an absolute of the unity of essence and appearance. Brecht, too, wants in the work of art the dialectical unity of the contradictory aspects; however, he doesn't erase the contradictions but sees them as serving to disclose social relationships.

Although this whole complex of problems may seem very theoretical, Brecht and Lukacs, each in his own way, deduce from it immediate practical consequences for art. Lukacs concludes from the unity of essence and appearance that the true and most profound relationship in a novel or a play can only be discovered at the end. "It is part of the essence of their construction and of their appeal," Lukacs writes, "that only at the end do we get the real and complete explanation to the beginning. . . . The essential definitions of the world which a work of literature represents are disclosed in elaborate succession and gradation. But this gradation must take place within an ever-present unity of essence and appearance; through intensified concretion it must make the unity of both more and more close and evident." From his own theory of representation Lukacs derives the Aristotelian structure which he represents and invokes repeatedly, that of an "organic, rounded and closed work of art." To the extent that Lukacs makes an absolute of the unity of essence and appearance and neglects the contradictions between them, he passes up the possibility of creating great, spacious and open forms. Such forms, however, are required by the social materials which the socialist authors are to handle.

Brecht's notions of effective representations are closely connected with his method of distancing. Out of the dialectic inherent in the process of representation he works out a practical artistic method. He points out that the creation of representations destined to contribute to the conquest of the world demands that the artist should use a new, modified technique, in accordance with the new, modified purpose.[9]

The contradictory character of the representations and the thing represented is used by Brecht to make obvious to the public what is natural and self-evident. "Only thus," Brecht writes, "can the laws of cause and effect be made apparent."

We are getting here to the central point of the Marxist theory of representation: the elucidation of the social relationships. Exact representations of reality must illuminate the dialectical law of motion of the social machinery, the causal nexus, in order to make it easier for man to control his own existence. Brecht held as primitive and careless representations which for one reason or another failed to perform this function. He emphasizes the hidden events which determine man's fate and points out: "The subject of the representation is thus a network of social relationships between men. Such a representation is unusual. The phenomenon cannot be understood, if it is not seen to be unusual."

Lukacs is also concerned with the reflection of the whole complex which he tries to interpret in terms of essence and appearance. While Brecht, through his stress on the contradictory nature of this unity, is in a position to show what direction the changes in social relationships must take in order to improve human existence, Lukacs' method can only give us a passive reflection of certain conditions, for example, how man is against his will entangled in the capitalist system. Whereas Lukacs' method underlines the coercive nature of the social process and thus is hardly able to stimulate a socialist impulse, Brecht's method shows clearly the potentialities for change, for intervention. Brecht attacked repeatedly the method of "empty reflection," which shows only what is and not at the same time what could be. "It is not asking enough of the theater," Brecht writes, "when one demands from it only perception, knowledge, informative illustrations of reality. Our theater must stimulate the *pleasure* in knowing, must organize the *excitement* of the process of changing reality. Our spectators have not only to hear how Prometheus was unbound, but must themselves learn the pleasure they may have in liberating him."[10] Here we see Brecht's partisanship, his commitment to the political struggles of his time. Lukacs, on the other hand, understands the partisanship of the socialist writer only "in the sense of the clarity and intelligibility" with which the artist organizes his material.

The Non-Aristotelian Conception of Art versus Aristotelian Structure

If further clarification is needed to show the opposite positions of Brecht and Lukacs, let us take the problem of catharsis. For both it is a starting point leading to wide-ranging conclusions. Brecht, the great opponent of Aristotelianism, himself characterized his plays as non-Aristotelian. Lukacs, on the other hand, attempts to base the central function of Aristotelian catharsis on life as well as art.

Incidentally, we ought to note that both did not care much about what Aristotle understood by catharsis. They were concerned with the force of the *effect* of the work of art on the public, which Aristotle discovered and was the first to formulate. Brecht, therefore, doesn't limit his anti-Aristotelian attitude to the drama, but extends it to a general principle of aesthetics. For Lukacs also, catharsis is a general category of aesthetics and is not restricted to tragedy. In his opinion, catharsis is the great exemplary process which takes place in the same way in each work of art. Starting with this position, he sees as the "innermost essence" the structure of the work of art, which remains the same through all times. This view is important because of the distinction Lukacs draws between form and technique. As he explains in *The Historical Novel*, the principles of great art are the same in Shakespeare and in the old Greeks. He is led to this concept by the importance he attributes to catharsis. In the first volume of his *Aesthetics*, he discusses this far-reaching generalization of catharsis: "It is the accepted custom in literary aesthetics to apply this (the theory of catharsis — W. M.), as it was in fact established by Aristotle, exclusively to tragedy, to the emotions of fear and pity. . . . As with all important categories of aesthetics, this one did not come from art into life but from life into art. Because catharsis was and is a permanent and significant motive in social life, its reflection must be not only an ever-recurring theme of artistic creation but it appears even among the formative forces of the aesthetic representation of reality."[1] In this way Lukacs works out the Aristotelian structure which he then raises to the level of an artistic norm.

In his essay on *Makarenko: Der Weg ins Leben*, he provides a solid base to his concept. For him, the Aristotelian theory of catharsis, as a cleansing of passions, is a heritage in which socialist society ought to be interested not only from the aesthetic point of view but also from the ethical. For Lukacs the cathartic process, which can be brought about by life as well as by art, consists in an explosion, a moral crisis when in the face of certain facts of life or of the work of art, one is shaken to such an extent that a change may take place in his thoughts and feelings. In his later years, Lukacs describes the process as follows: "Immediately, to the emotion stirred in the spectator by the new feelings which the author creates in him, a negative emotion is added: regret, even a kind of shame never to have been aware in his own life, in reality, of what the artistic creation presents so 'naturally.' It won't be necessary to discuss in greater detail the fact that there is contained in this contrast and shock both a previous fetishizing outlook on the world and its destruction by the de-fetishized image of the work of art. . . . Rilke gave us once a poetic description of the torso of an archaic Apollo. The climax of the poem—supporting the above considerations—is an appeal by the statue to the spectator: 'You must change your life.' "[12]

Elsewhere in the Makarenko essay, Lukacs adds that in class society the moral crises of its members are "resolved" by a pseudo-catharsis. With profound insight he explains how the late bourgeois theories, for instance depth psychology, transform the necessary public collision into a purely private, individual one. In class society the cleansing of passions then takes place at their own level. Under socialist conditions only the explosions do not any longer necessarily occur spontaneously, and if they do they can be evolved consciously. Also in a socialist society the collision can assume sharpness without necessarily or even typically bringing about a tragic, catastrophic end. Thus Lukacs sees in such an explosion a process through which a reaction is elicited leading to the cathartic "know thine own self."

"Catharsis is thus directed at the essence of man," writes the Hungarian critic.[13] In this sentence which apparently is non-problematic, the idealism of Lukacs' position is at its climax and the contrast with Brecht well defined. No matter how much emphasis Lukacs puts on the effect of catharsis acting only in a socio-historical concrete situation, he is really focussing on the inner ethical changing of man, not on the changing of society. According to him, man must with "a kind of shame" discover in the work of art what he has not found in reality and what challenges him to change his life. Uppermost with him are not the changing of society and the control of the economic conditions of existence but the individual within an idealistically conceived dialectic of "good and bad." Later in life, Lukacs explained why in his theory of catharsis he always speaks of a critique of *life* and not of society. If he presents these two concepts as "almost synonymous," this can only be understood from his philosophic position. Moreover, Lukacs goes on, certain aspects and appearances of life can bring about a stirring reaction without the public and even the creative artist being aware of the real social foundations.

Here lies the essential difference with Brecht, who developed an artistic method allowing him to bare precisely this awareness. He considers Aristotle's catharsis as a mystical process which has no place for a completely free, critical attitude intent on purely down-to-earth social solutions of difficulties. We don't have to concern ourselves here with the extent to which Brecht does justice in his polemic on Aristotle to the historic development of this category. What is of interest here is the contrast between these two positions and the motives which led to them. For Brecht catharsis does not offer any base, since it relates both the structure and effect of the work of art to the "inner space" of the individual in a one-sided way. Its mechanism results in the "know thine own self," not the knowledge of social conditions, the social causal nexus. Lukacs' theory is certainly not proof that the Aristotelian catharsis always means exposure to the danger of idealism and subjectivism; socialist authors have built their works on the effect of catharsis without succumbing to idealism. However, this is not the place to discuss the relationship of subject, plot and catharsis.

For Brecht, Aristotelian cathartic effect means primarily empathy.

The cleansing of passions takes place as a result of a properly speaking psychic act, namely empathy. In contrast Brecht developed a technique destined to prevent identification of the public with the hero. Readers and spectators must be led through various means—through distancing, for example, to follow what goes on critically. They must not dive into the story as into a river, but have to be given the opportunity to pause and pass judgment. Brecht's new technique of the drama has as its object to show social events as modifiable, as rid of the false glow of the eternal, the self-evident. An art that thus encourages a critical attitude doesn't impair in any way the aliveness of the characters, does not exclude great emotional effects, as Lukacs wrongly assumes. If Brecht with his method induces a critical distance from the events represented and prevents uncontrolled empathy, this doesn't mean that the author will ban any kind of empathy. He is rather concerned with the dialectical application. The spectator must be helped to identify emotionally with positive events, although not exclusively and absolutely. Brecht's method is based not only on distance but also on the dialectic of distance and empathy. What element will be used always depends on the social content and the effect aimed at.

If we follow the letter, and not the spirit, of Lukacs' statements, he turns out to be, even far more than Brecht, a strong opponent of the theory of empathy. However, his opposition does not go beyond the late bourgeois theories of art, that of Theodor Lipps, for instance, which results in a justification of psychological expressionism. The peculiar psychic act which comes out of catharsis and which Brecht calls empathy is for Lukacs not empathy but *re-living*. Later on Lukacs writes with Brecht in mind: "We can empathize with something whose objective essence is unknown or indifferent to us, but in the face of the obvious reality of its correct representation we can only be led to a re-living in which there is the consciousness that here we don't have to do with our subjectivity but with a 'world' that depends on it."[14] This, according to Lukacs, is the specific character of the re-living as opposed to the commonplace view of the theory of empathy, the cathartic effect being the strict opposite of any empathy. Brecht's passionate polemic against empathy would be based precisely on this modern prejudice which has led him to the "erroneous concept" of the distancing effect.

Only in the 60s did Lukacs take a position on the Brecht method of distancing. He did it in a rather detailed way, if one remembers his former reticence as to Brecht's work. However, he must hardly have noticed that we have here a kind of replica to his description of the artistic typical process, otherwise he wouldn't have so glaringly misrepresented Brecht's method.

We need here a rapid sketch of what Brecht understands by distancing. What he wants is to draw attention to daily life, so that the spectator can focus on it and wonder whether it couldn't be different. To behave toward reality as if it were familiar, that seemed to Brecht a fatal error. He therefore evolved a way of representation which removed from the portrayed events the obvious, the familiar, the plausible element. Things shouldn't have any longer the stamp of familiarity. What was known should be considered as strange—estranged—so as to make one aware of what had not yet been perceived, the possibility that the familiar might be changed. In the 42 theses of the *Kleines Organon*, Brecht gives us a brief definition of the distancing effect: "A distancing representation is one which lets us recognize the object but at the same time makes it appear strange." The spectator must have an event shown to him in its specificity so that he may thus recognize the possibilities of change. This, however, requires that the events be presented as historical phenomena, belonging to a certain social order. Distancing aims at destroying the false view that these social relationships are eternal conditions prescribed by nature itself. It draws attention to their contradictions and to the way they can be overcome, it is true, not by the individual since these contradictions do not have their cause and base in him, but by society, by the struggles within society."

In his controversy with Brecht, Lukacs asserts that Brecht is kicking at open doors with his distancing effect, that the old drama had without it brought about in the spectator not only the "surprise" but also the deep shock caused by the dramatic interpretation of the contradictions. Brecht would certainly not have denied it, but this doesn't affect the method of distancing. Its purpose is to point out certain social phenomena which are hard to identify and which have become "nature" for people in a capitalist society. The dramatist wishes to place them in a context that will show the influence of society. The drama of antiquity could not do it, not even with distancing, which incidentally Brecht doesn't claim to have discovered, as Lukacs seems to believe. Lukacs doesn't see that Brecht's method of distancing developed on the basis of dialectical materialism and thus offers altogether

new possibilities. In his later years Lukacs understands Brecht as little
as he did in the 30s. The only difference is that now he raises the
formalist whom he saw in Brecht to the level of a "realist against his
will" who created great works of art in spite of the distancing effect.
With complete misapprehension of Brecht's conception of art, he praises
him "for holding on to the kernel of catharsis." "In spite of his anti-
thetical position to Rilke, the latter's axiom: 'You must change your
life' governs Brecht's creative will."[15] Brecht was here more misunderstood by the Marxist Lukacs than by bourgeois critics. The obstacle
that lies in Lukacs' way is less of an aesthetic than of a conceptual and
political nature. It is rather tragic that a man who, in spite of his own
limits, made such an invaluable contribution in the domain of literature,
could not say a sensible word about the socialist classic author and the
greatest playwright of modern times.

The counterpart to Brecht's theory of distancing is Lukacs' analysis
of typification which he takes up repeatedly in his books. We cannot
here describe it in detail, especially since it went on evolving into the
60s. While Brecht developed his method in direct controversy with
the bourgeois view of art, we are struck by the fact that Lukacs sees
no essential difference between the typification of the critical realist
and that of the socialist realist. Lukacs confronts the realist with a
"double task," which he describes as follows in his book, *Probleme des
Realismus:* "Each important realist, even by abstract means, transforms
his own experience in order to get to the laws of objective reality, in
order to reach the deep, hidden conditions of social reality which
cannot be apprehended immediately. As these conditions do not lie
on the surface, as these laws are entangled and force their way to the
surface irregularly, the realist has a tremendous double task, both aesthetic and pertaining to the world view: first he has to discover the
idea content and the artistic forms of these conditions, then, his second task that cannot be separated from the first, is to cover over
through art the conditions that have been laid bare or abstracted, and
thus to achieve the 'Aufhebung' of the abstraction. Thanks to this
double action, a new immediacy emerges, a formed surface of life
which, while allowing the essence to shine in every impulse, as is not
the case in the immediacy of life, still appears as the immediacy, as the
surface of life."

In this statement we can already see Lukacs' attack on abstraction
and also the role which he ascribes to it in the process of artistic crea-

tion. His polemic against abstraction is an important support of his conception of realism. He uses it in his praise of the great masterpieces of the 19th century and in his rejection of all modern trends and technical innovations. His criticism is largely right, for example when he turns against bourgeois theories in which abstraction is used to "subtract," to do away with, all social conditions. We can only agree with his criticism of Wilhelm Worringer's famous book *Abstraktion und Einfühlung* as Worringer establishes with his concept of abstraction a mythical view of the world and of art leading to a complete devaluation of the development of art since the Renaissance. But Lukacs ignores totally the projected solutions which were proposed on the Marxist side, by Brecht for instance, who uses them to clarify the social causal complex. He does this because he sees abstraction within a certain field of tension which is basically mechanistic, even though he calls it dialectical. Within the "double task" proposed to realism, Lukacs affirms the role of abstraction without which perhaps no typification is possible. Abstraction, Lukacs explains, is used by the artist in the process of creation to penetrate through the surface in order to render visible the objective reality, the social conditions. This is also Brecht's concern. But Lukacs introduces the category of immediacy with which he raises abstraction to a new level. There is no question that abstraction must be understood within a dialectical relationship, as its absolute use would prevent a realistic creation. Lukacs, however, does not use it to show the spectator where the social attack must follow. Lukacs' "double task" is a mechanistic juxtaposition, not a dialectical process in the sense of the negation of the negation when the abstraction would be transformed by being raised to a higher level. He uses that "double task" to cover over again with a blanket of immediacy all the social relationships that had been disclosed. Immediacy is for him the expression of the abundance of outer appearances, of the multiplicity of individual connections. In this way Lukacs constructs the theoretical foundation for his postulate of "*the* realistic way of creation." Thus the "organic plot" originating in the complex psychological entanglement of the individual fate, becomes the essential criterion. Lukacs' process of typification is so structured as to exclude all new literary devices such as montage, parable, distancing, interruption of plot, etc., to make them appear as if they were strange bodies, anti-realistic elements.

New Artistic Devices

When Lukacs happens to mention montage, his tone which is generally measured and analytic becomes accusatory and dogmatic. The technique of montage is for him the cardinal sin of the modern artist. Furthermore, Lukacs uses the term montage as a kind of synonym for many other techniques developed in the last fifty years. In his book, *The Historical Novel*, he writes: "On the one hand montage as art is the culmination of the false trends of naturalism because it abandons that superficial reconstruction of verbal and emotional experience which the old naturalism had considered as its task; on the other hand montage is at the same time the culmination of formalism, as the linkage of particular points has nothing any longer to do with the objective dialectic of man's experience; on the contrary montage establishes merely external connections." It is no coincidence that the first criticism Lukacs makes of montage, although in terms of a definite basic tendency, is directed at the abandonment of the "verbal and emotional experience," for this is the logical consequence of his view of the process of typification and of the role which the category of immediacy plays in it. In his rejection of all new creative techniques, Lukacs even calls somewhere else on Friedrich Engels as a star witness to the unsuitability of "abstract literature of facts" and of montage. He derives the Marxist foundation of his theory of "organic narrative" from Engels' criticism of Karl Beck. When Ilya Ehrenburg, at the First Congress of Soviet Writers, proclaimed that socialist artists were greatly interested in reportage, short-hand notes, reports, protocols and diaries, Lukacs concluded: "This is precisely the description of the style of Dos Passos as seen by Sinclair Lewis."[16] Dos Passos is one of the writers with whom Lukacs "wipes the floor," as Brecht used to say. The reactionary turn taken by the Dos Passos of the 30s is no proof of the unsuitability of the montage technique he made use of, especially not from the point of view of Lukacs who knew how to derive realism from a reactionary attitude. Brecht is not concerned with the defense of Dos Passos' technique. At the time he remarked: "I don't see why I should propagandize on behalf of or against the Dos Passos technique of montage." The issue was the realistic use of new possibilities and the password was, not: back to before Dos Passos, but on, beyond Dos Passos. The new subject matter and new social aims required a different style both of plot and construction of characters from that which Balzac and Tolstoy had developed. Without naming Lukacs but with him in mind, Brecht writes in the 30s with bitterness: "When certain people see new forms, they start to yell accusingly: 'Formalism!' but they themselves are the worst formalists, worshipers of old forms at any price, people who only look at, only pay attention to the form, and make of it the sole object of their analyses."[17] For that matter the theatrical workers' groups in the 20s and 30s had already shown how montage can be practically adapted to the representation of great socio-political controversies.

For Brecht, the realist form results primarily from the questioning of reality and not from aesthetics. What was meaningful to him was not the description of the surface of the empirical world, but how things really are. He subordinates the choice of literary forms and of technical means to the requirements of the class struggle. That's why we encounter in his books the most varied forms and genres, the didactic play, the chronicle, the historical drama, the parable and both Aristotelian and non-Aristotelian techniques. For him the forms are not realistic or non-realistic "in themselves" but turn out to be one or the other when they aim at a certain goal, when they are used with a definite subject. "Anybody," Brecht writes, "who does not want to give a purely formalist definition of realism (as what was understood by realism in the epoch of the bourgeois novel of the 90's) can have all sorts of objections against such narrative techniques as montage, inner monologue or distancing, but he can't do it from the point of view of realism. Of course, there is a kind of inner monologue which must be described as formalistic, but we have also a realistic inner monologue; with montage we can show the world as crooked but we can also show it right, there is no doubt about that. On the question of pure form one should not speak lightly in the name of Marxism. That is not Marxist." Brecht did not make use of the new forms for their novelty's sake but because the old ones, as he says himself, were an encumbrance in the battles that had to be fought. He couldn't be satisfied with any statement which didn't take into consideration the great class conflicts.

Definition of Realism

Although Lukacs has always declared himself a supporter of socialist realism, he gives nowhere in his numerous writings a workable definition of this method. Surely this cannot be explained only by the scholar's reluctance to give a definition. His concept of realism remained oriented on the great realists of the 19th century whose creative art he tried to put in the service of the socialist writer, but in so doing he blurred the limits between socialist and critical realism. When Lukacs comes with detailed definitions, as in his book of essays *Balzac und der französische Realismus*, his starting point is always critical realism. He writes: "Realism is the knowledge that artistic creation is neither a dead average, as naturalism believes, nor an individual principle that falls apart and dissolves into nothingness, something mechanistic, forced, or occupied with the extremes of non-recurring events. The central category and criterion of the realistic concept of literature, the type in terms of character and situation, is a definite synthesis which links organically the general and the individual. What makes a type is not its average nature nor its individual character—no matter how profoundly seen—but the fact that in it all the human and the important social determining impulses of a historical period run together and cross each other, the fact that the creation of the type shows these impulses in the culmination of the possibilities they contain, in the most extreme representation of the extreme, showing concretely at the same time the summit and the frontiers of the totality of man and of the epoch."

Brecht, who was always trying to give working definitions of realism, stresses in contrast to Lukacs the new social conditions which the socialist writer has to take into account. In the 50's, Brecht summed up his thoughts on socialist realism in ten theses. In a way these represent the conclusion of the Brecht-Lukacs controversy. "What socialist realism is," Brecht says, "should not simply be derived from present works or styles. The criterion should not be whether a work of art resembles certain other works of art which pass as representations of socialist realism, but whether it is socialist and realistic:

1. Realist art is militant art. It combats false views of reality and forces which are contrary to the true interests of men. It makes possible correct views and supports the productive forces.

2. Realist artists stress the sensuous, the "earthly," what is in the widest sense of the word the typical (historically significant).

3. Realist artists emphasize the *becoming* and *disappearing*. They think historically.

4. Realist artists represent *contradictions* in men and in their relationships and show under what conditions these develop.

5. Realist artists are interested in *changes* in men and relationships, both the continuing changes and the sudden ones.

6. Realist artists represent the power of ideas and also their material base.

7. Socialist-realist artists are human, that is, friendly toward men; they represent relationships between men in such a way as to strengthen the socialist impulses. These are reinforced through practical insights into the social mechanism and by becoming enjoyable in themselves.

8. The socialist-realist artists maintain a realist attitude not only toward their theme but also toward their public.

9. The socialist-realist artists take into account the degree of education and the class background of their public as well as the condition of the class conflicts.

10. The socialist-realist artists view reality from the point of view of the working population and of the intellectuals allied to it, who are for socialism.

REFERENCES

1. Bertolt Brecht, *Schriften zur Literatur und Kunst,* Vol. II (Berlin and Weimar, 1966), p. 56. When there is no other indication, the Brecht quotations are from *Schriften zur Literatur und Kunst.*
2. Günter Fröschner, *Die Herausbildung und Entwicklung der gechichtsphilosophischen Anschauungen von Georg Lukacs.* PhD. dissertation, Institute of Social Sciences of the Central Committee of the German Unity Party, (Berlin, 1965).
3. Georg Lukacs, *Der historische Roman* (Berlin, 1955), p. 183.
4. Berliner Ensemble, *Theaterarbeit* (Dresden, o.J.), p. 253/4.
5. Georg Lukacs, *Wider den missverstandenen Realismus* (Hamburg, 1958), p. 96.
6. Bertolt Brecht, *Schriften zum Theater* (Berlin, 1964), Vol. III, p. 201.
7. Georg Lukacs, *Beiträge zur Gechichte der Aesthetik* (Berlin, 1954), p. 204.
8. George Lukacs, *Probleme des Realismus* (Berlin, 1955), pp. 13-14.
9. Bertolt Brecht, *Schriften zum Theater* (Berlin, 1964), Vol. III, pp. 116-117.
10. Bertolt Brecht, *Schriften zum Theater* (Berlin, 1964), Vol. VII, p. 76.

11. Georg Lukacs, *Die Eigenart des Aesthetischen* 1.Halbband (Berlin-Spandau/ Neuwied am Rhein, 1963), p. 811.
12. *Loc. cit.*, p. 818.
13. Georg Lukacs, *Die Eigenart des Aesthetischen* 2. Halbband, (Berlin-Spandau/Neuwied am Rhein, 1963), p. 868.
14. *Ibid.*, p. 187.
15. *Ibid.*, p. 825.
16. Georg Lukacs, *Probleme des Realismus* (Berlin, 1955), p. 142.
17. Bertolt Brecht, *Schriften zum Theater*, Vol. III (Berlin and Weimar, 1964), p. 135.

SOCIALIST REALISM

At the first annual conference of our Writers' Union (early November, 1966), we took stock of a whole epoch of literary development which began around 1959 and is about to end now. In this period, the discussion of aesthetic questions played a far greater role than before. Starting from the needs of our artistic development, the main effort was to define and to deepen the theory of socialist realism. This effort has received valuable impetus from the study of proletarian and socialist traditions in art.

For example, examination of the so-called "artist's aesthetic" has helped us to overcome in a considerable measure certain limitations of the concept of realism. I have in mind statements by Johannes R. Becher, Bertolt Brecht, Hanns Eisler, Anna Seghers, etc., written to throw light on their own work and the art of their times. The concept of realism which is incorporated in their writings has helped us to revise the views of Georg Lukacs, who had derived his criteria primarily from the laws of form and composition in the bourgeois realism of past centuries.

For socialist realism, it is irrelevant to set down which structure, which form, it uses. It is possible to give a true view of the world through the use of inner monologue or literary montage, but it is also possible to distort it, and the same applies to the Aristotelian dramatic rules versus the non-Aristotelian. What matters is that a work of art, to quote Brecht, "while laying bare the social causal nexus, should give us insight into the social machinery" and thus make us aware of the *socialist momentum*. In spite of occasional relapses, this concept has been adopted by us. This is then a dynamic concept of realism, open-ended in front—and capable of rendering all historical changes with all kinds of innovation in form and composition. Christa Wolf's narrative, *Divided Heaven*, and Konrad Wolf's moving picture of it, as well as Hermann Kant's *The Aula*, provide striking examples for the contention that formal criteria are not what makes a book socialist and realist.

If today we are placing great emphasis on formal criteria, this is mainly in response to a non-historical, hence abstract, conception of literary quality. Certain progressive writers from West Germany defend the thesis of a single, undivided German literature. For them literature is a language indifferent to classes and ideologies, deriving its standards from itself alone. To provide an illustration, Heinrich Böll is compared to Dieter Noll and the latter is declared not to make the grade, aesthetically speaking. But when we bring the two authors together, while Böll can certainly teach Noll a thing or two in language and form, it is certain that Noll is in advance in more important respects. Noll is attempting, especially in the second volume of *Werner Holt*, to master a subject which has not yet entered Böll's field of vision.

Not only the progressive West German authors but, even more, class antagonists present to us on a silver tray abstract judgments concerning literary quality; they offer norms intended to be valid for all Germany in which the common element, our language and its formal matter, is taken as an absolute, without regard to the concrete social content which this literature incorporates.

In our Republic also, some authors and critics had adopted this same formal aesthetic approach to literature, against which Anna Seghers has intervened several times in discussions. She has stressed repeatedly that each period in art—from antiquity to the present time —always begins with the discovery of a new reality, be it outside of or within man. "Our reality," she says, "here in the GDR is completely new, and for the first time it is being represented by German writers." Anna Seghers encourages our writers in their effort to give shape to the immediate presence of socialism and not to pay attention to any notice board that might stand at the entrance of this new poetic terra incognita. As we know, Brecht, when he went over to the position of the working class in his "Svendborg Poems," was also blamed for "a loss in aesthetic substance."

This does not mean that we abandon literary value judgments. But it is completely irrelevant to juxtapose two different phases of historical development like those of the Federal Republic and of the GDR, and to compare them only from the viewpoint of form and language. The development of aesthetic criteria may be continuous, but it may also be interrupted, as when a new object is to be represented.

In the annual conference of our Writers' Union, it has been pointed out, and rightly so, that in recent years a whole series of innovations in language and form have appeared, in lyrical as well as in epic works. But we are not yet satisfied with what has already been achieved.

As our socialist life does not develop evenly, so our literary evolution is not without its contradictions. There is nothing unusual in this; it is completely normal. Hence at the Writers' Conference a great many problems were discussed, certain results were achieved, certain agreements were aimed at. There are persisting differences of opinion—and how could it be otherwise?—on a few points, as well as a series of open questions.

"I can't forget for one minute," says Anna Seghers, "that the GDR stands before a new phase in the development of socialism. Its realization in a part of what was formerly Germany takes place in a terribly war-threatened world." This expresses very clearly our position and our responsibility in this discussion. Our artistic development and our debates on aesthetic problems have aroused strong interest—especially since 1961—in West German publications. This does not surprise us, since aggressive forces in the Federal Republic are always trying to do us injury wherever they can. What is more surprising is the willingness of a few Marxists to use these publications and to express through this means vehement criticism against our art and aesthetic concepts in particular as well as more generally against certain aspects of our social order. These attacks are made under the pretext of purifying Marxism from dogmatism. It seems to me that Ernst Fischer for example in his polemical writing on *Art and Co-existence* not only looks in the wrong direction but also in his purifying process throws out the baby with the bath water. In the future we shall go on to foster an art that helps man to find his way in our world. For the present it would undoubtedly be wrong, as Anna Seghers has said, to "conceal our shortcomings." Still, we do not believe that our main artistic task is, or ought to be, to give an account of these shortcomings.

I have chosen a few questions around which our recent discussions centered, without trying to be exhaustive and without assigning to them an order of importance.

At the center of our discussion on aesthetics is naturally the image of man as formed by our literature. With Ole Bienkopp we finally have a popular hero in the literal meaning of the term. His actions show us how far a simple man can go when his creative force is liberated. Ole belongs with those *who are erecting the house of socialism*. If it is not his lot to work with us in making this house livable, it is primarily because he gets caught in spontaneity, "the hereditary evil of the eternally dispossessed." The contradictory struggle toward an Aufhebung of alienation is presented here in a particularly striking way. It is true that next to Ole Bienkopp others have taken their place, Hannes Balla or Stephen Beck. One notes a certain evolution. Still, in our literary image of man, a certain something recurs, an element of spontaneity, a factor of disturbance between the "I" and the "we." Our writers themselves have sometimes criticized the fact that our literature gives a distorted picture of those men who day in and day out are working for the realization of socialism. The prototype of our historical change is a man who has not only got rid of his mistrust concerning his own strength but is also highly conscious of that strength. This well-informed man who possesses both creative initiative and familiarity with theory hardly appears in our literature. I don't want to be misunderstood. What is needed is not merely a more marked "intellectual physiognomy," with the so-called intellectual novel as a model. The great need now is for a *stronger artistic representation* of the psychospiritual process through which man comes to grips with his times and his world. Since activity and consciousness both represent the determining characteristics of the new man, the difference from the intellectuality of the critical-realist novel becomes obvious. Knowledge of the laws of development in society gives to man's activity its historical singleness of purpose. In the well-informed man we see the integration of his active side, as Marx described it in his eleventh thesis on Feuerbach. ["The philosophers have only *interpreted* the world, in various ways; the point, however, is to *change* it." Eds.]

Our discussion has also shown that it is necessary to clarify what is central to our notion of realism, the concept of applied humanism in a time when socialism is being built under the conditions of an expanding technical revolution. The creation of the new socialist reality, the education of the well-informed man who is not yet "the totally developed individual" of whom Marx spoke but who nevertheless represents an important step in the direction of this "total" man, all this is taking place here and today in an epoch of scientific advance. In the natural process of exchange between man and his world, the productive force of science serves as the mediating agent. This is also true, figuratively, for the relationship of art to reality. Shortly before his death, Brecht expressed the thought that the complicated tasks that our artists have to face demand a high degree of scientific clarity. Artistic work is a process that goes on in accordance with scientific methods and there's no escaping this fact. This does not mean that art is treated scientifically, but that the artist, if he wants to say something of significance about his world, has to take into consideration the results of science in a far greater measure than has been the case so far. One of our authors, Inge von Wangenheim, said recently: "The cosy idyll of $a^2 + b^2$ belongs to our past; now we have before us the peaks of differential calculus. In literature too."

There has been much discussion lately of the importance in the process of artistic creation to be attributed to the discoveries of modern natural science, medicine, cybernetics, semiotics and other disciplines. Surely, such influences are only at their beginning. No matter what fascination is exerted on the artist by these new discoveries, we should not lose sight of the other possibilities. Speaking of the theater in the "age of science," Brecht stressed the dominating role of the social sciences, primarily of Marxist-Leninism, in uncovering the "social causal nexus." For him, philosophy and psychology were of great importance. A sociology based on science could put an end to the situation in which writers find themselves even today, attempting to forge ahead with their books in terrain still predominantly anonymous, sociologically speaking. This is all the more to be deplored in that the discoveries writers make under these conditions are neglected for purposes of research, although they do indeed serve to supply materials for subjective reflections and for speculation. But there can be no substitute for scientific research dealing with the influence of art, something that would make possible the use of artistic means in the promotion of socialist man. The transformation of the public into a co-actor ("Ko-Fabulierer," Brecht) doesn't proceed at a steady pace. Exact knowledge on this subject can be of importance in determining how to address the public, how to gain access to it, even in the choice of genres and means. To clarify such questions our keenest attention is required since our class enemy, with the help of mass media such as TV and radio, is constantly trying to influence the population of the GDR in our common language.

The stage of development which our literature has just gone through is characterized by the thrust toward interpretation of our immediate present. The "commitment to socialism" as the predominating literary theme was soon combined with demonstrations of the workability of socialism. This concern with the immediate reality of socialism was pre-conditioned by the mastering of the past in the form of an anti-fascist orientation. The latter has not yet been in any way superseded or "exhausted." It can be recognized in the books that have a durable

impact as a basic force in the interpretation of the present and is, in
the best sense of the word, "aufgehoben" in them. At the same time, socialism has already its past in some of the recent works. (The clearest
example is *The Aula*.) Each artist is conscious of the fact that the historical development is three-dimensional, that is, that the present is
certainly sequence and result of the past and at the same time an in-
timation of the future, or, as Brecht says, "Today goes into tomorrow,
fed by yesterday." However the creation of the future, *the perspective*,
is the weakest point of the shaping of socialist life. On one hand these
are the natural growing pains of socialist experience. On the other hand
the individual writer, in order to create this perspective, must himself
acquire the "vision of the leader and planner" that would enable him
to survey the changes now taking place and to interpret them. As
Johannes R. Becher once said, "the only man who can speak of the
future is he who has one, and the only man who has a future is he
who can look ahead and see what is commonly called a perspective.
A perspective is the result of a concept." Still, writers are surely correct when they point to and criticize the Achilles heel of the social
sciences, their so far insufficiently developed prognostic capacity.
There is also the shortcoming of our not having worked out enough
theoretical models of our future social evolution. We should equally
accept the fact that whatever basic principles for our economy have
been worked out, much of it is not yet applicable in the sense of a
model for the social development in the next few years. What does
it mean when in the course of the technical revolution man steps out
increasingly from the manufacturing process? What patterns are there
for this general evolution? What will be the socio-psychological, spiritual, emotional repercussions on the behavior of the individual? These
and other similar questions are to be answered by theoreticians mainly,
but the writer is by no means free of a responsibility to give his own
answer also.

*   *   *

No realistic or humanistic work of the past or of the present is
only the mirrored image of its time, a mere reproduction of "what
is." In each artistic category, and in literature also, a contradiction
has to be solved between what is and what could or should be, between
ideal and reality, between the morrow which will see the realization
of our wishes and the today in which these wishes are born. The basic
question of socialist realism is the formation of the dialectic of the

immediately given reality and the possibility. That is, the socialist realist cannot be only concerned with an interpretation of reality. For him reality has many layers; it is constantly evolving. From his point of view, which corresponds to the objective dialectic of life, not everything has the same value, the same specific weight. In real life, the new and the old, what is becoming and what is decaying, coexist, often within the same social phenomenon. This doesn't make it any easier, even for one who stands on the right side of the social parallelogram of forces, to determine at first sight what a social phenomenon is like. For, as a general rule, the new element is not heralded by trumpets and cymbals and does not appear as something mature and complete. It always first emerges in human development as an actual possibility. So the main concern of a socialist realist cannot be the mere quest for factual data nor the simple representation of the immediately given. What he wants is to discover, select and shape the possibilities which inhere in reality and determine the development of life. What matters is not only that the individual participate through literature in the complex experience of man as a member of his species and thus become conscious of his place in the world, of his concrete historical position in society. He first of all wants to know where he is going. Questions like this—questions about the meaning of life—can be answered only by a literature that points beyond the here and now and knows how to explore the real possibilities of the human species. Of course when we try to shape today the form of tomorrow, we cannot follow an exact historical direction. What we do is play through, so to say, the real possibilities for man's actions. With such a concept of the path-breaking function of socialist literature, the work of art becomes the arena of the humanly possible, the display of the potentialities of the human species which have remained dormant and whose development —from germination to complete flowering—involves both present and future. This means not only orientation toward this goal but also the activation of all creative potential to attain it. Thus the socialist realist work is in a wider sense the artistic counterpart of a program of action, although in a many-sided and complex way.

The obstacles in this direction in the field of imaginative literature as well as in theory are many and varied. For a time in our literature (and the trait still exists here and there), stress was put on a simple—positivistic—display of facts. We are aware that, from the point of view of historical development, there are different shapes or sequences in the artistic conquest of a new object or a new theme. The first stage is most concerned with the mere enumeration of data. Johannes R. Becher remarks that to present reality simply as raw material, or at best as a "half-finished product," is typical of the new in "its first stammer. . . . The new can be recognized by its drunken babble, by the fact that it has not yet found its language. It has to learn how to talk." The naturalistic trends which appear then must be held as a transitional stage toward socialist realism. This is a point that socialist realism has in common with all literatures in formation. As Brecht says, "to throw to the public raw statements of facts, artificially provided with tendencies, this happens in the first phase of a socially ascendant epoch. There is often then a neglect of form." This phenomenon is the "natural" toll that has to be paid at the first stage of catching hold of new artistic themes. Another obstacle in the path of literary development in this area has been insufficient philosophic penetration of the process of historic development.

A further difficulty has been a tendency toward schematic transposition of conflicts from the antagonistic class society to our circumstances. The basic situation that got the hardest wear and tear was the model of alienation, the estrangement between the individual and the group, in both directions. The stress appearing now and then on errors and deficiencies in the construction of socialism led to an "anti-dogmatic neo-schematism." In extreme cases the actual dialectic of our development was reduced to an either-or proposition. An impassable wall was erected between the present and the future, the latter reprsented as clear and luminous against the grey daily reality of the present. This point of view finds its clearest expression in *Art and Coexistence* by Ernst Fischer. He supplements science, which he erroneously views as a mere reduction of reality to the factual (p. 222), with utopia, which means for Fischer what is not realized but factually possible. (Wasn't scientific socialism as created by Marx and Engels a factual possibility which became a reality after the October revolution? While Fischer rigs himself up a reduced set of conceptual tools, he necessarily has to have recourse to such "supplement." It's downright weird to observe how Fischer makes a scarecrow out of an object in order to impale it polemically. The process, however, matters less than the attitude.) According to Fischer, the dream (the utopia) comes before the thing, then the criticism (of the intellectuals) follows. How and by what means the thing (socialism) is realized, is apparently quite irrelevant. Bloch's principle, hope, is striven for in order to push ahead the utopia as an ideal state to be realized in some distant future. As Ernst Bloch says, "while the intellectual keeps before his eyes the utopian goal steady and true, he endeavors through criticism to prevent the utopia from being degraded to the level of something already reached, from being thrown like golden sand to blind men." (p. 79/80) No wonder that to Fischer socialism appears "deficient" in the countries that are building it. At the base of the tearing apart of reality from real possibility, we have not only confusion and doubts concerning the future realizability of the ideal but primarily the deep refusal to believe that it can be realized in daily life.

Those writers who in their books concentrate on the errors and deficiencies in socialist construction generally justify their attitude by quoting Hegel: "What is true is the whole." (Preface to the *Phenomenology of the Spirit*). However, they omit as a rule to quote what follows, "The whole, however, is only the essence becoming complete through its development." The cognitive aspect of socialist realism as it pertains to the problem of truth needs a more thorough elaboration. We must also investigate more closely the specific character of the truth relationship. We must see it, that is, in the context of axiologic considerations which in many of their aspects have been neglected in Marxist aesthetics; problems of the beautiful, noble, tragic, comic, etc. must be more than heretofore brought into the focus of scientific investigations. "Should one not tell the truth?" Bertolt Brecht asks. "That sounds a little as if only courage were needed, where none should be needed. But it takes also talent and knowledge . . . to tell the truth often may mean to exercise criticism. But the whole truth contains that which is coming into being."

The debates concerning interpretations and applications of the concept of myth by some Marxists (for example Roger Garaudy, Conrad Farner, Ernst Fischer) are related to these problems. While it is true that in some instances the concept of myth has been employed loosely, the ideological importance of the myth problem now requires a closer investigation of the assumption that with the help of the concept of myth socialist realism (or simply realism) can be made more precise. We are told, for example, that the creation of myths has been the main function of art from its beginning until today. The formative power of the myth and its capability to give us a visionary insight into the future contained in the present is being made an absolute and declared as the essence of the matter. We consider as completely legitimate the wish to give greater weight within the theory of socialist realism to an imaginative "dreaming ahead," as Lenin once put it. But we don't see why the concept of myth has to intervene. In this way one forgets that the myth has been and could only be "a valid expression of thinking and living" (Kerenyi) in a single historically limited period of the evolution of mankind, its infancy. Originally the myth constituted an historically necessary element of the mastering of practical life and as such cannot be separated from the belief in destiny. Myth is the adequate expression of a certain undeveloped social stage. Mythical thought is a form of cognition with a pre-scientific character. At the time of Euripides, it was already in decline in ancient Greece because of the rapidly increasing mastery over nature, bringing about the advance of philosophy and science. This again erased the conditions in which mythology and the belief in fate could thrive. Of course the degree of development of the productive forces was not yet high enough to do away with every mythical, even religious, disguise. Even within the monotheistic religions a certain survival of mythology can be traced. However, we have to keep clearly in mind that a complex society with its many social relationships and class interactions can no longer be represented in terms of myth. Our present cannot be adequately conceived and interpreted in yesterday's terms, with the myth as the "sacred" tradition of the tribe or the nation. The characteristic of the myth is that it is "pre-historical," and that it appears in the guise of "timelessness," of the "eternally human."

At the present level of our cognitive possibilities, whose complexity is the result of the total history of mankind, it is impossible to go back to mythic thinking without abandoning the heights of cognitive development that have been reached. As Marx said, "a man cannot be a child again without becoming infantile." The conscious return of imperialist ideologists to myth—in philosophy, art, daily life, etc.—serves only one purpose, namely, to disguise the loss of perspective which characterizes imperialist ideology. Irrational mythical thinking disbars a coherent view of our time and prevents the look into the future. It serves not only as a kind of ideological "appeasement" but also as an instrument of mobilization. Nietzsche, Stefan George, and Ernst Jünger are typical builders of myths having a nationalistic or racist character. Many bourgeois realists who in our time have professed belief in myth, like Thomas Mann, Hermann Broch, etc., used the traditional myths in the choice of material, motifs, symbols, characters, etc., but they themselves created none, although they may have believed they did (cf. Thomas Mann in *Joseph and his Brothers*). Most of these authors see in the untouched, immediate entity of the myth a sort of humanistic anti-world as a kind of preservative against the harmful influence of capitalist alienation in the epoch of imperialism. In my opinion, myth nowadays is only "viable" as irrationalistic mythologizing. Poetic generalizations centered around symbols like Moloch, Leviathan or Prometheus are not myths any longer. Therefore neither are Becher's Prometheus, nor Goethe's poem by the same title, nor Shelley's "Prometheus Unbound," nor Kafka's "The Vulture" myths properly speaking. Rilke's conversion of the symbolism of darkness and light in the Gospel according to St. John in his *Book of Hours* is equally no modern myth, although we shouldn't overlook certain mythical remains. Such mythical elements are also to be found in his "Duino Elegies." Rilke also considers Orpheus as a kind of mythical ancient metaphor which unites extremes and symbolizes for him "pure contradiction." In my opinion certain mythical remains are visible in Rilke's turning of images *into religious utopianism*. But I refuse to designate simply as irrationalism or myth whatever the humanist artist has not been able to cope with in his effort to throw light on the meaning of life. I also hold it as questionable when parables like Samuel Beckett's "Waiting for Godot" are described as myths simply because the flight into timelessness and the "eternally human" give them certain resemblance to myths.

I don't want to be misunderstood: the roots of our image of man reach deep into antiquity's world of myths and legends. The utilization of material, motifs, symbols, etc., stemming from this world has accompanied the humanist and artistic creation of each period since the Renaissance. Even in socialism such close connection is not only wholly legitimate or a matter of respect for that tradition but also one of the possible ways of making generalizations and statements of literary validity about our time with the help of previously created basic situations. Of course we always have to interpret anew the characters, symbols, etc., from the socialist point of view. Socialist writers like Johannes R. Becher, Anna Seghers, Georg Maurer, Franz Fühmann and others have proved abundantly that, if the tradition is properly understood, such motifs, metaphors and characters are not only decoration but a necessary artistic element in the interpretation of the present.

In our Conference the problem of the intelligibility of realistic art here and today was the focus for a whole series of questions concerning the use of parables, factual data (the principle of documentation in the art of the present), the creation of images, the guiding function of socialist art, etc. In the discussion of poetry, a position was taken against obscurity as a modern trait. But the question of the intelligibility of socialist art in our time has not been solved and theoreticians are still concerned with it. The complexity of structure of many works of art has often been explained by the complexity of present reality. The answer to this argument has been that each period has its own difficulties and none can be understood easily, since the artists always proceed from an historically given perspective of knowledge and of cognitive potentiality in their interpretation of reality. The refutation is essentially correct. But it does not answer the question: what special difficulties stand in the way of socialist artists today? What precisely are these difficulties? On one hand, we have the comparatively new flow of communications—movies, radio, television and other so-called mass media. The artist must be aware of them since they have altered the receptivity of his public. These media make possible and even favor new possibilities of interpretation because of the altered structure of space-time relationships (what has been called the time-aspect of space and the space-aspect of time) or the so-called problem of simultaneity which has been a concern of late bourgeois philosophy and art since Bergson.

On the other hand the cognitive potentialities have not only increased but we also know much more about our world than was known in the 19th century. So there has been both a qualitative and quantitative change. Our socialist understanding of the laws of historical change produces in man an entirely different way of thinking and behaving from that of people who doubt the meaning of life as a result of the loss of perspective characteristic of the crisis in imperialistic ideology (an expression of the loss of perspective of capitalism as a system).

Another phenomenon has been pointed out by many bourgeois humanist and realist artists, generally in a negative way. They question the possibility of portraying our present world. They base themselves, as for example Dürrenmatt, on the assumption that science has taken away from art a number of subjects, has reduced the domain of artistic subjects. True, this question is not properly answered, is not even properly posed. But the problem can be seen just the same, and it is that in our century social reality is less immediately apprehended in many respects. In contrast to the 19th century, direct comprehension and interpretation are often beyond our grasp. As Brecht once said, the situation has become complicated because "a simple reproduction of reality says less than ever about this reality. A photograph of a Krupp or AEG factory yields almost no information about them. Reality properly speaking slips into the functional." To give an example: in the 19th century, the capitalist was for the worker as a rule the head of the factory in which he worked, and was known to him. There was a direct confrontation of worker and capitalist. The situation changed somewhat with the emergence of the joint-stock company and more radically when the monopolies appeared. The board of directors of a particular enterprise is for today's working man an almost "depersonalized"—anonymous—governing apparatus whose members he as a rule does not know, although he may have seen their names or their pictures in the newspapers or on television. But this anonymous "apparatus" functions. It is exceedingly difficult to transpose into images these conditions and relationships which remain to the individual obscure and even abstract and eery. It is difficult to make these relationships and functions vividly clear, so that the reader or the spectator can see them and apprehend them. In most cases this is possible only through indirect presentation. We may have here one explanation for the frequent use of the parable and similar forms in the art of the 20th century.

However it may be, the fact is that the solutions to artistic problems—in poetry, in the drama and in the novel—are different from those of the 19th century. We do not propose to canonize any single artistic method. In art things are not simple as with logic: Aristotelian logic has been completely transformed and raised to a new level in the modern form of mathematical logic. In art, the non-Aristotelian as well as the Aristotelian theater continue to coexist (the latter in a modified, more developed form in comparison with the 19th century). One can write novels like Arnold Zweig but also like Hermann Kant (*The Aula*). As we know, Brecht also wrote Aristotelian plays when the subject demanded that form, as, for example, *Señora Carrar's Guns*. Sometimes, to retain traditional forms of representation and dramatic devices can also hinder the development of the conflict. Hero-anti-hero, action-reaction, these basic dramatic situations are still possible today. However, I am of the opinion that with the exception of the experi-

mental film, "Divided Heaven," our film and television industry does
not yet make use of all the potentialities we have at our disposal to
represent new conflicts through adequate means. This becomes clear
when we compare our production with some of the new Soviet movies,
like "Lenin in Poland," "Good Morning, Here am I," "The Last Month
of Autumn," etc. Statements by critics about the last-named movie,
for example, that there is here no solution, demonstrate how novel the
solution of the conflict is. For this film does have a solution but neither
as a traditional "ending" nor in the way of the so-called open-end
plays. The conflict is not built on the causal sequence of exterior
events. The old father who feels isolated carries the conflict within
himself—on the spiritual and psychical level. We have here no antagonist. The function of antagonist, or rather of co-actor, is taken
by the world of his children. His encounter with this world helps him
to overcome his loneliness and gives him the assurance that his sons
will have lives richer in content than his was. He goes home feeling
that he has not lived in vain.

Now concepts like "intelligible," even "popular," are very loose,
subject not merely to historical change and development. Their meaning has a relatively great elasticity which corresponds to life itself. A
great many factors, both immediate and historical, determine who will
understand what goes on in given social and personal conditions. When
Johannes R. Becher at the beginning of 1950 wrote his "New German
Volkslieder," which correspond to and are the expression of a very
definite single social situation (cf. Horst Haase, *Dichten und Denken*,
p. 66 ff.), he influenced the young poet Günter Kunert, who wrote
very differently from Becher in his lieder. Kunert at that time was—
and is still, partly—a difficult poet in many respects, and yet he can
be understood, only not by anybody at any time. This depends on
the degree of maturity of the public. Also our public has drifted away
from reading poetry and lacks the poetic experience—a repercussion
of capitalistic alienation. At school everyone studies his own language,
but access to poetry is more complex as the symbolic values and the
traditional motifs often go back to antiquity. A comparison with music
will make this clearer: the audience can penetrate fully the ideal spiritual content only with the knowledge of the language of form. In
literature this knowledge is sometimes considered superfluous but to
me this is an oversimplification.

In spite of everything, intelligibility remains a basic characteristic of any socialist art. If art is to have influence, if it is to achieve certain —socialist—goals, it has to be intelligible. For Brecht "realist," "intelligible" and "popular" were synonymous concepts. (And we ought to add that for Brecht "popularity" and "partisanship" were two sides of the same thing.)

These few hints are meant to give a degree of insight, as a kind of sample, into the problems that were discussed. I should still mention that scholars interested in literary theory and aesthetics since 1962/63 have been following our literary development with livelier discussions than previously. As a result new points of departure in method have been established. Sharing in this development is the study of "New Criticism" by the specialist in English and American literature, Robert Weimann. In the very recent discussions on realism authors have participated actively. One of the most interesting works concerning questions of creativity in our contemporary socialist literature is the essay by Inge von Wangenheim, *History and Our Histories, Thoughts of an Author.*

Elisabeth Simons

SOCIALIST REALISM—DEVELOPMENT OF THE THEORY IN THE GERMAN DEMOCRATIC REPUBLIC SINCE 1955

The theses below have been prepared by a literary working group in the Institute for Social Sciences of the Central Committee of the Socialist Unity Party. This group intends to analyze the German contribution to the theory of socialist realism, but will limit itself to the sphere of literary aesthetics. By theory of socialist realism the authors understand the scientific generalization of the relationships between literature and life in the epoch of transition from capitalism to socialism and of socialist construction. In examining the literary creative process and its aesthetic reflection, they go "far beyond the purely literary" (Johannes R. Becher). They consider their research as an appropriate way to work out scientific views for the planning and leading of activities in the literary community.

This cultural and political aim determined the choice of the period and the main problems under analysis. We are concerned with the historical process of the continuing development of Marxist-Leninist aesthetic theory and of its confirmation and creative correction in the practice of the socialist literary community.

The theory of socialist realism develops as the result of collective effort. This makes it difficult to do justice to the breadth and contradictory nature of the emergence of aesthetic awareness and to the accomplishments of eminent individuals.

The history of socialist realist literature and its aesthetic theory is causally and immediately linked in Germany with the struggle and the spiritual world of the revolutionary German working class and its Marxist-Leninist party. This is true both for the period preceding the taking over of political power and socialist change and for the one that followed. The historical and theoretical development is not to be separated from this context.

Since what we are to set forth below is presented in the form of brief theses, it is necessary to elucidate a few principles of method:

1. The development of a Marxist theory of aesthetics begins in Germany with Marx and Engels and continues through the more than a century long history of the revolutionary German working-class

movement. Our working collective cannot possibly propose to write an historical survey of this period. We shall restrict ourselves to the recent phase, that is, to the development of the theory of socialist realism after 1945 and what immediately preceded. [Treatment of the period 1945-1955 will be omitted here. Eds.]

2. Our description of the German contribution to the theory of socialist realism assumes that the particular case of Germany is to be regarded as an expression of the broad comprehensive process of literary and aesthetic development in the 20th century. This requires research into international ties and interrelationships, first of all into the close connection of the development of German theory with the history of socialist realist literature and literary aesthetics in the Soviet Union. The extent and complexity of these reciprocal relationships are well known; their systematic description is a special task for research which is outside of the scope of these theses.

3. The present work will be concerned with generalizations associated with socialist realism. The theses will make it clear, however, that neither the history of literature nor the development of the socialist literary community is to be regarded as the object of our investigation.

The present collective work does not intend to present a comprehensive history of the theory of realism in Germany. It attempts a preliminary investigation in this area which the literary theoreticians of the German Democratic Republic have not yet studied. A more thorough analysis of certain developmental phases, of the emergence of special categories and problems of Marxist-Leninist aesthetics as well as of the so-called "aesthetics of the writer" must be presented in monographs before a complete historical description can be attempted.

The authors are aware of the temporary nature of the positions they have reached so far. The discussion of the concept in a larger frame of reference (during the colloquium on questions of socialist realism which took place on April 16-17, 1967) has given them a number of valuable critical insights and has encouraged them to publish these theses. They hope that the discussion will be broadened and will be thankful for any comment.

The Development of the Theory of
Socialist Realism from 1955 to 1961

Distinctive features

1. The second phase of the socialist cultural revolution began in the German Democratic Republic with the systematic construction of the socialist order. The artistic practice and the aesthetic theory of socialist realism were confronted with new tasks and problems. The relationship of socialist production, which was becoming stronger, expanded the social base for the leadership of the state power and party of the working class in all areas of collective life. The economic and political phase of development brought about an ideological revolution. The aim was to reach a level of consciousness that would comprehend the laws of social development in the most far-reaching way and would give rise to behavior in conformity with these laws.

Among these tasks, socialist realist literature acquired a qualitatively new function as one of the most valuable media of communication. In this period all theoretical efforts centered upon the definition of this function and sought to define the conclusions that must necessarily follow for the process of literary creation.

The discussions about socialist realism became increasingly part of the ideological and theoretical interchange concerning the fundamental problems of socialist society and national perspective. Increasingly the participants were workers belonging to various segments of society, as these discussions were not limited to professionals, writers and critics. This participation even led to creative work. (Movement of writing workers; workers' festivals, etc.)

The working class began to realize that its historical task was not only to take possession of the national culture but also to take an active part in its development. Literary works started the process and the theory of socialist realism formulated it as the "Bitterfeld way" and came to speak of the historically important goals of the cultured nation.

2. The relationship of the socialist realist literature to the changing social reality and to the contemporary builders of socialism became the starting point for all theoretical discussions, the search for objectively based aesthetic standards, and the criteria for socialist realist literature.

The strengthening and widening of the socialist literary community exerted a decisive influence on the development of aesthetic theory. Increasingly theoretical questions ceased to be exclusively or primarily a matter of the aesthetic expression of artists and became instead the concern of collective discussions among writers, critics, cultural functionaries and plain people interested in literature. The major role was played by deliberations of the Socialist Unity Party of Germany, cultural conferences and plenary meetings on literary and cultural questions, as well as joint discussions of writers and critics (congresses and theoretical conferences of the Union of German Writers).

The most important major publications on the problems of socialist realism were the result of collective deliberations.

3. The continuing development of socialist realism in this period took the form of a bitter ideological class struggle. It was characterized by contradictory attempts at artistic appropriation of new tasks and the creative defense of the basic Marxist-Leninist positions in aesthetics. The recognition that the construction of socialism in the German Democratic Republic is a historical necessity and a question of vital importance for the nation prevailed only slowly and as a result of discussions of principles within the working class and by members of the artistic intelligentsia.

After the 20th congress of the C.P.U.S.S.R., there were renewed attempts at a revision of the socialist direction in the German Democratic Republic favoring greater economic, political and cultural closeness to imperialist West Germany. Their ideological expression in the literary sphere was a serious effort to direct Marxist-Leninist aesthetics and literary theory—as well as other areas of intellectual life —toward a "third way"through the propagation of bourgeois conceptions, to nullify their social orientation and to separate literary and artistic development, conceived as being an unpolitical activity, from the planning and guiding influence of the state and the party.

The Fourth Congress of German Writers held in January, 1956 had unanimously approved the requests of the Nachterstedt workers formulating the new aesthetic requirements of the most advanced part of the working class. After many clarifying discussions on ideological and artistic problems, these requests became in fact the guiding line of socialist literary development. In the great ideological offensive of the Socialist Unity Party, the program for a socialist German literature presented by the Fourth Congress of German Writers (Becher: "On the Greatness of our Literature"; Walter Ulbricht's speech) presented a constructive alternative to the revisionist compromises. This work was developed further in important cultural meetings (Cultural Conference of the German Unity Party in 1957; Fifth Parteitag, 1958; Bitterfeld Conference, 1959; Cultural Conference, 1960; Fifth Congress of German Writers, May, 1961).

This great theoretical impetus was linked with abandonment of schematic conceptions of the nature of socialist realism and with a struggle against a dogmatic interpretation of the social role and tasks of literature. In all this a large part was played by the discussion on ideological and political positions and the interpretation of the counter-revolutionary events in Hungary.

The new definition of the traditional contours and perspectives of socialist realist literature brought new life to the theoretical conception of socialist realism and of the process of literary creation. Most important of all, criteria concerned only with content were discarded.

Program of Socialist National Literature.

1. In the mid fifties, the theory of socialist realism widened into one of the special disciplines of Marxism, to be studied and taught in the universities and other scientific institutions of the German Democratic Republic. The majority of the published scholarly contributions were concerned with the specificity and the subject matter of socialist realist art and literature as well as with the limits that separate them from progressive trends in the cultural heritage. The most valuable achievements of scholarship consisted in the Marxist interpretation of classic humanist thought and of the recently analyzed traditions (German Jacobins, etc.). However, this primary concern with the past favored a tendency to discuss problems of aesthetics in isolation, with stress upon their philosophical implications and without relating them to contemporary literary activity.

Several Marxist scholars of the German Democratic Republic concentrated on the analysis of aesthetic categories in order to provide a theoretical base for socialist realism. Characteristic of this effort was Walter Besenbruch's study, published in 1956, *Zum Problem des Typischen in der Kunst*. In it he tried to elucidate the relationship between socialist literature and social change with the help of the historically conceived category of the typical. This book was the focus of a discussion by Marxist aestheticians in learned journals which had a determining influence in the years that followed. Wolfgang Heise and Erwin Pracht advanced particularly constructive positions.

2. At the Fourth Congress of German Writers in January, 1956, the perspectives for socialist realist literature in the German Democratic Republic were discussed concretely for the first time. In his report ("On the Greatness of our Literature"), Johannes R. Becher stressed the great revolutionary traditions of this literature ("Our literature grew . . . as a literature of the working class") and outlined its most important task, to give shape to the "new reality" for the "new reader." He spoke of the socialist literary community as of a great collective body which is destined to "go far beyond literature proper" because of the rich and varied formation of total literary development as well as its widened concept of artistic creativity. These thoughts were developed in the programmatic decisions and recommendations of the first Bitterfeld Conference aiming at bridging the gap between art and life. Anna Seghers supported in her report ("The Role of Literature in Forming the Consciousness of the People") the Marxist-Leninist concept of the active social role of socialist literature with an analysis of developments in the German Democratic Republic. From the agreement on principle with the demands of the Nachterstedt workers she derived important artistic criteria for the socialist writer: partisanship and ideological clarity, search for the most effective means of representation and especially for plots centered on real conflicts, occurring in real life; the first pre-condition to artistic development, the discovery of the "new subject matter," should be pressed further. In the resolution of the Congress, the writers expressed unanimous support for the method of socialist realism. ("Socialist realism . . . gives scope for varied forms of expression in all literary genres and requires closeness to life and true representation of man. Only the method of socialist realism makes it possible today to represent what is new in life, the new man equipped with power to transform society.")

3. Georg Lukacs, in his contribution to the Fourth Congress of German Writers ("The Problem of Perspective") analyzed the qualitative differences between socialist and critical realism, enlarging on thoughts previously published. In certain articles he had developed his conception of the Marxist theory of portrayal, particularly through the representation of the form and content relationship and of the category of totality in which he formulated the essential theses of

his own concept of realism: "form as the highest expression of content" is subject to definite objective laws which also determine "the media of aesthetic form" (1954); the objective truth content—a crucial characteristic of realism is gauged in terms of the category of particularity. A main feature of socialist realism, the category of partisanship, loses with Lukacs its class definition: "Partisanship is the attitude toward the represented world which is revealed in the work through artistic means." (1955)

In the "struggle against dogmatism," these revisionist tendencies played an important role. The discussions on the political and ideological position of Georg Lukacs during the counterrevolutionary events in Hungary made it possible to begin re-evaluating and refuting his doctrinaire conception of realism (1958 Conference).

4. Ernst Bloch's views on the philosophy of art, which appeared in various cultural publications of the German Democratic Republic (*Das Prinzip Hoffnung*, vol. I, 1954; vol. II, 1955), likewise reduced the qualitative difference between Marxist-Leninist aesthetics and bourgeois conceptions. His ideas concerning the followers of Hegel opened the way to ideological coexistence. His interpretation of the essence of art as a "foreshadowing" of an "eschatological humanum," which extends over the totality of an historically concrete social order, stimulated a deeper comprehension of the specificity of art. But it was also an attack on the Marxist-Leninist theory of reflection. His concept of "artistic day dream" is not bound to any historically fixed social basis, and that is why the criteria of a progressive art for mankind in general took the place of a definition of the essence of socialist realist art and literature. Expressing these views at the Fourth Congress of German Writers, Ernst Bloch warned of an undefined "feeling of superiority alien to art," which may damage permanently the "poetic impulse" because of "codified traffic regulations." Referring to these views Günter Zehn and Gerhard Zwerenz expressed in 1956 and 1957 counterrevolutionary opinions concerning the leading role of the working class in the domain of culture and the partisan character of socialist realist literature.

5. After the Fourth Congress of German Writers, its basic declarations were violently discussed in publications and in meetings. The counterrevolutionary events in Hungary contributed decisively to clarify the social responsibility and position of the socialist writer.

A radio talk by the literary critic Hans Meyer ("On the Present

State of our Literature") stirred new discussions on basic questions: evaluations of the artistic achievements of GDR literature, its relationship to today's international and bourgeois literature, primarily to literary developments in West Germany; the problem of tradition and of the literary models for young authors in the GDR as well as the assessment of "modern" literary currents influenced by Kafka and Joyce.

In this context and with the examples of some books published in the GDR (primarily Sartre, *Childhood of a Hero*, and Wolfgang Koeppen, *Tod in Rom*), there was discussion of the nature of decadence and its influence on the socialist literary community, but with more stress on the criteria of socialist realism than on getting at a deeper definition of literary decadence.

The supposed "opulence" of the 20s was rejected through energetic recall of the socialist literary tradition. Productions and memoirs of old members of the "Alliance of Proletarian and Revolutionary German Writers" appeared, proletarian books were republished, some of them in German for the first time. The literature of the GDR was seen, under the imprint of first or renewed acquaintance with literary and theoretical achievements of earlier stages of development, as a concrete phase of a necessary tradition which culminates in the perspective of a socialist national literature. The most important contributions in literary theory and criticism of the second half of the 50s bore upon research in and clarification of this problem. They represent a solid base for the historically understood theory of realism.

The rediscovery and objective appreciation of the revolutionary tradition in literature gave encouragement to the new artistic creativity of today's socialist realist literature. Many young authors showed in their artistic activity that they were paying heed to Bertolt Brecht's demand at the Fourth Congress of German Writers that new life be breathed into agit-prop art. Didactic sketches, drama groups and political and satirical poetry appear. At the first Cultural Conference of the Socialist Unity Party in 1957 and in the theoretical reports that followed, there is stress on the aesthetic legitimacy of "operative genres" (reportage, documentary films, television plays, etc.) which a rigid "formalist canon" had long undervalued, having regarded them as invalid forms of expression for socialist realism.

6. There were concrete contributions to the theory of socialist realism by eminent writers with long experience who, through their

creative work and in their theoretical writings, took a position as to the tasks and content of socialist realist literature. In the "Bemühungen" of Johannes R. Becher (especially in the "Poetisches Prinzip" which appeared in 1957) we find thoughts on the specific character of the aesthetical which go far beyond their intended meaning and which, in the self-critical re-assessment of certain of Becher's positions, represent a new conception of realism. These aphoristic statements penetrate to the basic questions of the concept of socialist realism (to the object, to the relationship of cognitive function and artistic truth, to the evaluation of single literary works and of varied currents). They are at the base of, and complete, Becher's programmatic speeches on the social function and significance of socialist national literature. His considerations on the aesthetic pre-conditions—especially in poetry—culminated in an orientation toward the "new object," that is, the socialist transformation of man's social life.

Bertolt Brecht raised his concept of realism to a new level in his writings on the drama and in his work with the Berliner Ensemble. The "Notate zu Katzgraben" contain theoretical remarks on the tasks of socialist realist literature under the new social conditions which even go specifically into the attitude of the writer and the solution to problems of artistic creation. He wanted the aim of socialist realist literature to inspire in the public the struggle of the new against the old, and as a pre-condition for such an art he wanted the artist to be full of enthusiasm for the new (Fourth Congress of German Writers).

7. In the ideological offensive of the party, a new study of the classics of Marxism-Leninism played a large part. The significance of the beginnings of Marxist literary theory in Germany, the contributions of Mehring, Liebknecht, Zetkin, Luxemburg and of the members of the Alliance of Proletarian and Revolutionary Writers, and primarily the works of Marx, Engels and Lenin were studied and valued. In this respect, special mention should be made of the writings of Hans Koch. His definition of the objective bases of the aesthetic essence of art, which determines the aims of socialist art, went beyond mere interpretation of the classics and enriched the theory of socialist realism (primarily *Marxismus und Aesthetik*, 1961). The encounter with the aesthetically and theoretically significant Early Manuscripts of Karl Marx contributed much to Alfred Kurella's volume of essays (*Der Mensch als Schöpfer seiner selbst*, 1958). Scientific articles on the contemporary literary situation (for instance, H. Koch: "Kultur in

den Kämpfen unserer Tage," 1959) offered theoretical analyses of the new work being produced in what Becher had called the "literary community."

8. The theory of socialist realism received a decisive impetus from the position taken on literature and politics by the Socialist Unity Party of the GDR. In cultural conferences, in writers' meetings and in joint sessions with writers attended by high functionaries of party and state, the close connection between general social questions and artistic development was established. The necessity was also explained for each writer of the GDR to make a decisive choice between capitalism and socialism and to implement his decision in his creative work.

The first Bitterfeld Conference, called in 1959 as a writers' conference of the Mitteldeutscher Verlag, became the climax of the effort to establish close bonds between literature and life in socialist society. It was marked by important statements concerning the subject matter and the social function of literature in the GDR. (W. Ulbricht: "What matters . . . is to give our literature a new, socialist content and to make it accessible to the whole nation.") Starting from the first experiences that writers had had in collaborating with socialist brigades, the conference discussed the leading role of the working class in the construction of socialism with particular reference to the assignment of social tasks and active participation in the building of socialist culture. The need for development of aesthetic sensitivity and artistic capacity in the working population gave rise to a consideration of how today's socialist literature could influence the masses. Much time and attention was given to the necessity for changing the writers' way of life and work, thus creating the pre-conditions for the exploration of the "new subject matter." The Conference urged that writers get to know everyday life in the GDR through constant contacts, talks in the factories, etc., with industrial workers and with the agricultural population. Thus it would be possible to find important material and human conflicts. These programmatic recommendations contributed to the obvious impetus of literary life and to the appearance of a series of books which the public acclaimed. They led to constructive theoretical generalizations concerning the laws that govern ideological change and the socialist cultural revolution.

9. In the period under examination all programmatic contributions to the theory of socialist realism shared a basic theme, namely, the importance for the nation of a decisive and consistent development in

socialist realist literature. This theme came under attack from different sides. Already at the Fourth Congress of German Writers there were polemical discussions about the various duties which devolve upon the writers of the GDR and of the Federal Republic in view of the continuing existence of two German states on different levels of social development (Walter Ulbricht's speech). Later on, there were attempts to postulate an ideologically co-existing "unified German literature" and to abandon partisan ties to the socialist GDR. A few literary critics saw GDR literature as part of a general "literature of the modern epoch," indifferent to social questions, and not taking into account the socialist character of life in the GDR. A definitely partisan polemic against all attempts to build up a unified German literature as a "true community" of the German people, East and West, was led at the Fifth Congress of German Writers (May, 1961) by the East Germans H. Kant, H. Nachbar and S. Hermlin. Günter Grass was their principal antagonist.

10. The Fifth Congress of German Writers analyzed the new impetus of literary development since the Fourth Congress. A generation of young writers had come upon the scene, rich in promise, some of them even with excellent publications to their credit.

In her report ("Breadth and Depth in Literature"), Anna Seghers refuted all those who doubt "that the Bitterfeld way unites the greatest possible diffusion of culture with the potentiality and necessity of great art." In describing the connection between literary quality and dissemination of artistic work, she came to the conclusion that artistic mastery is the inevitable pre-condition for the force that can transform consciousness in socialist realist literature. This view dispelled the illusions of those who had hoped that ideological clarity and relationships with the factories would automatically solve all the newly emerged problems of artistic creativity. From then on, the questions of realism were at the center of all aesthetic research and endeavor.

11. The Marxist-Leninist literary critics of the GDR were concerned to turn literature toward the social world and the main social problems of the time. Some conferences were noteworthy (on Socialist Realism, 1958; Peace, War and Militarism in Critical and Socialist Realism; theoretical conferences of the Writers' Union).

New forms of collective scientific discussion characterized the new stage of development. On single questions of artistic creativity, there was pressure for a systematic analysis and representation of the theory of socialist realism. The best critical contributions to the theory of socialist realism were evolved in the course of discussions with revisionist concepts on the relationships between literature and politics. Also critical evaluation of bourgeois methods of interpretation of literary development in the 20th century (Hans Kaufmann: *Ueber aktuelle Probleme der Literaturwissenschaft*, 1957; et al.) led to a more precise definition of the criteria and function of aesthetics and literary criticism in the GDR.

Shaping the Socialist Image of Man

1. The concept of a socialist national literature had given rise to the question of the heroes in our epoch and of the central figure of the socialist realist literature of our time.

As to the humanist outlining of a socialist image of man, some valuable insights had been gained in the mid-fifties with regard to the question of ties between art and the people (Volksverbundenheit). In literary history some research had been done on the problem of the positive hero (Edith Braemer, Ursula Wertheim, etc.) and questions of aesthetics had been posed concerning the harmonious personality under various historical conditions.

In the works of a great many writers also there was important material for the theoretical working out of this problem; examples are Johannes R. Becher (*Poetisches Prinzip:* Observations on *Roheisen* and other so-called industrial novels) and Bertolt Brecht (*Notate zu Katzgraben*). It is now recognized that the creative task of the new literature is to form the new type of German worker, the conscious builder of socialism. The Fourth Congress of German Writers pointed to this "real hero" as the true aesthetic central figure (Becher, A. Seghers, W. Ulbricht). The first Bitterfeld Conference gave him the central place in the discussions of literary theory (example of the collaboration of Regina Hastedt and Sepp Zach).

2. Revisionist distortions of the socialist character of GDR literature equated the "daily surroundings" in bourgeois and in socialist literature (H. Mayer); the "small truth" of the individual was detached from the general historic condition of social relationships. According to another variety of distortion, only the anomalous, the exceptional was declared fit for art. These theories were presented as part of the

literary situation and were to be raised to the level of principle. These were political attacks set forth as aesthetic principles; they were directed against the new literary concern with contemporary themes drawn from the life of citizens of the GDR; they were aimed primarily at the representation of the positive hero and of perspective (that is, awareness of laws of historical development) as it affects understanding of individual behavior. The first task of socialist realism was proclaimed to be the disclosure of the historic truth, that is, a biassed, unflattering representation of errors and weaknesses in socialist development, and the exclusion of the "new subject matter" (changes in man under socialist conditions). These views were published primarily by the magazine "Sonntag" (1956-1957).

In the discussions that followed, questions concerning perspective as an artistic expression of the objective direction of social development and of human progress were clarified. These theoretical analyses refuted the view, represented especially by Georg Lukacs, that the shaping of perspective, an important criterion of socialist realist literature, was equivalent to window-dressing.

3. In these years, the literature of the GDR, in its aesthetic comprehension of the image of socialist man, turned away slowly from the favorite subject of the protagonist of the class struggle and of resistance against inhuman conditions; the aesthetically central theme of the epoch was taken up: the historical decision for socialism as realized in millions of individual destinies. This was represented first in minor genres, later in longer works (A. Seghers, *Die Entscheidung;* E. Strittmatter, *Die Holländerbraut;* H. Baierl, *Frau Flinz,* etc.) Through the analysis of these literary achievements the theoretical discussions of the specific national task of the literature of the GDR became more concrete and more convincing. These works disclosed new problems of literary creativity which were bound together with the shaping of the socialist image of man. They are at the center of the debate concerning new structures of conflict emerging in a society based on non-antagonistic contradictions.

At the Fifth Congress of German Writers Anna Seghers called the grappling with true conflicts and their partisan interpretation the precondition for good writing, the only way to escape from schematic constructions derived from literary sources and "to bear clear and authentic witness for the specifically new in our reality." The discussions in the Congress analyzed the reluctance of some writers to handle such real conflicts and explained this unjustified reserve by ideological insecurity and deficient knowledge of life (E. Strittmatter, W. Ulbricht); at this point a warning was expressed against the danger of schematism.

In certain critical writings, especially in analytical examinations inspired by Soviet works such as *In the Battle* (Nikolayeva) and *Spring Storms* (Ovetchkin), the theory of the lack of conflict was constructively opposed. However, these studies were not developed to the point of systematic aesthetic investigations of the literary representation of conflict.

4. Theoretical research into the problems of the relationship of individual to society, into the productive sphere as the place where socialist man realizes himself and into the cultural function of work made an important contribution to aesthetic theory (H. Koch, A. Kurella, et al.) and to the overcoming of a mechanistic and vulgar-sociological concept of the typical.

The Fifth Congress of German Writers stressed the increased significance of the socialist image of man in the present literature of the GDR (E. Strittmatter, "Der Mensch bleibt das Wichtigste") and stated that "for Becher and for us, when 'man' is mentioned, it is, quite naturally, man working, man participating in history through his activity" (H. Kant). In the field of literature there appeared some figures of workers full of life and movement, principally as educators and mentors who help young intellectuals turn toward socialist life (Reimann, Fühmann, Jakobs, et al).

5. In attempts to achieve a precise delineation of the intellectual mood of their contemporaries, young authors searched primarily for effective means of representation. Consciously leaning on literary models, they often truly enriched socialist realist literature. However, their success was more doubtful when, along with techniques and means of expression, they also adopted the image of man of bourgeois writers.

Anna Seghers, at the Fourth Congress of German Writers, had called attention to the topical importance of the literary portrayal of World War II and of the fate of soldiers whose thinking had been changed by the war. At the end of the Fifties and especially in works that treated this theme, there was a tendency toward reducing the image of man to the basely physical, even to the barbarian. Some tried in plays and novels to adopt the "hard-boiled style of writing" in an attempt to imitate a misunderstood Hemingway. But almost all of them remained caught in empirical experience. A basic clarification of the relationship between realism and humanism and a theoretically based exposé of the potentialities in the use of varied forms of expression in the literature of socialist realism, had not yet materialized.

On the History of the Theory of Socialist Realism
1961-1965

1. In the Sixties, the discussion of socialist realism became more active. In the GDR there was an increase in the number of publications on literary criticism which presented the results of the new research. German departments and other literary disciplines took part in this discussion. At the same time other new methodological impulses contributed to literary aesthetics. In the GDR literary science and criticism began to play a larger role in social life. All these forces exerted a positive influence on literary criticism.

2. The new developments in the theory of socialist realism are directly and indirectly tied to the new phase in the construction of socialist society, to the emergence of a socialist international system, a system that has repercussions in almost all the aspects of collective life. They are also connected with the new trends in the communist international movement as well as with new forces in the class conflict between socialism and capitalism.

3. The theoretical debates on realism are marked by the fact that socialism developed certain characteristic forms in the GDR and also by the fact that theory and practice of the socialist literature in the GDR are tightly bound to the laws of evolution of the international socialist movement. Thus the dialectic of the national and the international is reflected in the debate on realism.

4. The first half of the Sixties marked a new phase in socialist construction. The measures taken by the Government of the GDR on August 13, 1961 [erection of Berlin Wall. Eds.] made it possible to create a national economy and culture free from the disturbing influence of West German imperialism exerted before the closing of the border. Now the elements of strength in socialist society could manifest themselves with less interference. This introduced a change in the relationships of man to man as also in those of man to state and society.

5. It became apparent that socialist society is not a transitory phase but an autonomous stage of social development with its own laws, its own material technical base and superstructure. With the introduction of the new economic system of planning and leadership in the national economy, the starting point for the economic system which constitutes the kernel of a developed socialist society, and also with the planned beginning of the technical and scientific revolution, important steps were taken in the construction of socialism.

In the course of this construction, more and more social processes came under the control of the members of society, and production and other spheres of activity were consciously put at the service of society and the individual, bringing an Aufhebung of alienation, although the dialectic of consciousness and spontaneity continues to exert itself.

6. Under these conditions the role of the individual and of the collective grew; the subjective factor acquired more importance, and a new relationship developed between individual action and modes of behavior required by a new socialist reality. These modes of behavior are not accepted blindly or spontaneously; they are associated with a new stage of social consciousness.

7. In this context the function and significance of the natural and social sciences changed. But literature was also subject to this same transformation of function; the "necessity of art" is not a rigid, unhistorical dimension. Socialist society based on modern industry and socially producing agriculture opened up new problems for the process of literary creation, for the guidance of the literary community and thus for the theory of realism. Any isolation of theoretical work from the new vital processes is to be overcome. Abstract theorizing, detached from real life, the adoption of late bourgeois theories and the "simple" defense of recognized Marxist positions cannot offer satisfactory solutions to the new problems.

8. Out of the further evolution of the socialist international system and the new strategy and tactics in the struggle of the international communist movement against an imperialism which in the most important countries had entered the state monopoly phase, there developed the necessity to work out a basic common concept of strategy (Moscow, 1960). Primarily as a component of the policy of alliance, the question relating to world literature in the past, present and future took on new aspects. The discussion centered on the concept of realism, while a series of new scientific queries was drawn into the com-

plex of realism. This subject received its most extensive treatment in the realism discussion in the Soviet Union. There the main points of the discussion bore upon the problems resulting from the new phase of socialist reality as well as problems of a new relationship to bourgeois literature of the 20th century. Certain theoretical debates showed a direct parallel with the GDR.

9. The Kafka Conference (1963) constituted the prelude to an international comprehensive debate on realism, devoting relatively little attention to the work of Kafka himself. It centered on the problem of alienation which, in the form Marx described, is linked to the capitalist mode of production and reaches its high point with imperialism. This phenomenon was unhistorically transferred to socialist society (Fischer); the main task of socialist art was said to be to wage a fight against alienation. This view did violence primarily to the principle of historical concreteness in artistic expression, reducing the particular quality of socialist realism as opposed to bourgeois realism and other bourgeois literary trends simply to the subjective attitude of the writer. Fischer's notion of art and his aesthetic concepts are linked to a separate strategy and tactics of the anti-imperialist struggle which lean on the intelligentsia and see in it the main social force, with a general orientation toward bourgeois democracy. Essentially, Fischer takes over the views of bourgeois social democratic theoreticians concerning modern industrial society; like them, he fails to take account of the concrete conditions that result from a specific social formation. His views (*Kunst und Koexistenz*) are not supported by any analyses of socialist society.

10. In the discussion one of the central problems was that of decadence, which remains one of the most important questions. Lukacs' narrow concept of decadence was attacked and its dubious character was demonstrated. Up to a point, however, realism and literature were made into equivalents, since literature is always connected with reality in some way. But this leads to a negation of the definition of realism itself, and it leaves us as little advanced as a narrow, unhistorical and unliterary definition of decadence which confines itself simply to the application of philosophical categories to the field of literature.

The most important conclusions of the debate so far are these: decadence is not a normative opposition to realism, it is not a generic characteristic of late bourgeois literature, there are no decadent forms of expression per se. The problem can be cleared up only by historically exact research which will take into consideration in each instance the historically concrete relationship of the literary work to reality. Furthermore, the concept of decadence—like our own concept of realism—is not to be understood normatively.

11. Garaudy stressed the creative element in the literary process and this signified, in comparison to Lukacs, a stronger aesthetic relationship to the literary work, but he abandoned certain criteria which are to be included in the definition of realism (the historical quality, etc.), defining them as outside the realm of aesthetics. Garaudy attempts to take hold of the specific of literary reflection through the concept of myth and thus lands cognitively in the vicinity of objective idealism, that is, he makes an absolute of certain forms of creation by considering them non-historically.

12. Although an inclination toward abstract theorizing detached from relevance to our social reality continues to manifest itself, one can now discern efforts to create a scholarly base for a concept of leadership of the literary community. In a certain respect, this is a new feature. It will open up new problems of the theory of realism, it will take under scrutiny a number of relationships that have to be seriously considered as components of a theory of realism (relationship between writer and society, between literary work and the public, between literary image and reality, writing and world view, etc.).

Theoretical Discussion of the Literary Representation of the Socialist Image of Man

1. The second Bitterfeld conference drew attention again to the dynamic character of our concept of realism; it urged us to analyze the new questions in the light of theory also. The main artistic and aesthetic orientation was directed toward the shaping of the socialist image of man. What was needed was a literature that would bring into consciousness the new elements of our social life rationally and emotionally and would have real influence on the formation of the socialist personality.

So the further development of the theory of socialist realism took the following directions: consistent debates with late bourgeois and revisionist conceptions, an attempt at a constructive solution of the new problems, and in association with this the effort to overcome cer-

tain constricting formulations. It is in this process that we find ourselves
now.

2. In these years a decisive step was taken in the make-up of literary works, in that there now moved into a central position protagonists
who had already made their decision for socialism and whose behavior
was defined by their activities on behalf of socialist society. This
brought an enrichment to the artistic representation of the socialist
image of man. This applies to all literary genres and types. But at the
same time new problems were raised in relation to the question of
the literary handling of new aspects of reality.

This development was not exempt from contradictions.

3. Literary works concerned with central problems of contemporary socialist humanism played an important role in the public discussion (novels like *Divided Heaven, Ole Bienkopp, Spur der Steine,
Die Aula, Die Alchemisten, Mein namenloses Land,* plays like *Kipper
Paul Bauch, Der Bau,* even though some did not reach the production
stage, volumes of poetry and single poems by Kunert, Maurer, Mickel,
etc.). The artistic solutions were not always accepted. But it became
clear that a meaningful unity between literature and reality, between
literature and the life of the people, can only be achieved when the
focus of literary efforts is the socialist image of man.

4. An essential point was the dialectic of the social and the individual as determined by our social conditions. Both in literary practice
and in theory it appeared that society and individual were seen only
in their opposition, sometimes antagonistically opposed. A "claim of the
individual" to assert himself in confrontation with the collective was
stressed. What was left out of consideration was the fact that the social
personality can only realize itself in the collectivity, in the society. In
fact the individual can only develop himself personally in the conscious formation of his life relationships. This dialectic is expressed in
reality through contradictory processes in which both spontaneity and
consciousness are active at present.

5. The literary character, be it a person in a novel or in a play or
the lyrical "I," cannot be represented realistically in opposition to the
social. It is equally true that it cannot be a pure representative of a
certain class or segment of society and can even less represent socialist
society as such. But such were the demands made on literature (discussion of the novels *Divided Heaven* and *Ole Bienkopp*). In literary
scholarship specialized research was undertaken aiming at shaping

a literary character and having a general relevance. It was made clear that the problem of the socialist image of man is not to be limited to the immediate creation of characters—in the meaning that it can be realized only through delineation of straightforward positive characters who embody all social norms. Satire and other means and techniques of expression which establish critical distance can also contribute to the formation of the socialist image of man to which they bring the correct, realistic detachment.

6. In literary aesthetics some important gains were made in overcoming an undialectical opposition between empathy and detachment. "In each novel, there must be at least one positive character, the author" (Strittmatter). It seems that the term "empathy" can only have a limited use in Marxist scholarship since it does not do justice to the dialectic of literary creation and aesthetic receptivity.

7. Socialist realism accomplishes its function of forming man above all through a realistic representation of the image of man. In novels and in plays this has immediate connections with the working out of plot and conflict. It was made apparent that an essential aspect of the representation of conflict is to make clear that contradictions can be solved through human action (Anna Seghers).

8. Successful achievements in literature (*Ole Bienkopp, Die Aula*) inspired a theoretical deepening of views of the function of the critical element in socialist realism under present conditions. This problem is of particular importance for the shaping of characters and the realistic representation of the socialist image of man.

The critical element and its inclusion in socialist realist literary creativity are conditioned by the historically concrete function of literature in social practice. Also, while socialist society is being built, the critical element remains a determining component of socialist realism. There is objectively no necessity to promote in socialist society a special critical realism devoted to the criticism of society. Any critical posture not originating in socialist partisanship is anachronistic.

The critical element does not grow today exclusively out of criticism of the past but also out of the incorporation of literature into practice in the context of the great social framework. The essence of the critical element rests in the indirect action of literature on social transformation, in the shaping of a new human community. It is not rooted in pure negation—in the same way as socialist realism is not pure halleluyah—but in a productive critical attitude toward reality.

Thus the critical element exerts its formative influence on literary work. It includes socialist partisanship and a materialist awareness of history.

9. As a reaction to the international discussion on realism but also to the development of socialist literature in our country, theory stressed more than ever before the creative element in the literary representation of reality. The specific nature of creative subjectivity and the specific problems encountered by the author received stronger theoretical consideration. The specific relationship between image and reality became in this way subject matter for research. It is true that in this context there were some simplifications, the process of literary creation being seen simply as the act of creating a new reality and the differences between spiritual and material activity being glossed over.

10. An important result of the theoretical considerations mentioned above is the fact that the criterion for realist writing is no longer the use of certain means of representation in literary technique. The measure of realism is more and more determined by the true understanding of the dialectic of the individual and the social and by the influence the literary work is likely to have on social reality and the direction of socialist development. This last element is the main criterion for socialist realism. Thus an important gain is won over earlier theoretical conceptions, namely, the exclusion of a normative standard. If the relationship between reality and literature is simplified, it is easy to introduce standards of vulgar materialism.

11. On this subject there was for the first time a start toward serious study of the factor of influence as a criterion of realism. Attempts were made to create a sociology of literature and to include aspects of information theory into the theory of realism. It was an attempt to reach objective standards. In so doing, the shooting was sometimes wide of the aim, as when the results of bourgeois literary sociology (Mierendorf-Tost) were uncritically adopted. One cannot successfully equate a systematic literary scholarship with a purely empirical criticism having affinities with the natural sciences. Also these trends implied a denial of the whole heritage of Marxist scholarship and criticism, particularly as regards methodology. Research in literary sociology, especially attempts to ascertain the real influence of a literary work, not the presumed one, cannot take the place of a semantic analysis of art. Properly handled, however, this research can add to the resources of the theory of realism.

Further Criteria of Socialist Realism

1. Further criteria of realist literary representation are generally held to be the truth of the literary image and the element of historic authenticity in the image. An advance has been made particularly in regard to the problem of historicity and perspective. These matters are being constantly explored in the analysis of literary material (Jena theses on perspective formation, etc.).

2. On the other hand, the treatment of the problem of truth in a particular literary statement is in part imprecise. This happens mostly because the relationship between reality, the literary work and practice is often seen from one side only, or because literary cognition is represented and treated in the same manner as philosophic cognition. Both criteria, historicity and truth, are, however, next to the image of man, real criteria of realism.

3. A new approach—one which does justice to the specificity of literature—manifests itself in the dialectic of function and content. A mechanistic dialectic of form and content that has been simply derived from philosophy does not explain adequately the artistic specificity. We can be thankful to criticism and scholarship for penetrating more deeply, in this respect also, into the specific of aesthetic structure.

4. One of the main concerns of literary scholarship was to analyze the traditions of socialist literature, the question of whence and whither. In several articles, the traditions and evolution of socialist realism in Germany were elucidated, while out of the analysis of historical processes criteria for realism were derived. Most valuable is the recognition of the uniqueness of socialist realism in Germany and at the same time of the variety of socialist realist styles.

The relationship of the socialist to the late bourgeois literary development has been repeatedly investigated, with special stress on the relationship between socialist and critical realism. It has been shown that certain forms of expression of bourgeois literature can be adapted for socialist purposes. It becomes increasingly clear that an important socialist realist national literature can only evolve in the context of reciprocal exchanges with the best examples of world literature. Exchange means here an Aufhebung that passes from negation to appropriation.

5. We have to mention first attempts to investigate the various literary currents in the GDR and their mutual relationships (literature based on a Christian humanism).

6. To sum up, new efforts have been made to solve the problem of socialist realism, and at the same time new methodological experience has been gained. The progress achieved in the field of literary scholarship since the Sixth Parteitag does not show any break with previous Marxist research. The distinctive feature has been that the problems we are encountering on our road to socialism are raised to the level of subject matter for theoretical research.

SOURCES – TRANSLATORS

I. Current Directions

Georg Lukacs, Appearance and Essence. Source: "Einführung in die ästhetischen Schriften von Marx und Engels." In *Schriften zur Literatursoziologie*, edited by Peter Ludz. Berlin-Spandau, 1963. Tr. by Eva LeRoy.

S. Petrov, Realism–The Generally Human. Source: S. Petrov, *Realism*, Moscow, 1964. Tr. by Mark Yaron.

Robert Weimann, Past Significance and Present Meaning in Literary History. Written in English by Robert Weimann.

Robert Weimann, Point of View in Fiction. Written in English by Robert Weimann.

N. K. Gay, Truth in Art and Truth in Life. Source: N. K. Gay, "Obraz i Chudoshestvennaya Pravda," in *Teoria Literatury*, Moscow, 1962. Tr. by Anne White.

II. Late Capitalism and the Humanist Image

Werner Mittenzwei, Contemporary Drama in the West. Source: Werner Mittenzwei, *Gestaltung und Gestalten im modernen Drama*, Berlin, 1965. Tr. by Eva LeRoy.

B. G. Zhantieva, On Joyce's *Ulysses*. Source: D. G. Zhantieva, "Dzheims Dzhois," in *Angliiskiy Roman XX Veka, 1918-1939*, Moscow, 1965. Tr. by Anne White.

III. The Arts and the Perspective of Socialism

Erwin Pracht and Werner Neubert, Partisanship. Source; *Neue Deutsche Literatur*, No. 5, Berlin, 1966. Tr. by Eva LeRoy.

Werner Mittenzwei, The Brecht-Lukacs Debate. Source: "Die Brecht-Lukacs Debatte," in *Sinn und Form*, Vol. 19, No. 1 (Feb., 1967). Tr. by Eva LeRoy.

Erwin Pracht, Socialist Realism. Source: *Humboldt Universität: Organ der SED Kreisleitung*. Tr. by Eva LeRoy.

Elisabeth Simons, Socialist Realism—Development of the Theory in the German Democratic Republic since 1955. Source: Unpublished manuscript prepared by the Institute for Social Sciences of the Central Committee of the Socialist Unity Party, GDR. Tr. by Eva LeRoy.

INDEX

271